The Boston Putford Story

PART ONE

PUTFORD ENTERPRISES LTD., WARBLER SHIPPING CO. LTD., BREYDON MARINE LTD.

By
Malcolm R. White

Coastal and Maritime Heritage Series
2003

INFORMATION

Published by Malcolm R. White
Coastal Publications
71 Beeching Drive
Lowestoft
NR32 4TB
England, UK

Printed by Microvpress Printers Ltd.
27 Norwich Road
Halesworth
Suffolk
IP19 8BX
England, UK

First Published May 2003

ISBN 09532485 8 5

Every effort has been made to ensure the information contained in this review and comprehensive fleet list is accurate and for this reason many sources of information have been consulted. These include personal accounts of events, official documentation, local diaries, media resources, and numerous accredited research works. However, when considering such a complex, variable and historical subject, 100% accuracy cannot be guaranteed. By popular request, all measurements, dimensions and distances in this book are stated in British Imperial. Books in this series are part of the National Published Archive, and as such are included in the library collections of the British Library, the National Library of Scotland, the National Library of Wales, the Universities of Oxford and Cambridge, Trinity College, Dublin, and when appropriate, The National Museum of Science & Industry.

Other titles in the Coastal and Maritime Heritage Series: -

DOWN THE HARBOUR 1955-1995	40 years of fishing vessels, owners, the harbour and shipyards at Lowestoft	ISBN 09532485 0 X
A CENTURY OF FISHING	Fishing from Great Yarmouth and Lowestoft 1899-1999	ISBN 09532485 1 8
FISHING WITH DIVERSITY	A portrait of the Colne Group of Lowestoft	ISBN 09532485 2 6
CROWNIES OF LOWESTOFT	The steam trawler fleet of Consolidated Fisheries	ISBN 09532485 3 4
DRIFTING, TRAWLING & SHIPPING	A portrait of Small & Co. (Lowestoft) Ltd.	ISBN 09532485 4 2
GREETINGS FROM LOWESTOFT	A picture book of old postcards and photographs	ISBN 09532485 5 0
THE LOWESTOFT TRAIN	The railway at Lowestoft and scenes on the lines to Norwich, Ipswich and Yarmouth	ISBN 09532485 6 9
LOWESTOFT ANTIQUITY	A picture book of once familiar scenes	ISBN 09532485 7 7

Front Cover
Top - One of the present day Boston Putford fleet, the 1976 built dual role safety standby and cargo vessel *Putford Achates*.
Bottom - In 1948, the steam drifter/trawler *LT56 Sedulous* became the first vessel to be purchased for the fishing fleet of Putford Enterprises. She is seen here shortly after conversion from steam to diesel propulsion. *Sedulous* remained in the fleet until 1961.

Title Page
This rare photograph shows the *Sedulous* as a Scottish steam drifter, whilst in the ownership of Mrs. A. Jack and W. Jack of Hopeman.

Opposite Page
After being purchased for the Putford fleet, the Yarmouth drifter/trawler *Hilda Cooper* was converted to diesel propulsion and renamed *Specious*. She served as a trawler for over 10 years until sold for scrapping in 1967. *Specious* is seen leaving Lowestoft for the fishing grounds.

CONTENTS

ACKNOWLEDGEMENTS

My grateful thanks to Mr. George Catchpole for considerable assistance during the preparation of this publication, and for providing substantial in-depth information about the Company and their ships. Without his help, the task of compiling this work would have been much more difficult.

Much appreciated has been the cooperation and support offered during the preparation of this book by several kind people, interested in researching and recording the diverse history and heritage of the Lowestoft area. These include in particular, Mr. Stuart Jones BA, who has provided editorial support for all the titles in this popular series. Assisting or participating in this complex project have been Mr. Peter Catchpole, Mr. Robert Catchpole, Mr. Bryn Colton, Mr. Tom Drew, Mr. Stanley Earl, Mr. Peter Hansford, Mr. Peter Killby, Mr. Peter Parker, Mr. Terry Reeve, Mr. Parry Watson, Mr. David White, Louise Clarke and the staff of the Suffolk Record Office, and the staff of Boston Putford Offshore Safety Ltd. Last but not least, I would like to thank my wife, Cathryn, for the patience, support and understanding she has shown during the long hours I spend writing, publishing and distributing books in this series.

PHOTOGRAPHIC OWNERSHIP AND COPYRIGHT

Mr. Frederick E. Catchpole and his wife Muriel at Richards shipyard in Lowestoft, on the occasion of the launch of the *Valiant Star,* which later became the *Monkleigh.* This fine drifter/trawler was completed in 1959, having taken 12 weeks to build. The Catchpole family have traditionally been associated with ship owning at Lowestoft. In 1902, in addition to sailing trawlers, the early steam drifters *Doris* and *Berry Head* were part of their fleet.

Later renamed *Putford Blazer* in the Boston Putford fleet, the *Dawn Blazer* was Lowestoft owned for almost 20 years, having been acquired in 1976 by Small & Co. (Lowestoft) Ltd. as the *Aberdeen Blazer*. Renamed in their fleet *Suffolk Blaze*, she was sold to Warbler Shipping in 1987, and became the *Dawn Blazer*. Built as the supply ship *Lady Alison* in 1965 at Aberdeen, *Putford Blazer* left the Boston Putford fleet in 1995, but later returned to Lowestoft under new ownership for an extensive refit as the *Sea King*.

Introduction

The Lowestoft based Boston Putford Offshore Safety Ltd. organisation was set up by a group of companies comprising Boston Deep Sea Fisheries, Putford Enterprises, Warbler Fishing Co. Ltd., the Great Yarmouth based shipbuilders and repairers Breydon Marine, and Mr. A. F. T. Jenson, founder of North Sea Divers, and a stock holder of oil dispersants. From the very early days of oil and gas exploration in the southern North Sea, the group set out to meet the needs of the offshore companies by providing comprehensive and professional safety services to the industry, which often works in a hostile and dangerous environment. This book details the vessels owned by some of the companies before and after the setting up of the organisation.

Boston Deep Sea Fisheries was one of the largest fishing companies in the UK with a major base at Lowestoft, and others at Hull, Grimsby, Fleetwood and Penzance. The company owned and operated a large fleet of fishing craft in addition to safety standby ships. The Putford Enterprises/ Warbler consortium, at one time both fishing concerns with several vessels at Lowestoft and Grimsby, has since the mid 1960s, been one of the largest operators of safety standby vessels in the UK.

Eventually operating all round the British coast, the group's fleet has always been in the forefront of offshore safety activities, with the ships and crews establishing an enviable record for reliable service. In the 21st century, this includes supply and cargo carrying in addition to the well-established safety work, and as a result of the ongoing policy of upgrading the fleet, it now consists of a range of large modern quality ships. In the early days, the standby fleet consisted of converted drifters and trawlers. These however, were very restricted in their range of activities, and could prove somewhat uncomfortable for their crews, when spending substantial periods at sea.

Long standing Boston Deep Sea and Putford Enterprises' experience, obtained through working the seas initially in fishing vessels, has proved a major advantage in providing support to the offshore industries, especially when shifting sands and fierce tides are encountered, as in the southern North Sea.

Since early in 2000, Putford Enterprises Ltd, trading with associated companies as Boston Putford Offshore Safety Ltd., has been part of Seacor Smit Inc. This leading American organisation operates a fleet of over 300 ships supporting oil and gas exploration and production, on a global scale.

The registered office of Boston Putford Offshore Safety Ltd. is at Columbus Buildings, originally built in 1907 by Mr. Harry Adams. It is situated in Waveney Road, Lowestoft, opposite the entrance to the docks. Designed by Mr. R. Scott Cockrell, it was unusual at the time, being the first local building with a steel frame. This unique and historic building, with the glazed earthenware façade representing the ships of Columbus, has a long history associated with maritime activities being at one time a marine store with a net making establishment above. It underwent a major renovation in 1926 and again in 1951, and was for many years the offices of Consolidated Fisheries and later Boston Deep Sea Fisheries. The Consolidated was a major fishing company operating from several ports, similar to Boston Deep Sea Fisheries.

Details of the local history and the vessels of Boston Deep Sea Fisheries, and a later participant in the Boston Putford organisation, Britannia Marine Ltd., will be considered in a future work. This volume deals with Breydon Marine Ltd., Putford Enterprises Ltd., the Warbler Shipping Co. Ltd. and associates.

Malcolm White
Lowestoft
June 2003

The *Homocea*, seen here entering Lowestoft, was one of three steam drifters/trawlers purchased in the 1940s and 50s by Putford Enterprises for conversion into diesel-powered trawlers. *Homocea* was built by A. Hall at Aberdeen, and delivered on the 11th September 1919. She was intended for naval auxiliary patrol duties as *HMD Waterfall* (No. 4132), but was sold soon after delivery for use as a fishing vessel. In 1953, *Homocea* was acquired, converted and renamed, and went on to give over 10 years service as the diesel powered trawler *Strenuous*.

The Origins of Boston Putford
Part One-Putford Enterprises Ltd., Warbler Shipping Co. Ltd., Breydon Marine Ltd.

The roots of the Lowestoft based Boston Putford Offshore Safety Ltd. lie in the 1960s when the fishing industry was in rapid decline and the offshore oil and gas industry was becoming well established in the North Sea. Boston Deep Sea Fisheries, at that time the largest local trawler owning and managing company, and Putford Enterprise Ltd. set up the group to provide the required offshore safety services, initially by utilising former fishing vessels. Later, the majority of Boston Deep Sea Fisheries vessels passed to a new company, Britannia Marine.

During the late 1970s and early 1980s, vessels owned by other operators including Breydon Marine joined Putford Enterprises, Warbler Shipping and Britannia Marine in the group. Details of the local history and the vessels of Boston Deep Sea Fisheries and associated owners, and Britannia Marine Ltd. will be considered in a later work. This section deals with Breydon Marine Ltd., Putford Enterprises Ltd. and the Warbler Shipping Co. Ltd.

Within the Boston Putford Offshore Safety group, the Breydon Marine fleet consisted of three former trawlers, one of Scottish origin and two Lowestoft built. All had been converted for offshore safety work. No other vessels such as former supply ships were purchased to upgrade the fleet, and by the end of 1992, Breydon Marine had disposed of these three vessels, and was no longer part of Boston Putford Offshore Safety Ltd.

Putford Enterprises Ltd. was established in 1948, when John Hashim and Anthony Rainey, who had become close friends during the Second World War in the Special Boat Service, joined up with Bob Mitchell to form a small fishing company in Brixham.

Columbus Buildings in Lowestoft, the head office of Boston Putford Offshore Safety Limited.

Also that year, John Hashim purchased the steam drifter/trawler *Sedulous* and had her converted to diesel power, with the intention of fishing her from Lowestoft.

Four years later, in 1952, John Hashim himself moved to East Anglia and more conversions of steam drifters/trawlers such as the *Homocea (Strenuous)*, *Hilda Cooper (Specious)* were made until 1960, when the first of two new diesel trawlers for the Putford fleet, the *Woodleigh,* was completed at the local shipyard of Richards Ironworks. Having been converted and re-engined, this vessel remained in the Putford standby fleet until early in 1993. *Bickleigh* was the other trawler built at this time, and she was later sold to Aberdeen owners. Putford Enterprises went on to earn the reputation of having owned the most varied and interesting fleet of drifters and trawlers, used both for fishing and offshore support work, to be seen anywhere in the British Isles.

The Sedulous

Builder/Built Philip & Son., Dartmouth. 1912
Official No.   132952
Construction Steel
Dimensions   88.9ft x 19.1ft x 8.7ft
Tonnage   Registered 42.10   Gross 99.55
Engine   Philip & Son Ltd., Dartmouth - Triple Expansion
             35hp   10.25ins. & 16ins. & 26ins. x 20ins.
Boiler   185lb. Central Marine Engineering Works,
             West Hartlepool

FIRST WORLD WAR SERVICE
Requisitioned: January 1915 Released: 1920

SECOND WORLD WAR SERVICE
Requisitioned: May 1940   Released: October 1945

A very interesting vessel with a notable past, the *Sedulous* was well qualified and worthy to be the first vessel in a fleet, which would become in the future, a major force in British shipping and the offshore industry. She was first registered as *LT1168* in May 1912 at Lowestoft in the ownership of James and Walter Pye, and Robert Green. *Sedulous* was sold on during February 1914 to T. W. Moore (64 Shares) of Great Yarmouth for £3,200 and

registered at Yarmouth as *YH2*. One of four vessels to leave Lowestoft during World War One on the 2nd January 1915, to form the nucleus of the Dover Net Drifter Flotilla, she was allocated the identifying number *158* and equipped with a 47mm gun by the Admiralty during her naval service. On return to commercial fishing in 1920, she was insured for £5,000. In January 1924, the *Sedulous* went to new owners at Inverness, becoming *INS3,* but still retaining her original name. After valuable service in World War Two from May 1940 until October 1945, during which time she served as a boom defence vessel, examination vessel and barrage balloon vessel, she returned to Lowestoft in the ownership of Shire Trawlers Ltd., Water Lane, London, as *LT56,* a registration she was to retain for the rest of her fishing career. In 1948, ownership passed to John R. Hashim, a director in Putford Enterprises. That same year, her steam machinery was stripped out by the well-established Lowestoft engineering firm of George Overy Ltd., and replaced by a four-cylinder Petter diesel engine, which developed 306shp at 600rpm. This engine was replaced in 1958 by a 400hp Petter engine. In 1961, the *Sedulous* was sold to another Lowestoft fishing company, Merbreeze Ltd., and continued to fish from her long-standing homeport. Her orange painted funnel complete with a blue flag with the letters "PE" on, would no longer be seen in the harbour at Lowestoft. By 1963, her fishing days were over, and she was sold to Konstanin Zuis of London, and left Lowestoft.

The first contract for oil or gas related work was obtained in 1967, and three years later in 1970, Fred Catchpole joined the company by acquiring the interests of Bob Mitchell. From then on, attention was focused on the offshore safety aspect of the business, particularly as the southern gas fields became an area for more intense development. Many additional ships were bought for safety standby work including the Podd trawler fleet of *Mincarlo, Ada Kerby,* and *W.F.P.* Because of her locally built A. K. Diesels main engine, and also having been Lowestoft built, the *Mincarlo,* later renamed *Putford Merlin,* was given by Putford to the Lydia Eva Trust when she came to the end of her useful standby vessel life. She is now preserved by the Trust, which has plans to restore the vessel to her former fishing state as an outstanding example of a Lowestoft trawler of the early 1960s.

The first vessel built for Putford was the trawler *Woodleigh*. She gave over fifteen years service fishing, followed by a further eighteen as a safety standby vessel. Truly a remarkable record. *Woodleigh* is seen here off Lowestoft heading for the fishing grounds.

The company continued to be involved in fishing until the mid 1970s, during which time they purchased many trawlers including *Boston Sea Dart, Eta, Dreadnought, Granton Harrier, Iago, Margaret Christina, Suffolk Punch, Suffolk Craftsman* and also larger vessels such as the *Idena* and *Boston Seafoam*.

Of special interest, the *Suffolk Craftsman* and *Suffolk Punch* were two of five similar vessels built in 1961 by Richards Ironworks at Lowestoft as additions to the large drifting and trawling fleet of Small & Co. (Lowestoft) Ltd. Disposal of the five by Smalls in October 1974, saw three going to Boston Deep Sea Fisheries and the remaining two to Putford. These five quality vessels were all renamed, and in the case of the Putford two, the *Craftsman* became *Winkleigh* and the *Punch* the *Hatherleigh*. By January 1975, all five could be seen in the harbour at Lowestoft displaying their new names and owner's colours.

For several years the two fished successfully, however, by the early 1980s, the economics of fishing were becoming questionable and the decision was taken to transfer them to offshore support work.

Prior to the implementation in 1993 of the new code of practice concerning the calibre and capability of offshore safety standby vessels, ships such as the *Winkleigh* and *Hatherleigh* were typical of dozens of vessels employed on this work. However, after 1993, these would have to be replaced by more suitable ships and the former trawlers disposed of. For *Winkleigh*, this meant travelling to southern Africa after being sold for further service. For the *Hatherleigh*, her future use was destined to be somewhat unusual. She was purchased in late 1992 by the chairman of Pindar plc; a Scarborough based printing and communications company. After a refit at Whitby, she headed for her new homeport of Scarborough, where initially she would become a tourist attraction in the harbour there. A change of use soon occurred when the *Hatherleigh* became a Maritime Voluntary Service training ship, and in the following years as a certified passenger vessel, she was to be seen all around the British Isles.

Following the run down and final closure of the fishing side of the business, many vessels from the Boston and Putford trawling fleets followed the *Hatherleigh* and *Winkleigh*, and transferred to safety standby work for a few years in the booming offshore support market in which Putford already had a major presence, before they too were sold off.

An interesting project undertaken by Putford around this time was working with the Ministry of Defence in assisting in the recovery of aircraft lost at sea around the coasts of the British Isles. The skipper, who was particularly successful in this department, was George Outlaw with the *Dreadnought* (*Putford Harrier*). His prowess in these operations earned him an MBE for his efforts. George was still working for Putford in 1992 when the company celebrated 25 years of offshore support work.

In 1968 Fred Catchpole and John Hashim, together with George and Peter Catchpole, set up the Warbler Shipping Company to acquire and operate the *Warbler* as a safety standby vessel. This former steam trawler, built in 1912 and converted to diesel power in 1958 with the installation of an AKD engine built in Lowestoft, was the first vessel in the Warbler Fleet.

The vessels in that fleet later had the prefix "Dawn" added to their names, and the more recent *Dawn Warbler*, a former supply ship built locally at Brooke Marine as the *Lady Claudine*, looked very different to the first.

In the early days of standby, when Putford were still active in fishing with as many as seven trawlers, Boston Deep Sea Fisheries looked after Putford fishing vessels and arranged for Putford to develop and manage the standby business of both companies. Fred Catchpole and John Hashim, who achieved contracts throughout the North Sea, did this very successfully. The northern areas were eventually shed to jointly form the Safetyships Company of Aberdeen when it was realised that the offshore companies in the north preferred to deal with locally based contractors.

In the southern North Sea, the business continued to be developed based on converted trawlers, with George Catchpole joining the company on a permanent basis as Marketing Director in 1977.

As Boston Putford continued their expansion at Lowestoft and

The first vessel in the Warbler Shipping fleet was built as the Hull steam trawler *H587 Warbler* in 1912 at Goole. She worked out of Lowestoft as *LO251* and was converted to diesel power there in 1958, when she was also re-registered as *LT63*. *Warbler* is seen leaving Lowestoft for a further spell of standby duty.

added more ships to the fleet, a shortage of crews developed as the pool of former fishermen was absorbed into the fast developing new safety standby industry. Hull and Grimsby had suffered a similar decline in their fishing fleets to Lowestoft, but were slow to recognise the opportunities in the new safety standby market. There were many good deep-sea skippers and fishermen unemployed and available on the Humber, and Boston Putford were happy to tap into this pool of skilled seamen who with intense training, soon adapted to the new activities. Even some of the top "Don" skippers made this transition. George Catchpole recalls the time when he and John Hashim watched the great Wally Boden who had skippered some of the large distant water Icelandic trawlers take the drifter/trawler *Monkleigh* to sea in atrocious conditions to maintain the safety cover in the Leman field.

It was late on a dark winter's evening and the ship was pinned on the North Quay by a southerly gale with driving sleet, when Wally manoeuvred her off the quay and away through the bridge to demonstrate ship handling of the highest order.

Wally later became the Putford flag skipper of the *Sir Fred Parkes* when she was the lead guard ship protecting the barge laying power cables from England to France. This large Hull freezer stern trawler was bought in 1982 for conversion into a diving support vessel.

However, for technical reasons the *Putford Skua*, formerly the *Suffolk Service* and one of four supply ships purchased in 1985, was substituted into that project. The task of the *Sir Fred Parkes* together with three other guard ships was to warn off shipping that might have collided with the trenching and lay barge, which was proceeding slowly across the very busy English Channel shipping lanes.

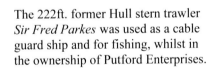

The 222ft. former Hull stern trawler *Sir Fred Parkes* was used as a cable guard ship and for fishing, whilst in the ownership of Putford Enterprises.

This operation went on for three years, during which for some of the time the *Parkes* was joined by two other large stern trawlers, the *Putford Protector,* built at Lowestoft as the *Ranger Apollo,* and the *Boston Lincoln.*

After a period of fishing in UK waters the *Sir Fred Parkes* was sold to Spanish owners to fish South Atlantic waters around the Falkland Islands after the war there had ended. The ship was later sold on to a company in Argentina!

The *Putford Skua* continued the diving project and worked well for three years until overtaken by new diving requirements whereupon she moved back to the safety standby market.

Trinity House, who were overseeing the cable laying project in the Channel, were particularly impressed with the skill and ship handling qualities of the Putford Masters in close quarter's situations; skills learnt in the Icelandic cod wars!

In fact, it says a great deal for the guard ships and their crews who protected the cable laying operations that during the three-year period no vessels hit the lay barge.

This achievement was underlined in the year 2003, when the car carrier *Tricolor* sank after a collision in the Channel, and no less than two ships grounded on the wreck even after a safety zone and guard ships had been put in place.

Amongst the other illustrious Humber skippers who successfully changed to safety standby duties were Tom Sawyer whose Greenland fishing activities were legendary, Paddy Macarthy who was frequently top skipper in the Grimsby "Cat" class trawlers that worked primarily off the west coast of Scotland and Faeroe, Mac Hastie, Colin Spall, John Stevens, David Woods, Dave Venney, Charlie Johanson, Frank Powdrill and Bill (the Colonel) Smith. They carried out their new duties for Boston Putford in a capable and efficient manner, with many notable rescues and achievements to their credit.

When Peter Catchpole, who had been manager of Boston Deep Sea Fisheries at Lowestoft in the early days of standby, returned to Lowestoft in 1979 he led Warbler Shipping on a diversification into surveying. Spearheaded by skippers Colin Spall and John Stevens in the *Dawn Sky*, and Tom Sawyer and Paddy Macarthy in the *Dawn Flight*, this proved successful, and these ships and their crews established an enviable reputation in the survey market.

The safety standby vessel *Oakleigh*, at one time the Aberdeen trawler *Wilronwood*, arrives at Grimsby on the 15th August 1979.

The *Dawn Sky* was formerly the Lowestoft built and based fisheries research vessel *Corella* that was purchased by Warbler when she was replaced by the MAFF. When the ready supply of Lowestoft fishing vessels for conversion to safety standby duties dried up, Putford/Warbler started to scour the other major fishing ports for suitable vessels for conversion and Aberdeen was a good hunting ground, with many including the *Dreadnought, Northleigh, Oakleigh, Dawn Cloud, Gem, Pearl, Monarch* and *Saviour* coming from there. The *Oakleigh* was a sister ship to the *Mincarlo,* later to become the *Putford Merlin,* both trawlers having been built by the Brooke Marine shipyard at Lowestoft. *Dawn Gem* was of particular interest, having been specifically built for great lining as the *Glenstruan.* The line fishing vessels prospered for a

In addition to many fishing vessels, a number of supply ships have been acquired for use in the Boston Putford fleet and later sold on, as part of the ongoing policy of continuous improvement of the fleet. One such vessel was the *Pacific Shore*, seen here leaving Great Yarmouth in the 1970s. She was purchased in 1991 as the *Pacific Service*, and after conversion entered service as the safety standby vessel *Putford Teal*. In 1996 she was sold, and left Lowestoft on the 18th January.

while after the Second World War and the fleet fishing the Faeroe banks, Iceland and Greenland numbered about a dozen vessels, catching primarily halibut, cod, ling and tusk on the 20 miles of line shot each day. The Lowestoft drifter *Friendly Star* also engaged in this fishery for a while but with limited success.

In 1983 Simon Hashim joined the company, bringing with him a number of years experience in the offshore field, having worked for several of the major drilling companies in the North Sea and other parts of the world. A very significant milestone was reached in 1985 when Putford and Warbler bought a number of supply boats from the Zapata/Offshore Marine Fleet and the *Norfolk, Essex, Kent* and *Suffolk Service* became the *Dawn Shore, Putford Guardian, Putford Tern* and the already mentioned *Putford Skua.* These vessels were built for the North Sea and because of their

twin screws, bow thrusters and large open aft decks lent themselves ideally to the standby role, as they were highly manoeuvrable in the safety mode and were also able to move small pieces of equipment from platform to platform and hold reserve supplies of fuel and water in the field. Although there were no specific contracts for these ships when they were bought it was considered that they should find a niche in the future, and that the morale of crews would be enhanced by their more obvious role of giving a service to an installation, as well as improving crew comfort in the more spacious living quarters on a supply ship, which had been considerably upgraded.

These ships sparked another Putford innovation in the development of Daughter craft rescue boats.

A Boston Putford Daughter craft.

MOTHER/DAUGHTER STANDBY VESSELS
HISTORICAL BACKGROUND

There were three reasons for Putford pursuing the Daughter craft concept.

FIRSTLY, they had been asked on a number of occasions to station the standby vessels in a position to look after one platform whilst its rescue boat was sent away to look after divers/scaffolders at another platform. John Hashim and George Catchpole resisted this practice as it seemed unreasonable to keep boat crews away in small open boats for long periods and furthermore it restricted the operational efficiency of the standby boat to respond to a "man overboard" at a third or fourth platform.

SECONDLY, as more and more platforms were being installed in the Gas Basin, Putford foresaw that there would be more and more seasonal maintenance work and standby vessel owners would not be prepared to hold ships over the winter for just a few weeks or months work. Thus there would in the long term be insufficient standby vessels to cover the work, but a suitable daughter craft could do so in a very cost effective manner.

THIRDLY, the trawler standby boats were limited in the services that they were able to offer the oil companies, whereas a former

15

supply ship could offer a positive service in addition to the safety standby function, by holding supplies of fuel and water in the field, offering spare deck space for storage for the installations, as well as having the ability to move stores and equipment around within the field.

Above all, they would provide an ideal stable platform for launching Daughter craft. As a result of these factors Putford took the decision in 1985 to pioneer a Mother/Daughter project even though at the time there was no contract in view. In 1986 they achieved the hoped for break through when British Petroleum (BP) realised the potential in what they were doing and chartered the *Putford Tern* for their 1986 summer maintenance season on West Sole. The ship and PR 30 Daughter craft performed well and they re-chartered for 1987. In 1988, they uprated the vessel with fire fighting and increased survivor capacity to give extra safety cover during the West Sole platform modifications. BP at Easington was well pleased with the vessel and the overall Mother/Daughter concept.

Meanwhile, the *Putford Guardian*, built as a sister supply ship to the *Putford Tern*, had performed well for two years as a straight supply and standby vessel for Hamilton Brothers, servicing and moving equipment between the Esmond, Forbes and Gordon platforms. British Gas were made aware of the two vessels, so that when they were renewing their Rough Field standby contract, they specified a Mother/Daughter standby vessel based on a supply ship and a PR 30 Daughter craft. Putford therefore bought a further supply ship, the Star Offshore Services vessel *Star Pegasus,* and invited Boston Deep Sea to join them in the project. The contract was eventually awarded to Boston Putford with the *Star Pegasus,* by then converted and renamed *Blue Flame 1*. The *Blue Flame 1* became a very high specification standby vessel of overall length 204ft., beam 47.5ft., draught 15.5ft., 4800hp twin screws, 6.3tons bow thrust, Becker rudders, Poscon Joystick control, and full FF1 Fire Fighting capability.

The vessel went to work in April 1987 and was operated in the way that the *Putford Tern* and *Putford Guardian* had been used, and met with ready acceptance as she performed excellently the tasks that British Gas envisaged. A further change of identity occurred in 2000, when she became the *Putford Viking,* thus bringing her into line with the Putford naming policy and identifying Viking Standby Ltd. as the other part owner.

In 1988, Shell UK Exploration and Production at Lowestoft adopted the Mother/Daughter principle for their multi-installation Leman Field, and Boston Putford operated the Warbler Shipping owned former supply ship *Dawn Shore* in this role. Such was the satisfaction with the Mother/Daughter principle, that Shell called for another vessel for 1989, and the *Nova,* another former Offshore Marine supply ship, joined the *Dawn Shore* to give this very specialised cover in Shell's Indefatigable Field.

A further Mother/Daughter vessel, the Lowestoft built *Dawn Warbler*, followed in 1990.

In the same year, Putford added three newer and larger supply ships to their fleet in anticipation of a more stringent era in the standby safety vessel market and pursuing their policy of uprating their fleet.

These three supply vessels, which became the *Putford Apollo, Putford Ajax,* and *Putford Achates,* were all built for North Sea operations and joined the seven former supply ships that the Boston Putford group were already operating as safety vessels in the U.K. Gas Basin. These ships are particularly well suited to operating Daughter craft standby boats, which is the specialist safety system, developed and pioneered by Putford Enterprises. The ability of this type of vessel to manoeuvre up to a rig or platform in a safety role was well proven when the *Blue Flame 1* 'dry evacuated' the crew of the stricken drilling rig *Glomar Labrador One.*

This rescue was viewed with interest by a number of oil companies as well as the DOT and DOE as the evacuation could not be carried out by helicopters because the rig was so severely damaged.

The *Putford Apollo, Putford Ajax,* and *Putford Achates* were later joined by the *Putford Achilles,* which was the largest and most powerful Putford vessel at the time. They went into service in the fourth quarter of 1990 and early 1991, and were soon placed on their own dedicated contracts. During 1991, Putford acquired further vessels to improve and upgrade their fleet. These were again supply ships and became the *Putford Snipe* and *Putford Acasta,* and were followed in 1992 by the *Putford Athena* and *Putford Artemis* and a new PR 33 Daughter craft. The PR33 is a development and improvement on the PR 30 and was on charter before the end of 1992. Also, during 1991, Warbler Shipping acquired the Smit salvage vessel, *Smit Barracuda,* and she was their first conversion to the new standby code as the *Dawn Patrol.*

These ships were all acquired to meet the new and more stringent Standby Regulations prompted by the Cullen enquiry into the Piper Alpha disaster, which were published in July 1991, for full implementation by January 1993. Crews were trained for these ships and to meet the new regulations. There was no shortage of enthusiastic volunteers as the new role gave added interest for both those who man the ships themselves, and the specialist daughter craft rescue boats. With crews working one trip on and one trip off the whole job became more attractive in every way.

In 1992, it was estimated that the North Sea Oil and Gas Fields had at least a further 25 year life and therefore Putford and Warbler could look forward with great confidence.

For most of the first 25 years of Putford Enterprises Ltd., Graham Walford, as Superintendent Engineer, put together some ingenious conversions and kept the fleet well maintained and running reliably.

Ian Palmer joined in 1991 from Stirling Shipping as General Manager, to help lead them forward into the 21st century, supported by Robert Catchpole who joined in 1989 to become the third generation Catchpole to enter the business.

Keith Cowan, a very experienced supply ship Engineering Director, also joined the Company around this time and continued the task of converting and upgrading supply ships for the dual role service.

During 1993/4, it was decided to merge the Warbler Shipping and Putford Enterprise fleets, a result of which saw the renaming of vessels of the Warbler fleet. In the great majority of cases, the prefix "Dawn" was replaced by the prefix "Putford", which since the mid 1980s had been in use on Putford Enterprises vessels, including the now replaced converted trawlers, such as the *Putford Dart*, the former trawler *Boston Sea Dart*. One Warbler vessel not to see a change of prefix, but a completely new name was the *Dawn Patrol*,

The supply ship *Auriga Tide* was purchased in 1990, and after conversion became the *Putford Achilles*. Shortly after arriving at her new home port of Lowestoft, and before conversion had commenced, she is seen in the colours of Tidewater Mediterranean Inc., her previous owners. *Putford Achilles* was built as the tug/supply ship *Lady Vivien* by Allied Shipbuilders, North Vancouver in 1973.

which became the *Putford Puffin*. This was necessary because *Putford Patrol* would have been confused with another Putford vessel, the *Putford Petrel,* formerly the MAFF research vessel *Clione*.

Many vessels in the present Putford fleet are capable of dual role working, operating as safety vessels in addition to cargo carrying. Further development in safety operations continues, one of which is the introduction of larger stand-alone Daughter craft, able to operate without the immediate close support of a mother ship.

In 2000, Putford Enterprises was taken over by the large American offshore supply and service boat owner Seacor Smit Inc. They retained the management staff and added their own Veesea vessels to the fleet operated, managed, and marketed from the Lowestoft office of Boston Putford Offshore Safety Ltd. At that time, Seacor had a global fleet of over 300 ships and employed around 1750 people worldwide. Seacor went on in 2001, to buy a large British supply ship fleet, that of Stirling Shipping. Four of their modern top quality ships were also added to the Boston Putford fleet. Three underwent conversion to full dual role status for carrying out both safety standby and cargo work. These vessels were equipped with Daughter craft fast rescue boats and had a complete refit to meet the very latest Offshore Regulations.

The fourth vessel continued as a dedicated supply ship working for Boston Putford in the southern North Sea. These ships became *Putford Enterprise, Putford Protector, Putford Provider* and *Putford Voyager*. Registered at Lowestoft, they entered service with Boston Putford Offshore Safety Ltd. during 2002; three of the four are the largest vessels ever to serve in the fleet, even exceeding in length, the large stern trawlers which once played an important part in the evolution of Boston Putford.

In 2003, Seacor/Boston Putford was operating and managing a

The Lowestoft registered dual role *Putford Apollo* was an addition to the fleet in 1989, and entered service in 1990. She was visiting her homeport when this scene was recorded. Complete with her Daughter craft, *Putford Apollo* was taking a break from cable guard duties on which she was employed at the time. She has had a number of identities during her life including *Rig Mate, Mohamed* and *Mansel 23*.

fleet of 27 dual and single role vessels, some of which were on charter in the north, central and southern North Sea and also off the west coast. It remains one of the three largest fleets involved in offshore supply and standby work. Boston Putford ships are major users of the ports of Great Yarmouth and Lowestoft, where usually a few of the fleet can be seen daily. With their main office at Lowestoft, they have brought investment and employment, directly and indirectly, to Lowestoft and Great Yarmouth. The ships from their substantial fleet have in part replaced the vast fleets of herring drifters and trawlers which were once seen at these East Anglian ports and which are now just part of history, and to younger generations, something which was in the distant past. As with the drifters and trawlers of yesterday, today's offshore supply and standby vessels of the Boston Putford fleet are similarly dedicated to the harvest of the sea and seabed.

In 2000, in order to reflect more accurately the important work carried out by standby ships, the industry association was renamed The Emergency Response and Rescue Vessel Association, and the safety standby vessels themselves would in the future be known as Emergency Response and Rescue Vessels (ERRV's).

In September 2000, following a review of offshore rescue and recovery arrangements, BP Amoco put forward proposals, named Project Jigsaw, for consultation within the industry. If carried out these would replace ERRV's with four Super Puma helicopters stationed offshore and two onshore, with fast rescue craft provided on the offshore structures. Much concern was raised by these proposals which were seen as a major dilution and backward step in the offshore rescue capability, with cost reduction, not enhanced safety, being seen by many as the main reason for these proposals. The ERRV fleets of ten companies, including Boston Putford, totalling some 115 ships and around 3,000 personnel would be directly affected if Project Jigsaw were to be implemented .

One of the fine ships to join the Boston Putford fleet in 2002, the supply ship *Putford Provider* heads for Great Yarmouth on the 13th January 2003. This ship was previously the Bridgetown registered *Stirling Vega,* and transferred to the British flag following purchase and renaming. Prior to June 1996, *Putford Provider* was well known at Lowestoft, initially as the *Star Vega* and later as *Stirling Vega*, when she operated from the Shell base on Lake Lothing.

ASSOCIATED COMPANIES VESSELS

The following list gives details of some of the steam and diesel powered vessels that have been owned by four of the original five member companies of **Boston Putford Offshore Safety Ltd.**

This log should not be considered as being conclusive. There may be other vessels that have been owned, or partly owned, by companies or individuals which are now or have been associated with the organisation. It should be noted that details of smaller Warbler or Putford owned craft such as *BCK150 Ocean Reward, GY314 Maxwell, GY420 Quiet Waters, LK187 Celerity, Putford Progress, Putford Fulmar* and the many ship carried daughter and other fast rescue craft are not included. A number of vessels appear more than once, but with a different identity, this may reflect a change of ownership, a change in the naming policy of the company, or change of the identity before and after conversion from steam to diesel power. Please note that as with other maritime titles in this series, the date given for the selling, transferring between subsidiaries, or disposal of a vessel, may only be approximate; for business reasons the actual date may be subject to commercial confidence.

Explanation of columns

Name	The name carried by the vessel whilst part of the Boston Putford fleet, their associated companies or individual owners.
Fishing Registration	The fishing registration consisting of port letters and numbers. Explanation of the different port registrations can be found below in the "History" section.
Port Registration	The port of registration for vessels other than drifters and trawlers.
Vessel Type	As originally built
Official No.	The official number or identity of the vessel.
Call Sign	The registered radio call sign.
Gross/Net Tonnage	As recorded in official or company documentation. Given in British Imperial units and rounded to the nearest ton.
Dimensions	As recorded in official or company documentation. Given in British Imperial units and rounded to the nearest foot.
Construction	The type of material used for the construction of the majority of the vessel.
Propulsion Unit(s)	Main engine information.
Build Date	The year the vessel was completed.
Yard	The yard at which the vessel was built.
Location	The location of the yard. By request, the building yard number where known, has been included.
History	Highlights of the vessel's life, including changes in use. Particular emphasis is placed upon the time when she was Lowestoft owned, registered, or based. Included in this column may be the following: -

PORT DISTINGUISHING LETTERS				ABBREVIATIONS	
A	Aberdeen	AR	Ayr	AKD	A. K. Diesel
BCK	Buckie	BM	Brixham	BDSF	Boston Deep Sea Fisheries
FD	Fleetwood	GN	Granton	BUT	British United Trawlers
GW	Glasgow	GY	Grimsby	GMT	Grandi Motori Trieste
H	Hull	HD	Helder (Holland)	HMD	His Majesty's Drifter
HL	Hartlepool	IJM	Ymuiden	MAFF	Ministry of Agriculture, Fisheries & Food
INS	Inverness	J	Jersey	MFV	Motor Fishing Vessel
KY	Kirkcaldy	KW	Katwijk	MVS	Maritime Voluntary Service
LH	Leith	LK	Lerwick	PE	Putford Enterprises
LO	London	LT	Lowestoft	SSV	Safety Standby Vessel
M	Milford Haven	SN	North Shields		
YH	Yarmouth				

Name / Fish Registration / Port Registration	Vessel Type / Call Sign / RSS/ON	Gross Tonnage / Net Tonnage	Dimensions (ft) / Construction	Propulsion Unit(s) / Make	Build Date / Build Yard / Build Location	History
Ada Kirby LT72 Lowestoft	Drifter/ Trawler MBAF 187037	126 49	95 x 23 x 10 Wood	Diesel 1 x 3cyl 300hp AKD	1958 Summers Fraserburgh Yard No. 105	Built for Inshore Trawlers Ltd., Lowestoft 1968 Transferred to White Fish Authority 1969 Purchased by Putford Enterprises Ltd. 1969 Fishing registration cancelled 1969 Converted for use as a SSV 1976 Sold to Ada Kirby Charterers (CI) Ltd. 1976 In use as a cargo vessel / yacht 1981 Arrested off Corunna whilst smuggling 1981 Laid up in Corunna 1983 Registered as a ferro concrete/general cargo vessel 1983 Sank, raised and broken up at Corunna
Admiral Hawke A520	Trawler MEFG 302244	225 74	108 x 24 x 12 Steel	Diesel 1 x 5cyl 670hp National	1961 Hall Russell Aberdeen Yard No. 893	Built for Mannofield Fishing Co. Ltd., Aberdeen 1965 Transferred to Parbel-Smith Ltd., Aberdeen 1966 Transferred to Aberdeen Motor Trawlers Ltd. 1971 Sold to Bruce Stores Ltd., Aberdeen 1977 Sold to Hewett Fishing Co. Ltd., London 1981 Purchased jointly by PE and BDSF 1981 Sold to T. Cato, W. Clarke and W. Clarke Jnr. 1983 Sold to Scupham and Lace, Lowestoft 1983 Registered in the ownership of Scupham and Raven 1983 Became LT43 Diane-Elizabeth 1984 Sold to Breydon Marine Ltd. 1984 Fishing registration cancelled 1984 Renamed Breydon Eider 1984 Converted for use as a SSV 1992 Vessel sold to Marcial Lopez Lojo, Vigo 1992 Left Breydon Marine yard on 3rd April for Corunna.
Anna Christina Kirkcaldy	Trawler MXKS 187015	130 54	91 x 22 x 11 Steel	Diesel 1 x 6cyl 360hp Ruston	1957 Richards Lowestoft Yard No. 435	Refer to Putford Falcon for history
Ardenlea Kirkcaldy	Trawler/ Liner MHGR 302493	206 71	106 x 23 x 12 Steel	Diesel 1 x 8cyl 660hp Blackstone	1963 Livingstone Peterhead Yard No. 10	Refer to Dawn Cloud for history

Name Fish Registration Port Registration	Vessel Type Call Sign RSS/ON	Gross Tonnage Net Tonnage	Dimensions (ft) Construction	Propulsion Unit(s) Make	Build Date Build Yard Build Location	History
Arduous LT400	MFV GFXY 166717	116 49	88 x 22 x 10 Wood	Diesel 1 x 4cyl 240hp Crossley	1944 Richards Lowestoft Yard No. 326	Built as MFV 1506 for the Admiralty 1948 Sold to G. D. Claridge 1948 Arrived at Lowestoft 13th May for conversion 1948 Became LT400 Eta 1949 Transferred to Colne Fishing Co. Ltd. 1952 Transferred to Huxley Fishing Co. Ltd. 1952 Length reassessed to 92.5ft 1954 Used for drifting 1956 Purchased by Putford Enterprises Ltd. 1957 Renamed Arduous 1958 Re-engined with a 6cyl 360hp Ruston unit 1966 Advertised for sale 1968 In use as a SSV 1968 Laid up in November 1969 Sold for use as a houseboat, later hulked and buried at Oulton Broad
Bannockburn LT302	Trawler MXXL 187024	178 59	103 x 22 x 10 Steel	Diesel 1 x 6cyl 440hp Crossley	1957 Richards Lowestoft Yard No. 438	Built as Sutton Queen for Talisman Trawlers Ltd. 1971 Purchased by Putford Enterprises Ltd. 1971 Renamed Bannockburn 1972 Sold to Keithly Enterprises Ltd. 1972 Sold to Safetyships Ltd., Aberdeen 1972 Registered at Aberdeen 1972 Converted for use as a SSV 1977 Transferred to Christian Salvesen Ltd., Aberdeen 1979 Sold to Kitson Vickers & Sons, Blyth for scrapping
Bickleigh LT444	Trawler GJBE 302410	164 56	94 x 22 x 11 Steel	Diesel 1 x 6cyl 450hp Crossley	1962 Richards Lowestoft Yard No. 467	Built for Putford Enterprises Ltd 1971 Sold to Bickleigh Fishing Co. Ltd., Aberdeen 1971 Fishing registration changed to A201 1986 Sold to Demco Marine Co. Ltd., Pembroke Dock
Blue Flame I Aberdeen	Supply Ship GVOY 359109	1456 654	200 x 48 x 19 Steel	Diesel 2 x 12cyl 4800hp British Polar	1976 Ysselwerf Capelle (aft) Yard No. 166 Holliandsche Grootammers (fwd)	Refer to Putford Viking for history

Name Fish Registration Port Registration	Vessel Type Call Sign RSS/ON	Gross Tonnage Net Tonnage	Dimensions (ft) Construction	Propulsion Unit(s) Make	Build Date Build Yard Build Location	History
Boston Mosquito LT373	MFV MLDZ 185731	115 48	90 x 22 x 10 Wood	Diesel 1 x 4cyl 240hp Crossley	1943 Richards Lowestoft Yard No. 324	Built as MFV1504 for the Admiralty 1948 Sold to G. W. B. Leslie, Cults, Aberdeenshire 1948 Became LK497 Betty Leslie 1960 Sold to BDSF 1960 Modernised and re-engined with 5cyl 375hp Ruston 1961 Became LT373 Boston Mosquito 1966 Transferred to Looker Fishing Co. Ltd. 1967 In use on SSV work 1967 Transferred to joint ownership of Looker Fishing Co. Ltd. and Putford Enterprises Ltd. in December 1970 In use on SSV work 1972 Sold to Mrs. L. Rodger, Blofield 1973 Became April Diamond 1973 Detained by Dutch Authorities at Scheveningen 1976 Sold for scrapping
Boston Sea Dart LT94	Stern Trawler GQEQ 342103	312 109	109 x 27 x 11 Steel	Diesel 1 x 6cyl 910hp Ruston	1972 MacLean Renfrew Yard No. 5008	Refer to Putford Dart for history
Boston Whirlwind LT454 Lowestoft	Trawler GHVQ 303678	165 61	93 x 22 x 11 Steel	Diesel 1 x 5cyl 475hp National	1962 Richards Lowestoft Yard No. 466	Built for F & T Ross Ltd., Hull 1974 Ownership transferred to BDSF 1974 Used as a SSV 1979 Fishing registration cancelled 1979 Transferred into joint ownership of PE and BDSF 1986 Sold to Parafleet Ltd., Plymouth 1986 Allocated fishing registration of LT 454 1987 Sold to John Swift, Scarborough 1988 Owned by Parafleet Ltd. 1995 Sold to Erida Ltd. 1996 Sold to Jovina Ltd. 1996 Became TN32 Sea Venturer
Boston Widgeon LT427	Trawler GHTL 302408	165 61	93 x 22 x 10 Steel	Diesel 1 x 5cyl 475hp National	1961 Richards Lowestoft Yard No. 464	Refer to Breydon Widgeon for history

Name Fish Registration Port Registration	Vessel Type Call Sign RSS/ON	Gross Tonnage Net Tonnage	Dimensions (ft) Construction	Propulsion Unit(s) Make	Build Date Build Yard Build Location	History
Breydon Eider Aberdeen	Trawler MEFG 302244	225 74	108 x 24 x 12 Steel	Diesel 1 x 5cyl 670hp National	1961 Hall Russell Aberdeen Yard No. 893	Refer to Admiral Hawke for history
Breydon Mallard Lowestoft	Trawler GHVP 302409	165 61	93 x 22 x 10 Steel	Diesel 1 x 5cyl 475hp National	1962 Richards Lowestoft Yard No. 465	Built as LT445 Boston Beaver for BDSF 1966 Transferred to Looker Fishing Co. Ltd 1978 Sold to Breydon Marine Ltd. 1978 Fishing registration cancelled 1978 Converted for use as a SSV 1978 Renamed Breydon Mallard 1987 Sold to Anglo Spanish owner Pamora Ltd. 1987 Left Gt.Yarmouth for Grimsby on 12th March 1987 Converted back to a fishing vessel 1987 Allocated fishing number LT131 2001 Owners reported to be in receivership

Breydon Widgeon
LH80
Leith
	Trawler
	GHTL
	302408
		165
		61
			93 x 22 x 10
			Steel
				Diesel
				1 x 5cyl
				475hp
				National
					1961
					Richards
					Lowestoft
					Yard No. 464
						Built as LT427 Boston Widgeon for Major A.
						    Suddaby MBE and B. Parkes OBE
						1965 Transferred to Near Water Trawlers Ltd.
						1973 Sold to Joe Croan, Leith
						1973 Allocated fishing registration LH80
						1974 Sold to Breydon Marine Ltd.
						1974 Renamed Breydon Widgeon
						1976 Fishing registration cancelled
						1976 Converted for use as a SSV
						1987 Allocated fishing registration LH141
						1990 Operated by Wherry Fish Selling Co. Ltd.
						1990 Advertised for sale
						1992 Port registry changed to Lowestoft
						1992 Sold and left Lowestoft on 4th September
						1994 Sold to Greek owners and converted to
						    yacht Navi

Chudleigh LT231 Lowestoft	Trawler GHYH 302492	219 71	109 x 24 x 12 Steel	Diesel 1 x 6cyl 785hp Ruston	1962 Livingstone Peterhead Yard No. 9	Built as GN77 Granton Harrier for W. Carnie Ltd. 1970 Transferred to BUT (Scotland) Ltd. 1976 Purchased by Putford Enterprises Ltd. 1976 Became LT231 Chudleigh 1986 Fishing registration cancelled 1986 Fully converted for use as a SSV 1993 Sold to Holland for use as a charter vessel 2001 Reported to be at Ijmuiden

Name Fish Registration Port Registration	Vessel Type Call Sign RSS/ON	Gross Tonnage Net Tonnage	Dimensions (ft) Construction	Propulsion Unit(s) Make	Build Date Build Yard Build Location	History

Dauntless Star
LT367
	Drifter/
	Trawler
	MAUH
	166711
		133
		42
			97 x 21 x 9
			Steel
				Diesel
				1 x 6cyl
				350hp
				Crossley
					1948
					Cochrane
					Selby
					Yard No. 1332
						Built as LT 377 Sunlit Waters for F. E. Catchpole
						    and equipped with an engine recovered from
						    a minesweeper obtained for that purpose
						1951 Sold to BDSF
						1952 Renamed Boston Swift
						1952 Re-engined
						1954 Transferred to Mercury F. Co., Halifax, NS
						1954 Allocated fishing registration Halifax 2
						1957 Sold to Craig Stores Ltd., Aberdeen
						1957 Became A143 Swiftburn
						1958 Sold to Star Drift Fishing Co. Ltd., Lowestoft
						1958 Became LT367 Dauntless Star
						1960 Re-engined with 6cyl 474bhp Crossley unit
						1961 Star Drift merged with BDSF
						1966 Left Lowestoft in October under charter to
						    Triton Savage & Towage Co. Ltd.
						1968 Sold to United Towing Co. Ltd.
						1969 Sold to G. F. West and A. & F. Reid
						1970 In the ownership of John Reid, Gardenstown
						1971 Sold to P. Catchpole, J. Hashim and others
						1976 Sold to R. J. Brookes, Ipswich
						1977 Vessel taken to the United Arab Emirates for
						    use by Mohammed Ali as a water carrier
						    to the oil industry in Dubai.

Dawn Blazer London	Supply Ship GOYN 307975	854 387	188 x 38 x 11 Steel	Diesel 2 x 8cyl 1600hp Blackstone	1965 Hall Russell Aberdeen Yard No. 927	Refer to Putford Blazer for history

Name Fish Registration Port Registration	Vessel Type Call Sign RSS/ON	Gross Tonnage Net Tonnage	Dimensions (ft) Construction	Propulsion Unit(s) Make	Build Date Build Yard Build Location	History
Dawn Cloud Kirkcaldy	Trawler/ Liner MHGR 302493	206 71	106 x 23 x 12 Steel	Diesel 1 x 8cyl 660hp Blackstone	1963 Livingstone Peterhead Yard No. 10	Built as GN75 Jarlshof for Buchan Motor Trawlers 1966 Sold to Craig Stores (Aberdeen) Ltd. 1966 Became A805 Ardenlea 1975 Fishing registration cancelled 1975 Converted for use as a SSV 1976 Transferred to BUT (Aberdeen) Ltd. 1980 Sold to Robert C. M. Patrick and others 1980 Converted back to a fishing vessel 1980 Allocated fishing registration KY194 1984 Sold to Seaward Safetyships Ltd. 1984 Fishing registration cancelled 1984 Fully converted for use as a SSV 1986 Sold to Warbler Shipping Co. Ltd. 1986 Renamed Dawn Cloud 1987 Sold to Paolo Giacalone and renamed Rosalba G
Dawn Flight Aberdeen	RoRo Ferry GYIO 377908	468 156	187 x 31 x 10 Steel	Diesel 1 x 6cyl 800hp Atlas MaK	1967 Felszegi Trieste Yard No. 86	Built as Rapillo for Det Forenede Dampskib Selskab A/S 1967 Renamed Tumlingen 1974 Sold to Rederiet Lindinger N/S 1974 Became Lindinger Surveyor 1979 Sold to Salvesen Offshore Services Ltd., Aberdeen 1979 Renamed Falkirk 1979 Converted for use as a SSV 1984 Sold to Warbler Shipping Co. Ltd. 1984 Renamed Dawn Flight 1991 Sold to new owners in Holland. 1992 Became Albatros (of Kingston)
Dawn Gem Aberdeen	Trawler/ Liner MYBL 300357	183 62	106 x 23 x 11 Steel	Diesel 1 x 6cyl 540hp Ruston	1958 Mitchell Peterhead Yard No. 1	Built as A200 Glenstruan for Glenstruan Fishing Co. Ltd. 1972 Sold to P.F., G.A. & F.E.Catchpole, & J.R.Hashim 1975 Transferred to Warbler Fishing Co. Ltd. 1976 Fishing registration closed 1976 Fully converted for use as a SSV 1981 Renamed Dawn Gem 1984 Transferred to Wavetask Ltd. 2002 Reported as being moored on the River Medina and owned by Dawn Gem Endeavours Ltd.

Name Fish Registration Port Registration	Vessel Type Call Sign RSS/ON	Gross Tonnage Net Tonnage	Dimensions (ft) Construction	Propulsion Unit(s) Make	Build Date Build Yard Build Location	History
Dawn Hunter Lowestoft	Research MDIV 301534	40 16	51 x 17 x 7 Wood	Diesel 1 x 4cyl 114hp Gardner	1960 Jones Buckie	Built as LT242 Tellina for the MAFF 1982 Sold to Warbler Fishing Co. Ltd. 1982 Renamed Dawn Hunter 1982 In use as an inshore survey vessel 1984 Sold to J. C. Cole, Whitby

Dawn Monarch
 	
Aberdeen
	Trawler
	MEDZ
	303202
		237
		67
			115 x 25 x 12
			Steel
				Diesel
				1 x 8cyl
				660hp
				Blackstone
					1961
					Harris
					Appledore
					Yard No. 505
						Built as A525 Jacamar for Ashley Fishing Co. Ltd.
						1963 Sold to P. & J. Johnstone Ltd.
						1965 Transferred to Johnstone Motor Trawlers Ltd.
						1970 Transferred to Glenstruan Fishing Co. Ltd.
						1973 Transferred to Forward Motor Trawlers Ltd.
						1975 Fishing Registration cancelled
						1975 Fully converted for use as a SSV
						1980 Purchased by Warbler Fishing Co. Ltd. in March
						1981 Renamed Dawn Monarch
						1992 Sold and left Lowestoft for Plymouth on
						    10th January
						2002 Reported as being converted into a houseboat and
						    moored near Exeter

Dawn Patrol Lowestoft	Salvage Ship PHOI 426722	661 198	149 x 39 x 15 Steel	Diesel 2 x 6cyl 1441hp Deutz	1970 Bodewes Foxhol Yard No. 168	Refer to Putford Puffin for history
Dawn Pearl Aberdeen	Trawler MEEY 302247	214 77	106 x 23 x 12 Steel	Diesel 1 x 8cyl 550hp Blackstone	1961 Lewis Aberdeen Yard No. 302	Built as A554 Eredene for Glendee Fishing Co. Ltd. 1971 Sold to Beaconhill Fishing Co. Ltd. 1974 Re-engined 1981 Sold to N.P.F. Ltd., Lowestoft 1981 Renamed Dawn Pearl 1981 Fishing Registration cancelled 1981 Converted for use as a SSV 1986 Sold to Vincentpride Ltd., Milford Haven 1987 Converted for use as a fishing vessel 1987 Allocated fishing registration A554 1987 Renamed Uxia 1993 Became AR864 Shark 1996 Sold to Floatmate Ltd.

Name Fish Registration Port Registration	Vessel Type Call Sign RSS/ON	Gross Tonnage Net Tonnage	Dimensions (ft) Construction	Propulsion Unit(s) Make	Build Date Build Yard Build Location	History
Dawn Saviour Lowestoft	Trawler GHBU 301593	281 94	121 x 26 x 13 Steel	Diesel 1 x 4cyl 640hp British Polar	1960 John Lewis Aberdeen Yard No. 293	Built as A417 Clova for Clova Fishing Co. Ltd (BUT) 1975 Fishing registration cancelled 1975/6 Converted for use as a SSV 1982 In the ownership of George Craig and Sons Ltd 1982 Sold to Colne Shipping Co. Ltd 1982 Renamed Saltrou, port of registry Lowestoft 1987 Sold to Warbler Shipping Co. Ltd. in December 1987 Renamed Dawn Saviour 1987 Re-engined with 8cyl 660hp Blackstone 1993 Sold to Middle East interests 1993 Renamed Seaguard 1993 Left Lowestoft on 4th July bound for Israel
Dawn Shore Rochester	Supply Ship GVXE 333522	499 173	160 x 35 x 13 Steel	Diesel 2 x 6cyl 1599hp Blackstone	1967 Ijsselwerf Rotterdam Yard No. 132	Refer to Putford Shore for history.
Dawn Sky Lowestoft	Research Vessel GWMA 309505	459 117	132 x 32 x 12 Steel	Diesel 2 x 6cyl 1060hp Allen	1967 Brooke Marine Oulton Broad Lowestoft Yard No. 325	Refer to Putford Sky for history

| Name | Vessel Type | Gross Tonnage | Dimensions (ft) | Propulsion | Build Date | History |
| Fish Registration | Call Sign | Net Tonnage | Construction | Unit(s) | Build Yard | |
Port Registration	RSS/ON			Make	Build Location	
Dawn Spray Lowestoft	Drifter/ Trawler GQBK 185677	114 46	88 x 20 x 10 Steel	Diesel 1 x 6cyl 360hp Ruston	1952 Richards Lowestoft Yard No. 410	Built as YH61 Ocean Starlight for Bloomfields Ltd. 1963 Purchased by Small & Co. (Lowestoft) Ltd. 1963 Allocated fishing registration LT465 1967 Sold to J.Beok (of Ijmuiden) 1967 Became KW38 Neptunus 1970 Sold to J. Van Lear (of Ijmuiden) 1970 Fishing registration cancelled 1970 Converted for use as a SSV 1972 Sold and became Dolphijn 1972 Sold to P.F., G.A. & F.E.Catchpole & J.R.Hashim 1972 Became LT465 Stoic 1975 Transferred to Warbler Fishing Co. Ltd. 1976 Fishing registration cancelled 1976 Fully converted for use as a SSV 1981 Renamed Dawn Spray 1987 Sold to Norrard Trawlers Ltd., Milford Haven 1987 Allocated fishing registration LT465 1992 Under detention and for sale at Milford Haven 1995 Sold for scrapping
Dawn Warbler Lowestoft	Trawler GHMF 302398	198 62	107 x 23 x 9 Steel	Diesel 1 x 6cyl 550hp Crossley	1961 Brooke Marine Oulton Broad Lowestoft Yard No. 280	Built as LT363 Carlton Queen for Talisman Trawlers 1971 Re-engined with 6cyl 900hp British Polar unit 1975 Sold to Warbler Shipping Co. Ltd. 1975 Renamed Warbler 1976 Fishing registration cancelled 1976 Fully converted for use as a SSV 1981 Renamed Dawn Warbler 1986 Sold to Laira Fishing Co. Ltd. 1986 Allocated fishing registration LT363 1986 Renamed Autumn Swallow 1986 Allocated fishing registration FD363 1993 Sold to Searanger Ltd. 1994 Became M363 Sea Horse 1999 Renamed Dawn Warbler 2001 Transferred to ownership of Crystal Fishing Co. Ltd. 2001 Renamed Crystal

Name Fish Registration Port Registration	Vessel Type Call Sign RSS/ON	Gross Tonnage Net Tonnage	Dimensions (ft) Construction	Propulsion Unit(s) Make	Build Date Build Yard Build Location	History
Dawn Warbler London	Supply Ship GOYO 308166	697 228	158 x 36 x 15 Steel	Diesel 2 x 8cyl 1600hp Blackstone	1966 Brooke Marine Oulton Broad Lowestoft Yard No. 332	Refer to Putford Warbler for history

Dawn Waters
LT377
	Beam
	Trawler
	GUCX
	362625
		99
		35
			85 x 20
			Steel
				Diesel
				1 x 6cyl
				500hp
				Kromhout
					1967
					Visser
					Den Helder
					Yard No. 53
						Built as HD26 Hoop Op Zegen for Bakker Bros.,
						       Den Helder
						1973 Sold to BDSF
						1973 Became FD263 Boston Islander
						1976 Sold to Paul & Gibbs, Lowestoft
						1976 Renamed PG Islander
						1977 Sold to Warbler Fishing Co. Ltd.
						1977 Became LT377 Dawn Waters
						1979 Sold to Isle of Man owners
						1979 Allocated registration AR72
						1982 Sold to A.M. Seafoods Ltd., Fleetwood
						     and G. Burns, Kirkcudbright
						1982 Allocated registration J472

Dreadnought A377	Trawler GGWH 301590	163 54	94 x 22 x 10 Steel	Diesel 1 x 6cyl 486hp Ruston	1960 Herd & Mackenzie Buckie Yard No. 174	Refer to Putford Harrier for history
Eastleigh LT76	Trawler GZJR 189036	238 81	111 x 24 x 12 Steel	Diesel 1 x 6cyl 660hp Widdop	1956 John Lewis Aberdeen Yard No. 260	Laid down as Boston Britannia for BDSF 1956 Completed as Acadia Snowbird for Acadia Fisheries Ltd., Halifax, Nova Scotia 1960 Allocated fishing registration St. Johns 45 1968 Transferred to BDSF 1968 Allocated fishing registration LT76 1968 Renamed Boston Harrier 1972 Purchased by Putford Enterprises Ltd 1972 Became Eastleigh 1972 In use on SSV duties 1976 Sold to Scott Marco Ltd., Dundee for scrapping

| Name | Vessel Type | Gross Tonnage | Dimensions (ft) | Propulsion | Build Date | History |
| Fish Registration | Call Sign | Net Tonnage | Construction | Unit(s) | Build Yard | |
Port Registration	RSS/ON			Make	Build Location	
Eredene	Trawler	214	106 x 23 x 12	Diesel	1961	Refer to Dawn Pearl for history
	MEEY	77	Steel	1 x 8cyl	Lewis	
Aberdeen	302247			550hp	Aberdeen	
				Blackstone	Yard No. 302	
Eta	MFV	116	88 x 22 x 10	Diesel	1944	Refer to Arduous for history
LT400	GFXY	49	Wood	1 x 4cyl	Richards	
	166717			240hp	Lowestoft	
				Crossley	Yard No. 326	
Glenstruan	Trawler/	183	106 x 23 x 11	Diesel	1958	Refer to Dawn Gem for history
A200	Liner	62	Steel	1 x 6cyl	Mitchell	
	MYBL			540hp	Peterhead	
	300357			Ruston	Yard No. 1	
Granton Harrier	Trawler	219	109 x 24 x 12	Diesel	1962	Refer to Chudleigh for history
GN77	GHYH	71	Steel	1 x 6cyl	Livingstone	
Granton	302492			785hp	Peterhead	
				Ruston	Yard No. 9	
Granton Merlin	Trawler	235	108 x 24 x 12	Diesel	1960	Refer to Umberleigh for history
GN72	GHDD	77	Steel	1 x 5cyl	Hall Russell	
Granton	300604			705hp	Aberdeen	
				Ruston	Yard No. 886	
Granton Osprey	Trawler	230	109 x 24 x 12	Diesel	1960	Refer to Putford Osprey for history.
GN19	GFPH	78	Steel	1 x 6cyl	Scarr	
Granton	300603			720hp	Hessle	
				Ruston	Yard No. 769	
Hatherleigh	Trawler	202	107 x 23 x 12	Diesel	1961	Built as LT395 Suffolk Punch for Small & Co. (LT) Ltd.
LT395	MEET	66	Steel	1 x 6cyl	Richards	1974 Purchased by Putford Enterprises Ltd.
Lowestoft	302400			550hp	Lowestoft	1975 Renamed Hatherleigh
				Ruston	Yard No. 461	1981 Converted for use as a SSV
						1981 Fishing registration cancelled
						1992 Purchased by Pindar plc
						1993 Port registration changed in Sept. to Scarborough
						2001 In use as a hospitality vessel, and by the MVS
						2002 Reported as being at Portsmouth and for sale
						2003 Visited Lowestoft during April

Name Fish Registration Port Registration	Vessel Type Call Sign RSS/ON	Gross Tonnage Net Tonnage	Dimensions (ft) Construction	Propulsion Unit(s) Make	Build Date Build Yard Build Location	History
Iago BM20	MFV MGNS 166928	112 48	92 x 22 x 11 Wood	Diesel 1 x 4cyl 240hp Crossley	1946 Rowhedge Wivenhoe Yard No. 47	Refer to Moreleigh for history

Idena
A793
Aberdeen
	Trawler
	GNWY
	185288
		296
		102
			128 x 27 x 13
			Steel
				Diesel
				1 x 7cyl
				773hp
				Mirrlees
					1953
					Cook, Welton
					& Gemmell
					Beverley
					Yard No. 856
						Built as FD136 for J. Marr & Son Ltd., Fleetwood
						1959 Lengthened to 136ft, with new tonnages of
						    317gross and 108nett
						1967 Transferred to Ranger Fishing Co. Ltd., Aberdeen
						1968 Fishing registration changed to A793
						1971 Purchased by Putford Enterprises Ltd.
						1972-74 Used for both fishing and SSV work from
						    Lowestoft
						1974 Sold for scrapping to Pounds Shipbreakers &
						    Shipbrokers Ltd., Portsmouth
						1974 Sold to Safetyships Ltd., Aberdeen
						1974 Work in hand to fully convert for use as a SSV
						1975 Renamed Falkirk
						1978 Sold to George Craig & Sons Ltd., Aberdeen
						1980 Renamed Grampian Falcon
						1986 Sold to Clipper Promotions and associates, for
						    conversion to a sailing vessel
						1986 Renamed Miami Clipper, later arrested at Penzance
						1988 The remains of the vessel broken up at Penzance

Jacamar A525 Aberdeen	Trawler MEDZ 303202	237 67	115 x 25 x 12 Steel	Diesel 1 x 8cyl 660hp Blackstone	1961 Harris Appledore Yard No. 505	Refer to Dawn Monarch for history
Jean-Marthe FD233	Trawler MCHY 301880	187 67	117 x 23 x 15 Steel	Diesel 1 x 6cyl 450hp Burmeister & Wain	1948 Bath Iron. Bath, Maine USA	Built for French Government under Marshall Aid Scheme 1950 Sold to Societe Les Doris, Boulogne 1960 Sold to Dalby Steam Fishing Co. Ltd., Fleetwood 1960 Allocated fishing registration FD233 1960 Re-engined with 6cyl 450hp Ruston unit 1971 Purchased by Putford Enterprises Ltd. 1976 Sold to T. G. Darling Ltd for scrapping

Name Fish Registration Port Registration	Vessel Type Call Sign RSS/ON	Gross Tonnage Net Tonnage	Dimensions (ft) Construction	Propulsion Unit(s) Make	Build Date Build Yard Build Location	History
London Town LO70	Trawler GFRU 301043	228 79	108 x 24 x 12 Steel	Diesel 1 x 6cyl 484hp Mirrlees	1960 Cook, Welton & Gemmell Beverley Yard No. 955	Built for Hewett Fishing Co. Ltd., London 1981 Purchased jointly by PE and BDSF 1981 Sold to G. Antoniazzi, Milford Haven 1984 Sold to Huxley Fishing Co. Ltd. Lowestoft 1984 Fishing registration cancelled 1984 Converted for use as a SSV and renamed Guana 1987 Sold to Pesca Fisheries Ltd. Milford Haven 1987 Allocated fishing registration LT 378 1987 Left Lowestoft on 30th July

Lord Keith
LT181
	Drifter/
	Trawler
	GYQD
	149243
		124
		51
			92 x 20 x 9
			Steel
				Diesel
				1 x 4cyl
				360hp
				Ruston
					1930
					Goole SBR
					Goole
					Yard No.292
						Built for Lowestoft Steam Herring Drifters Ltd.
						1939 Requisitioned by Admiralty for auxiliary patrol use
						1939 Allocated pennant number FY1884
						1943 Sold to St. Andrews Steam Fishing Co. Ltd.
						1945 Returned to owner in December
						1947 Sold to W. H. Kerr (Ship Chandlers) Ltd.
						1957 300hp triple Burrell steam engine and associated
						    boiler replaced by a 4cyl 360hp Ruston diesel at
						    Richards Ironworks Ltd.
						1957 Tonnages changed to 124 gross and 51 net
						1971 Sold to Keithly Enterprises Ltd.
						1971 In use on SSV duties
						1975 Sold to Cypriot owners and later reported as being
						    converted to a refrigerated stern trawler

Margaret Christina LT331 Lowestoft	Trawler GHDY 302388	137 48	92 x 22 x 9 Steel	Diesel 1 x 6cyl 360hp Ruston	1960 Richards Lowestoft Yard No. 459	Built for East Anglian Ice & Cold Storage Co. Ltd. 1969 Transferred to Small & Co. (Lowestoft) Ltd. 1970 Sold to Southern Marine Ltd., Malahide 1970 Fishing registration cancelled, registered at Dublin 1971 Sold to Putford Enterprises Ltd. 1971 Allocated fishing registration LT331 1975 Converted for use as a SSV 1975 Fishing registration cancelled 1983 Sank near Leman Bank on 12th September 1983 Wreck raised due to being near undersea gas pipe 1983 Taken to Rotterdam for scrapping by Taklift 4 1983 Arrived on 22nd October
Mincarlo LT412 Lowestoft	Trawler GHXB 303677	166 56	98 x 22 x 9 Steel	Diesel 1 x 5cyl 500hp AKD	1962 Brooke Marine Oulton Broad Yard No. 281	Refer to Putford Merlin for history

Name Fish Registration Port Registration	Vessel Type Call Sign RSS/ON	Gross Tonnage Net Tonnage	Dimensions (ft) Construction	Propulsion Unit(s) Make	Build Date Build Yard Build Location	History
Monkleigh Hartlepool	Drifter/ Trawler MCBU 301520	160 57	97 x 22 x 9 Steel	Diesel 1 x 8cyl 405hp Blackstone	1959 Richards Lowestoft Yard No. 450	Built as LT277 Valiant Star for Star Drift Fishing Co. Ltd 1972 Renamed Boston Valiant 1972 Sold to Albert Fishing Co. Ltd., West Hartlepool 1972 Became HL10 Cleveland 1978 Sold to Putford Enterprises Ltd. 1979 Fishing registration cancelled 1979 Converted for use as a SSV 1979 Renamed Monkleigh 1989 Sold for further non-fishing use.
Moreleigh LT170	MFV MGNS 166928	112 48	92 x 22 x 11 Wood	Diesel 1 x 4cyl 240hp Crossley	1946 Rowhedge Wivenhoe Yard No. 47	Built as MFV 1545 for Admiralty 1946 Completed as BM20 Iago for Fleetwood Drifters 1951 Transferred to Torbay Trawlers Ltd., Brixham 1958 Sold to Putford Enterprises Ltd. 1958 Re-engined with 6cyl 335hp Ruston 1959 Became LT170 Moreleigh 1965 Sold to Albert Fishing Co. Ltd., West Hartlepool 1965 Fishing registration changed to HL160 1972 Sold to Edith Szlukovinyi, Darlington 1974 Sold to E. Salthouse and J.R. Bracenbury 1978 Hulked at Fleetwood
Northleigh Aberdeen	Trawler GVXR 300167	211 75	107 x 23 x 12 Steel	Diesel 1 x 6cyl 540hp Ruston	1957 Livingston Peterhead Yard No. 2	Built as GW4 Teresa Watterton for Inch Fishing Co. Ltd. 1958 Sold to Inch Motor Fishing Co. Ltd., Granton 1958 Became GN17 Granton Kestrel 1963 Sold to George Wood (Aberdeen) Ltd. 1963 Became A735 Emma Wood 1974 Sold to Putford Enterprises Ltd. 1974 Fishing registration cancelled 1974 Renamed Northleigh 1974 Fully converted for use as a SSV 1987 Sold to Jay MacKay, Scrabstar 1987 Converted back to a trawler 1987 Allocated fishing registration A43 1990 In the ownership of Northleigh Fishing Co. Ltd. 1993 In use as a SSV, with fishing registration A43 2000 Used as a cableguard vessel, registered at Aberdeen 2002 Reported to be at Poole during September

Name Fishing Registration Port Registration	Vessel Type Call Sign RSS/ON	Gross Tonnage Net Tonnage	Dimensions (ft) Construction	Propulsion Unit(s) Make	Build Date Build Yard Build Location	History
Nova London	Tug/Supply Ship GZKG 337908	677 272	177 x 38 x 15 Steel	Diesel 2 x 12cyl 2400hp Blackstone	1969 Cochrane Selby Yard No. 1525	Built as Nova Shore for Offshore Marine Ltd. 1980 Offshore Marine taken over by Zapata Corp. 1980 Renamed Nova Service 1988 Purchased jointly by Britannia/Putford/ Warbler 1988 Renamed Nova 1988 Converted for use as a SSV 2002 Vessel jointly owned by Viking/ PE 2002 Working as a single role SSV
Oakleigh Aberdeen	Trawler MEDF 303208	166 56	98 x 23 x 9 Steel	Diesel 1 x 5cyl 500hp AKD	1961 Brooke Marine Oulton Broad Yard No. 285	Built as A546 Wilronwood for G.Wood (Aberdeen) 1978 Purchased by Putford Enterprises Ltd. 1978 Fishing registration closed 1978 Converted for use as SSV 1979 Renamed Oakleigh 1981 Re-engined with a 8cyl 438hp Lister unit 1992 Sold to Marcial Lopez Lojo, Vigo 1992 Arrested for smuggling off Brazil in June
Ocean Scimitar Lowestoft	Trawler GCKH 301514	135 45	92 x 22 x 10 Steel	Diesel 1 x 6cyl 360hp Ruston	1959 Richards Lowestoft Yard No. 446	Refer to Putford Scimitar for history
Paramount A309 Aberdeen	Trawler GFGE 301575	250 80	115 x 25 x 13 Steel	Diesel 1 x 6cyl 760hp Mirrlees	1959 Mitchison Gateshead Yard No. 94	Refer to Putford Eagle for history
Planter London	Tug	38	55 x 15 x 8 Steel	Diesel 1 x 8cyl 420hp Rolls Royce	1967 Cook Wivenhoe	Built as Planter for Port of London Authority Later sold and became Batty 1984 Purchased by Putford Enterprises Ltd 1984 Arrived at Lowestoft on 29th July 1985 Renamed Planter during March
Putford Acasta Lowestoft	Supply Ship MPNX2 720162	878 263	185 x 39 x 17 Steel	Diesel 2 x 12cyl 1400hp MWM	1972 Baatservice Arendal Yard No. 605	1972 Built as Ellerntor 1989 Sold and became Cumbrae 1991 Purchased by Putford Enterprises Ltd. 1991 Arrived at Lowestoft on 6th June 1991 Renamed Putford Acasta 2002 Sold to Al Dowari, Kuwait 2002 Left Lowestoft on 26th October

Name Fishing Registration Port Registration	Vessel Type Call Sign RSS/ON	Gross Tonnage Net Tonnage	Dimensions (ft) Construction	Propulsion Unit(s) Make	Build Date Build Yard Build Location	History
Putford Achates Lowestoft	Supply Ship MLDJ9 714610	1043 312	176 x 39 x 18 Steel	Diesel 2 x 6cyl 2400hp MaK	1976 Danneborg Aarhus Yard No. 165	Built as Maersk Leader 1983 Sold and became Bin Jabr 1 1987 Sold and became Maersk Tanis 1989 Purchased by Putford Enterprises Ltd. 1989 Renamed Putford Achates 1989 Converted for use as a SSV 2002 Working as a dual role SSV/cargo vessel
Putford Achilles Lowestoft	Tug/Supply Ship MMNK8 720130	1179 353	191 x 43 x 20 Steel	Diesel 4 x 6cyl 4198hp Polar	1973 Allied N. Vancouver Yard No. 183	Built as Lady Vivien 1974 Became Vivien Tide 1984 Became Auriga Tide 1988 In the ownership of Tidewater Mediterranean Inc. 1990 Purchased by Putford Enterprises Ltd. 1990 Arrived at Lowestoft on 22nd April 1990 Renamed Putford Achilles 1990 Major refit carried out by Richards at Lowestoft 1990 Converted for use as a SSV 2002 Working as a dual role SSV/cargo vessel
Putford Ajax Lowestoft	Supply Ship MLRD6 714611	1043 312	176 x 39 x 18 Steel	Diesel 2 x 6cyl 2400hp MaK	1976 Danneborg Aarhus Yard No. 166	Built as Maersk Logger 1983 Sold and became Bin Jabr 2 1987 Sold and became Maersk Tanta 1989 Purchased by Putford Enterprises Ltd. 1989 Renamed Putford Ajax 1999 Converted for dual role working 2002 Working as a dual role SSV/cargo vessel
Putford Apollo Lowestoft	Tug/Supply Ship MHPX7 714609	868 260	185 x 36 x 16 Steel	Diesel 2 x 6cyl 2310hp Nohab Polar	1975 Voldnes Fosnavaag Yard No. 14	Built as Rig Mate 1979 Sold and became Mohamed 1987 Became Mansel 23 1989 Purchased by Putford Enterprises Ltd. 1989 Renamed Putford Apollo 2002 Working as a dual role SSV/cargo vessel
Putford Aries Lowestoft	Supply Ship GWAS 369115	1829 548	220 x 48 x 19 Steel	Diesel 2 x 12cyl 4800 hp British Polar	1977 Ysselwerf Capelle Yard No. 167	Built as Star Aries for Star Offshore Services 1996 Sold and became Stirling Aries 1996 Purchased by Putford Enterprises Ltd. 1996 Renamed Putford Aries 1996 Vessel upgraded 2002 Working as a dual role SSV/cargo vessel

Name Fishing Registration Port Registration	Vessel Type Call Sign RSS/ON	Gross Tonnage Net Tonnage	Dimensions (ft) Construction	Propulsion Unit(s) Make	Build Date Build Yard Build Location	History
Putford Artemis Lowestoft	Supply Ship MQSW9 722481	1190 357	193 x 39 x 19 Steel	Diesel 2 x 9cyl 6001hp Wichman	1975 Scheepswerf Waterhuizen Yard No. 308	Built as Ibis Five 1980 Sold and became Secco Supply 1987 Sold and became Aomjai III 1990 Sold and became Moon Lady 1990 Sold and became Coral Sea 2 1992 Purchased by Putford Enterprises Ltd. 1992 Renamed Putford Artemis 1992 Re-engined with 1800hp Nohab Polar units 2002 Working as a dual role SSV/cargo vessel
Putford Athena Lowestoft	Tug/ Supply Ship MQDW9 722492	1188 356	191 x 39 x 19 Steel	Diesel 2 x 16cyl 6161hp Nohab Polar	1975 Nieuwe Noord Groningen Yard No. 385	Built as Siddis Mariner for I/S Savanger Offshore 1990 Sold and became Severn Mariner 1992 Purchased by Putford Enterprises Ltd. 1992 Arrived at Lowestoft on 31st January under tow 1992 Renamed Putford Athena on 6th November 2002 Working as a dual role SSV/cargo vessel
Putford Blazer London	Supply Ship GOYN 307975	854 387	188 x 38 x 11 Steel	Diesel 2 x 8cyl 1600hp Blackstone	1965 Hall Russell Aberdeen Yard No. 927	Built as Lady Alison for International Offshore Marine 1974 Sold to Sea Services Shipping Co. Ltd. 1974 Became Aberdeen Blazer 1976 Sold to Small & Co. (Lowestoft) Ltd. 1976 Renamed Suffolk Blazer 1987 Sold to Warbler Shipping Co. Ltd. 1987 Converted for use as a SSV 1987 Became Dawn Blazer 1994 Warbler Shipping and PE fleets merged 1994 Renamed Putford Blazer 1995 Sold to Reed Heavy Lift Marine Ltd. 1995 Renamed RV Sea King (of Kingston) 1995 Left Lowestoft on 27th October 2000 Returned to Lowestoft and underwent conversion work at former Brooke Marine shipyard 2001 Work completed and left Lowestoft during July as the Sea King

Name Fishing Registration Port Registration	Vessel Type Call Sign RSS/ON	Gross Tonnage Net Tonnage	Dimensions (ft) Construction	Propulsion Unit(s) Make	Build Date Build Yard Build Location	History
Putford Dart LT94 Lowestoft	Stern Trawler GQEQ 342103	312 109	109 x 27 x 11 Steel	Diesel 1 x 6cyl 910bhp Ruston	1972 MacLean Renfrew Yard No. 5008	Built as LT94 Boston Sea Dart for BDSF 1983 Purchased by Putford Enterprises Ltd. 1985 Fishing registration cancelled 1985 Converted for use as a SSV 1985 Renamed Putford Dart 1988 Sold to Gronlando Hjemmestyrese (Trawlervikommed) Godthab 1988 Renamed Naleraq (of Godthab) 1996 Sold to Hanstholm Burserservice 1996 Became Gorm (of Hanstholm)
Putford Eagle Aberdeen	Trawler GFGE 301575	250 80	115 x 25 x 13 Steel	Diesel 1 x 6cyl 760hp Mirrlees	1959 Mitchison Gateshead Yard No. 94	Built as A309 Paramount for P. & J. Johnson Ltd. 1972 Transferred to J. Marr & Sons (Aberdeen) Ltd. 1976 Converted for use as a SSV 1980 Purchased by Putford Enterprises Ltd. 1980 Arrived at Lowestoft during November 1984 Renamed Putford Eagle 1986 Sold to Takis Fisheries Ltd., Milford Haven 1986 Converted to a fishing vessel 1986 Became A309 Pitufo 1993 Sold to Interpesco UK Ltd. 2000 Sold to Ramosa Ltd. 2000 Became Grampian Avenger II
Putford Enterprise Lowestoft	Supply Ship VSXA3 701173	1704 654	223 x 51 x 21 Steel	Diesel 2 x 6cyl 5000hp Allen	1985 Cochrane Selby Yard No. 128	1985 Built as Star Altair 1996 Acquired by Stirling Shipping Co. Ltd. 1996 Renamed Stirling Altair 2002 Sold to Seacor Smit 2002 Renamed Putford Enterprise 2002 Upgraded to a dual role SSV/supply ship
Putford Falcon Kirkcaldy	Trawler MXKS 187015	130 54	91 x 22 x 11 Steel	Diesel 1 x 6cyl 360hp Ruston	1957 Richards Lowestoft Yard No. 435	Built as LT295 Suffolk Maid for Small & Co. 1970 Sold to Skipper James Wilson, Cellerdyke 1970 Became KY338 Anna Christina in May 1980 Purchased by Putford Enterprises Ltd. 1980 Fishing registration cancelled 1980 Converted for use as a SSV 1984 Became Putford Falcon 1991 Advertised for sale at £84,000 1992 Sold and became Jolly Roger I 1992 Left Lowestoft on 8th January for the Isle of Wight

| Name | Vessel Type | Gross Tonnage | Dimensions (ft) | Propulsion | Build Date | History |
| Fishing Registration | Call Sign | Net Tonnage | Construction | Unit(s) | Build Yard | |
Port Registration	RSS/ON			Make	Build Location	
Putford Guardian Rochester	Supply Ship GXVR 333533	499 184	167 x 37 x 14 Steel	Diesel 2 x 8cyl 2000hp Blackstone	1967 Ijsselwerft Rotterdam Yard No. 133	Built as Essex Shore for Offshore Marine Ltd. 1980 Offshore Marine taken over by Zapata Corp. 1980 Renamed Essex Service 1984 Sold to Putford Enterprises Ltd. 1984 Renamed Putford Guardian 1985 Converted for use as a SSV 2002 Working as a single role SSV
Putford Harrier Aberdeen	Trawler GGWH 301590	163 54	94 x 22 x 10 Steel	Diesel 1 x 6cyl 486hp Ruston	1960 Herd & Mackenzie Buckie Yard No. 174	Built as A377 Dreadnought for Grampian Fishing Co 1968 Ownership transferred to the White Fish Authority 1970 Purchased by Putford Enterprises Ltd. 1970 Arrived at Lowestoft during May 1975 Fishing registration cancelled 1975 Fully converted for use as a SSV 1984 Renamed Putford Harrier 2000 In the ownership of Mrs. Andrew Lawrence & partners
Putford Hawk Lowestoft						Name considered for Young Elizabeth, but not used.
Putford Merlin Lowestoft	Trawler GHXB 303677	166 56	98 x 22 x 9 Steel	Diesel 1 x 5cyl 500hp AKD	1962 Brooke Marine Oulton Broad Lowestoft Yard No. 281	Built as LT412 Mincarlo for Diesel Trawlers Ltd. 1968 Ownership transferred to the White Fish Authority 1969 Purchased by Putford Enterprises Ltd. 1969 In use as a trawler and occasionally a SSV 1976 Fully converted for use as a SSV 1984 Renamed Putford Merlin 1992 Handed over to the Lydia Eva Trust on 9th Dec. for preservation as the Mincarlo
Putford Osprey Granton	Trawler GFPH 300603	230 78	109 x 24 x 12 Steel	Diesel 1 x 6cyl 720hp Ruston	1960 Scarr Hessle Yard No. 769	Built as GN19 Granton Osprey for W. Carnie Ltd. 1970 Transferred to BUT (Scotland) Ltd. 1977 Purchased jointly by PE and Whapload Engineering 1977 Arrived at Lowestoft on 31st May 1977 Fishing registration cancelled 1977 Converted for use as a SSV 1984 Renamed Putford Osprey 1984 Re-engined with 500hp Ruston unit 1993 Sold and became Ford Osprey 1993 Left Lowestoft on 2nd July for Lisbon 2001 Existence of vessel in doubt

Name / Fishing Registration / Port Registration	Vessel Type / Call Sign / RSS/ON	Gross Tonnage / Net Tonnage	Dimensions (ft) / Construction	Propulsion Unit(s) / Make	Build Date / Build Yard / Build Location	History
Putford Petrel Lowestoft	Research Vessel GHJY 302394	482 144	140 x 29 x 14 Steel	Diesel 1 x 6cyl 1060hp Ruston	1961 Cochrane Selby Yard No. 1458	Built as LT421 Clione for the MAFF 1987 Sold to Putford Enterprises Ltd. 1988 Fishing registration cancelled 1988 Renamed Putford Petrel 1988 Converted for use as a SSV 1999 Sold and renamed Lynn on 1st December 1999 Taken to former Brooke Marine shipyard on 2nd December where name was amended to Lynn G 1999 Left Lowestoft for Plymouth on 10th December 2000 In the ownership of Mr. William Barbour 2001 Reported as being for sale at Plymouth for the sum of £145,000 2001 Located at Amsterdam
Putford Protector Lowestoft	Stern Trawler GRMA 187946	741 318	155 x 32 x 19 Steel	Diesel 1 x 12cyl 1270hp English Electric	1965 Brooke Marine Oulton Broad Lowestoft Yard No. 318	Built as SN148 Ranger Apollo for Ranger Fishing Co. 1973 Transferred to White Fish Authority 1973 Sold to British United Trawlers Ltd. 1973 Became H233 Turcoman 1977 Sold to Salvesen Marine (Offshore) Ltd. 1977 Became Kilsyth, registered at Aberdeen 1977 Converted for use as a SSV 1983 Sold to Putford Enterprises Ltd. 1983 Became Putford Protector, registered at Lowestoft 1987 Sold to Glover Associates Ltd., London 1987 Converted back to stern trawler 1987 Became LO75 Port King 1991 Sank in Vigo Bay on 24th November
Putford Protector Lowestoft	Supply Ship VSUE3 701153	1822 546	224 x 53 x 21 Steel	Diesel 2 x 12cyl 5076hp British Polar	1983 Ferguson Bros Port Glasgow Yard No. 488	Built as Star Capella 1996 Acquired by Stirling Shipping Co. Ltd. 1996 Renamed Stirling Capella 2002 Sold to Seacor Smit 2002 Renamed Putford Protector 2002 Upgraded to a dual role SSV/supply ship
Putford Provider Lowestoft	Supply Ship VSRN4 701152	1599 521	224 x 53 x 21 Steel	Diesel 2 x 12cyl 5076hp British Polar	1983 Ailsa Troon Yard No. 558	Built as Star Vega 1996 Acquired by Stirling Shipping Co. Ltd. 1996 Renamed Stirling Vega 2002 Sold to Seacor Smit 2002 Renamed Putford Provider 2002 Working as a single role cargo vessel

Name Fishing Registration Port Registration	Vessel Type Call Sign RSS/ON	Gross Tonnage Net Tonnage	Dimensions (ft) Construction	Propulsion Unit(s) Make	Build Date Build Yard Build Location	History
Putford Puffin Lowestoft	Salvage Ship PHOI 426722	661 198	149 x 39 x 15 Steel	Diesel 2 x 6cyl 1441hp Deutz	1970 Bodewes Foxhol Yard No. 168	Built as Barracuda 1987 Renamed Smit Barracuda (of Rotterdam) 1991 Purchased by Warbler Shipping Co. Ltd. 1991 Arrived at Lowestoft on 6th December 1991 Converted for use as a SSV 1991 Became Dawn Patrol (of Lowestoft) on 3rd June 1993 Warbler Shipping and PE fleets merged 1994 Renamed Putford Puffin on 10th May 2002 Working as a single role SSV
Putford Rover Lowestoft	Supply Ship MWUS6 729384	1294 388	211 x 45 x 20 Steel	Diesel 2 x 16cyl 6960hp GMT	1982 Esercizio Viareggio Yard No. 659	Built as AGIP Gryphaea 1989 Renamed Gryphaea 1993 Sold and became Al-Mojil XXXIV 1996 Purchased by Putford Enterprises Ltd 1997 Vessel handed over on 24th January to PE at the Lowestoft Shell Base after a major refit 2002 Working as a dual role SSV/cargo vessel
Putford Sea Mussel Lowestoft	Supply Ship GUHN 361642	699 299	182 x 39 x 15 Steel	Diesel 2 x 8cyl 2500hp Allen	1974 Cochrane Selby Yard No. 1553	Built as Stirling Brig for Royal Bank Leasing Ltd. 1986 Sold and became Sea Mussel 1986 Converted to a diving support vessel 1993 Purchased by Putford Enterprises Ltd. 1993 Renamed Putford Sea Mussel 1993 Converted for use as SSV 2002 Sold to Al Dowari, Kuwait 2002 Left Lowestoft on 19th October
Putford Scimitar Lowestoft	Trawler GCKH 301514	135 45	92 x 22 x 10 Steel	Diesel 1 x 6cyl 360hp Ruston	1959 Richards Lowestoft Yard No. 446	Built as LT100 Boston Scimitar for BDSF 1962 Transferred to Carry On Fishing Co. Ltd. 1970 Transferred to Aberdeen Near Water Trawlers Ltd. 1974 Sold to Scimitar Trawlers Ltd. (A.Lincoln & I.Lace) 1974 Renamed Ocean Scimitar 1976 Sold to Putford Enterprises Ltd. 1976 Fishing registration cancelled 1976 Converted for use as a SSV 1984 Renamed Putford Scimitar 1992 Sold and left Lowestoft on 8th January for the Isle of Wight

Name Fishing Registration Port Registration	Vessel Type Call Sign RSS/ON	Gross Tonnage Net Tonnage	Dimensions (ft) Construction	Propulsion Unit(s) Make	Build Date Build Yard Build Location	History
Putford Shore Rochester	Supply Ship GVXE 333522	499 173	160 x 35 x 13 Steel	Diesel 2 x 8cyl 1599hp Blackstone	1967 IJjsselwerft Rotterdam Yard No. 132	Built as Norfolk Shore for Offshore Marine Ltd. 1980 Zapata Corporation acquired Offshore Marine 1980 Renamed Norfolk Service 1984 Sold to Warbler Shipping Co. Ltd. 1985 Converted for use as a SSV 1985 Renamed Dawn Shore 1994 Warbler Shipping and PE fleets merged 2002 Working as a single role SSV
Putford Skua Rochester	Tug/Supply Ship GWGE 333527	684 241	172 x 38 x 14 Steel	Diesel 2 x 8cyl 1600hp Blackstone	1967 Cochrane Selby Yard No. 1512	Built as Suffolk Shore for Offshore Marine Ltd. 1980 Zapata Corporation acquired Offshore Marine 1980 Renamed Suffolk Service 1984 Purchased by Putford Enterprises Ltd. 1985 Became the diving support vessel Putford Skua 1988 Converted for use as a SSV 2000 Sold and renamed Scan Warrior 2000 Left Lowestoft on 16th January 2000 In the ownership of EchoScan
Putford Sky Lowestoft	Research Vessel GWMA 309505	459 117	132 x 32 x 12 Steel	Diesel 2 x 6cyl 1060hp Allen	1967 Brooke Marine Oulton Broad Lowestoft Yard No. 325	Built as LT767 Corella for the MAFF 1983 Sold to Warbler Shipping Co. Ltd. 1983 Renamed Dawn Sky 1984 Fishing registration cancelled 1984 Converted for use as a SSV, and on diving support 1991 Extensively upgraded and modernised 1993 Warbler Shipping and PE fleets merged 1994 Renamed Putford Sky 2002 Working as a single role SSV

Name	Vessel Type	Gross Tonnage	Dimensions (ft)	Propulsion	Build Date	History
Fishing Registration	Call Sign	Net Tonnage	Construction	Unit(s)	Build Yard	
Port Registration	RSS/ON			Make	Build Location	

Putford Snipe	Tug/Supply Ship	708 322	177 x 38 x 13 Steel	Diesel 2 x 12cyl 1200hp Blackstone	1969 Adelaide SC Adelaide Yard No. 61	Built as Cook Shore for Osmarine (Australia) Ltd.
Lowestoft	GUHV 332997					1975 Transferred to Offshore Marine Ltd
						1975 Port registration changed from Sydney to London
						1978 Sold to Small & Co. (Lowestoft) Ltd.
						1978 Renamed Suffolk Kinsman
						1986 Sold to Eurosalve Ltd., Hastings
						1986 Renamed Eurosalve II
						1990 Sold to Captain Oates and others
						1990 Became Cornishman
						1990 Transferred to Western Ocean Towage Co Ltd.
						1991 Purchased by Putford Enterprises Ltd.
						1991 Arrived at Lowestoft on 3rd May
						1991 Renamed Putford Snipe
						1991 Converted for use as a SSV
						1995 Sold to HLS Offshore Ltd.
						1995 Renamed Stella Dena (of Port Vila)
Putford Teal	Tug/Supply Ship	678 249	177 x 38 x 15 Steel	Diesel 2 x 12cyl 1600hp Blackstone	1969 Cochrane Selby Yard No. 1523	Built as Pacific Shore for Offshore Marine Ltd.
Aberdeen	GYVA 337058					1980 Zapata Corporation acquired Offshore Marine
						1980 Renamed Pacific Service
						1985 Sold and became Kinnaird (of Inverness)
						1987 Converted for use as a SSV
						1988 Sold to George Craig & Sons Ltd.
						1988 Renamed Grampian Kestrel (of Aberdeen)
						1991 Purchased by Putford Enterprises Ltd.
						1991 Renamed Putford Teal
						1991 Further work undertaken for use as a SSV
						1996 Sold and became Seven Haleluyah
						1996 Left Lowestoft on 18th January
Putford Tern	Tug/Supply Ship	769 230	172 x 38 x 15 Steel	Diesel 2 x 8cyl 1599hp Blackstone	1967 Cochrane Selby Yard No. 1511	Built as Kent Shore for Offshore Marine Ltd.
Aberdeen	GWDU 333523					1980 Zapata Corporation acquired Offshore Marine
						1980 Renamed Kent Service
						1984 Sold to Nomis Ltd., Aberdeen
						1984 Renamed Victoria Kent
						1985 Purchased by Putford Enterprises Ltd.
						1985 Renamed Putford Tern
						1985 Converted for use as a SSV
						2000 Sold in February and became Lynn B
						2000 Sold in May and became Cape Endurance (of Panama)

Name / Fishing Registration / Port Registration	Vessel Type / Call Sign / RSS/ON	Gross Tonnage / Net Tonnage	Dimensions (ft) / Construction	Propulsion Unit(s) / Make	Build Date / Build Yard / Build Location	History
Putford Trader Aberdeen	Tug/Supply Ship GBDW 377915	1329 398	187 x 43 x 22 Steel	Diesel 2 x 6cyl 4200hp MaK	1976 Kaarbos Harstad Yard No. 82	Built as Seaway Jura 1990 Sold and became Safe Truck 1995 Sold to Putford Enterprises Ltd. 1995 Converted for use as a SSV 1995 Renamed Putford Trader 2002 Working as a dual role SSV/cargo vessel
Putford Viking Aberdeen	Supply Ship GVOY 359109	1456 654	200 x 48 x 19 Steel	Diesel 2 x 12cyl 4800hp British Polar	1976 Ysselwerf Capelle (aft) Yard No. 166 Holliandsche Grootammers (fwd)	Built as Star Pegasus for Star Offshore Services 1978 Converted to a pipe-carrier/supply ship 1981 Converted to a diving support ship 1981 Converted to fire-fighting/safety ship 1987 Purchased jointly by Linegift Ltd. and PE 1987 Renamed Blue Flame I on 29th April 1987 Converted for use as SSV 1988 Registered as owned by Britannia Putford Enterprises Ltd. 2000 Renamed Putford Viking 2002 Working as a dual role SSV/cargo vessel
Putford Voyager Lowestoft	Supply Ship GFGR 701091	1403 560	211 x 46 x 20 Steel	Diesel 1 x 8cyl 4800hp Yanmar	1985 Teroka Nandan	Built as Stirling Dee for Scotts of Greenock (Est. 1711) Ltd. 2001 Sold to Seacor Smit 2002 Renamed Putford Voyager 2002 Upgraded to a dual role SSV/supply ship
Putford Warbler London	Supply Ship GOYQ 308166	697 228	158 x 36 x 15 Steel	Diesel 2 x 8cyl 1600hp Blackstone	1966 Brooke Marine Oulton Broad Lowestoft Yard No. 332	Built as Lady Claudine for P & O Offshore Services Ltd. 1966 Launched on 31st January 1973 Sold to Decca Navigator Ltd. 1974 Renamed Decca Engineer 1983 Sold to Jesmar Shipping Co. Ltd. 1983 Renamed Engineer 1984 Sold to Gardline Shipping Co. Ltd 1984 Renamed Researcher in April. 1989 Sold to Warbler Shipping Co. Ltd. in November 1990 Renamed Dawn Warbler 1990 Underwent extensive refit and conversion to SSV 1994 Warbler Shipping and PE fleets merged 1994 Renamed Putford Warbler 1994 Due to storm damage new wheelhouse fitted 1994 Sold to Norway and renamed Torungen 1994 Left Lowestoft in December

Name Fishing Registration Port Registration	Vessel Type Call Sign RSS/ON	Gross Tonnage Net Tonnage	Dimensions (ft) Construction	Propulsion Unit(s) Make	Build Date Build Yard Build Location	History
Putford Worker London	Supply Ship GVHQ 366218	1417 518	214 x 46 x 19 Steel	Diesel 2 x 6cyl 3200hp MaK	1976 Scheepswerf Waterhuizen Yard No. 325	Built as Maersk Piper for The Maersk Co. Ltd. 1985 Renamed Maersk Worker 1994 Purchased by Putford Enterprises Ltd. 1994 Renamed Putford Worker 1994 Underwent extensive refit and conversion to SSV 2002 Working as a dual role SSV/cargo vessel
Rae-Elizabeth LT501	Stern Trawler GJPH 187940	246 76	114 x 25 x 13 Steel	Diesel 2 x 4cyl 792hp Maybech	1962 Mitchison Gateshead Yard No. 514	Built as the twin engined SN58 Sailfin for Pelagic Trawling Co. Ltd., North Shields 1964 Transferred to Pelagic (Realisations) Ltd. 1965 Converted to side trawler 1965 Became LT501 Yoxford Queen 1966 Transferred to Talisman Trawlers (North Sea) Ltd. 1967 Existing engines replaced with another pair 1969 Engines replaced with a single 6cyl 850hp Ruston 1983 Sold to Scupham Fishing Co. Ltd. 1983 Renamed Rae-Elizabeth 1985 Sold to Putford Enterprises Ltd. 1985 All valuable equipment removed from vessel 1985 Sold for scrapping
Royalist LO50	Trawler GHFL 301171	212 79	108 x 23 x 12 Steel	Diesel 1 x 6cyl 484hp Mirrlees	1960 Cook, Welton & Gemmell Beverley Yard No. 960	Built for Hewett Fishing Co. Ltd., London 1981 Purchased jointly by PE and BDSF 1982 Advertised for sale at £25,000 1982 Sold to W. D. Ansell & B. S. Cato, Fleetwood 1983 Fishing registration changed to FD24 1983 In the ownership of Frederick Oldham Ltd. 1989 In the ownership of William Ansell & Brian Cato Later sold to Anglo Spanish interests

Name Fishing Registration Port Registration	Vessel Type Call Sign RSS/ON	Gross Tonnage Net Tonnage	Dimensions (ft) Construction	Propulsion Unit(s) Make	Build Date Build Yard Build Location	History

Sedulous
LT56
	Drifter/
	Trawler
	MFYG
	132952
		98
		42
			89 x 19 x 9
			Steel
				Steam
				Triple
				35hp
				Phillips
					1912
					Philips
					Dartmouth
					Yard No. 405
						Built as drifter/trawler LT1168 for Page and Green
						1914 Sold to T. W. Moore, Yarmouth
						1914 Fishing registration changed to YH2
						1924 Sold to W. Backie and J. Jack, Hopeman
						1924 Fishing registration changed to INS3
						1940 Requisitioned by Admiralty for barrage balloon,
						    and later examination vessel uses
						1945 Returned to owner
						1945 Sold to Shire Trawlers Ltd., London
						1945 Fishing registration changed to LT56
						1948 Sold to J. R. Hashim
						1948 Transferred to Putford Enterprises Ltd.
						1948 Phillips 35hp compound steam engine removed
						1948 Converted to diesel power with the installation of a
						    Petter 4cyl 340hp engine by George Overy Ltd.
						1961 Sold to Richards Ironworks Ltd.
						1961 Sold to Merbreeze Ltd.
						1963 Sold to Konstantin Zuis

Sheriffmuir LT313	Trawler GPZQ 183987	180 66	102 x 22 x 11 Steel	Diesel 1 x 6cyl 350hp Crossley	1952 Scarr Hessle	Built for West Hartlepool Steam Navigation Co. Ltd. 1962 Transferred to Talisman Trawlers Ltd. 1967 Transferred to Talisman Trawlers (North Sea) Ltd. 1968 Sold to P.F., G.A. & F.E.Catchpole and J.R.Hashim 1969 In use on SSV work 1973 Sold to Safetyships Ltd., Aberdeen 1976 Grounded near Aberdeen, vessel a total loss and broken up
Sir Fred Parkes H39 Hull	Stern Trawler GSDE 308533	1550 465	222 x 41 x 15 Steel	Diesel 1 x 8cyl 2350hp Mirrlees	1966 Hall Russell Aberdeen Yard No. 928	Built as H385 Sir Fred Parkes for BDSF 1982 Sold to Putford Enterprises Ltd. 1983 Converted for use as a cable guardship (Guard 1) 1983 Fishing registration cancelled 1986 Converted back to stern trawler 1986 Allocated fishing registration H39 1986 Transferred to joint ownership of PE and Interpesco Securities (UK) Ltd. 1987 Renamed Waveney Warrior 1987 Sold to SFP Fishing Co. Ltd. 1989 In the ownership of SFP Atlantic Fisheries Ltd. 1992 In the ownership of Perquera Santa Elena S.A.I.C.

| Name | Vessel Type | Gross Tonnage | Dimensions (ft) | Propulsion | Build Date | History |
| Fishing Registration | Call Sign | Net Tonnage | Construction | Unit(s) | Build Yard | |
Port Registration	RSS/ON			Make	Build Location	
Southleigh KY377 Kirkcaldy	Drifter/ Trawler GRFS 183995	115 46	88 x 21 x 11 Steel	Diesel 1 x 5cyl 300hp Ruston	1953 Richards Lowestoft Yard No. 417	Built as LT387 Young Duke for Small & Co. (LT) Ltd. 1967 Sold to Marinex Gravel Ltd., London 1967 Fishing registration cancelled 1967 Converted for dredger support work 1969 Sold to James Corson, Kirkcaldy 1969 Converted back to a fishing vessel 1969 Became KY377 Spes Aurea 1973 Sold to Putford Enterprises Ltd. 1974 Became Southleigh, registered at Kirkcaldy 1977 Fully converted for use as a SSV 1987 Sold to Eurosalve Ltd., Folkestone 1987 Renamed Eurodive I 1987 Converted for use as a diving support vessel 1990 Seen in Malta as Falcon, registered at Valetta
Specious YH392	Drifter/ Trawler GWTM 144158	132 53	98 x 20 x 12 Steel	Steam Triple 46hp Holmes	1928 Cochrane Selby Yard No. 1019	Built as drifter/trawler Hilda Cooper for Bloomfields Ltd., Great Yarmouth 1939 Requisitioned by Admiralty for use as an examination vessel 1939 Allocated pennant number FY1949 1944 Returned to owner in October 1956 Sold to Putford Enterprises Ltd. 1957 Holmes 46hp triple steam engine removed 1957 Converted to diesel power with the installation of a AKD 3cyl 300hp engine by LBS Engineering Ltd. 1957 Renamed Specious in July 1967 Laid up in April 1967 Sold to T. G. Darling Ltd., for scrap in December
Spes Aurea KY377 Kirkcaldy	Drifter/ Trawler GRFS 183995	115 46	88 x 21 x 11 Steel	Diesel 1 x 5cyl 300hp Ruston	1953 Richards Lowestoft Yard No. 417	Refer to Southleigh for history
Stoic LT465 Lowestoft	Drifter/ Trawler GQBK 185677	114 46	99 x 20 x 10 Steel	Diesel 1 x 6cyl 360hp Ruston	1952 Richards Lowestoft Yard No. 410	Refer to Dawn Spray for history

Name Fishing Registration Port Registration	Vessel Type Call Sign RSS/ON	Gross Tonnage Net Tonnage	Dimensions (ft) Construction	Propulsion Unit(s) Make	Build Date Build Yard Build Location	History
Strenuous LT112	Drifter/ Trawler GYKJ 137617	97 44	86 x 19 x 9 Steel	Steam Triple 42hp Hall	1919 A. Hall Aberdeen	Built as HMD Waterfall (4132) for the Admiralty 1919 Completed as YH214 Homocea for E. A. Baker 1922 Sold to A. Maxyon, Boulogne, France 1930 Sold to Alvargonzalez, San Sebastian, Spain 1930 Renamed Niyu 1932 Sold to W. Barnard, Lowestoft 1932 Became LT112 Homocea 1953 Sold to Putford Enterprises Ltd. 1953 Hall 42hp triple steam engine removed 1953 Converted to diesel power with the installation of a AKD 3cyl 300hp engine by LBS Engineering 1953 Renamed Strenuous 1964 Sold for scrapping at Milford
Umberleigh Granton	Trawler GHDD 300604	235 77	108 x 24 x 12 Steel	Diesel 1 x 5cyl 705hp Ruston	1960 Hall Russell Aberdeen Yard No. 886	Built as GN72 Granton Merlin for W. Carnie Ltd. 1970 Transferred to BUT (Scotland) Ltd. 1977 Sold to Howard I. Williams, Clwyd 1978 Purchased jointly by PE and Whapload Engineering 1978 Fishing registration cancelled 1978 Converted for use as a SSV 1978 Renamed Umberleigh Sold for conversion to a yacht Re-engined and substantially rebuilt 2000 Conversion in progress
Vanessa Ann Fleetwood	Trawler GNPF 183981	168 55	103 x 22 x 11 Steel	Diesel 1 x 6cyl 540hp British Polar	1951 Richards Lowestoft Yard No. 403	Built as LT254 for Consolidated Fisheries Ltd. 1955 Transferred to Rhondda Fishing Co. Ltd. 1957 Sold to Dalby Steam Fishing Co. Ltd. 1958 Registration changed to FD133 1971 Sold to Putford Enterprises Ltd. 1971 Fishing registration cancelled 1971 Converted for use as a SSV 1972 Sold to Keithly Enterprises Ltd. 1973 Sold to F. E. Catchpole and re-engined 1982 Sold to Clipper Promotions Inc. for conversion to a topsail schooner. Registered in Fleetwood.

Name Fishing Registration Port Registration	Vessel Type Call Sign RSS/ON	Gross Tonnage Net Tonnage	Dimensions (ft) Construction	Propulsion Unit(s) Make	Build Date Build Yard Build Location	History
Vigilance A204 Aberdeen	Trawler GXRL 300363	149 66	102 x 23 x 110 Wood	Diesel 1 x 6cyl 454hp Ruston	1958 Herd & Mackenzie Peterhead	Built as A204 for the Devotion Fishing Co. Ltd. 1969 Sold to Vigilance Fishing Co. Ltd., Aberdeen 1973 Sold to DAM Trawlers Ltd., Plymouth 1978 Transferred to DAM Engineers Ltd., Plymouth 1980 Purchased jointly by PE and Whapload Engineering 1980 Arrived at Lowestoft during September 1980 Valuable items removed from vessel 1981 Hulked on south side of Lake Lothing 1981 Hull purchased by Crompton Marine 2001 Remains of vessel still at Lake Lothing
Warbler LT63	Trawler GJRZ 133409	195 72	110 x 22 x 12 Steel	Diesel 1 x 5cyl 500hp AKD	1912 Goole SB Goole	Built as steam trawler H587 for Kelsall Bros & Beeching 1940 Sold to Brandon Fishing Co. Ltd., London 1958 Brandon Fishing merged with Robert Hewett Ltd. 1958 Brandon Fishing sold to AKD. 1958 Converted to diesel power by LBS Engineering Ltd. 1968 Sold to P.F., F.E., & G.A.Catchpole & J.R.Hashim 1968 Converted for use as a SSV 1972 Sold to T. G. Darling Ltd for scrapping
Warbler Lowestoft	Trawler GHMF 302398	198 62	107 x 23 x 9 Steel	Diesel 1 x 6cyl 550hp Crossley	1961 Brooke Marine Oulton Broad Lowestoft Yard No. 280	Refer to Dawn Warbler for history
Waveney Warrior H39	Stern Trawler GSDE 308533	1550 465	222 x 41 x 15 Steel	Diesel 1 x 8cyl 2350hp Mirrlees	1966 Hall Russell Aberdeen Yard No. 928	Refer to Sir Fred Parkes for history

Name Fishing Registration Port Registration	Vessel Type Call Sign RSS/ON	Gross Tonnage Net Tonnage	Dimensions (ft) Construction	Propulsion Unit(s) Make	Build Date Build Yard Build Location	History
Westleigh FD42	Trawler MWMS 187843	398 134	139 x 28 x 14 Steel	Diesel 1 x 6cyl 960hp British Polar	1956 Scarr Hessle Yard No. 726	Built as FD42 Boston Seafoam for BDSF 1968 Transferred to Parbel-Smith Ltd. 1970 Arrived at Lowestoft on 19th February 1974 Sold to Putford Enterprises Ltd. 1974 Renamed Westleigh 1976 Sold to Safetyships Ltd., Aberdeen 1976 Fully converted for use as a SSV 1976 Renamed Arkinholme 1978 Sold to George Craig & Son Ltd. 1979 Renamed Grampian Castle 1987 Vessel ashore near Caernarfon 1987 Reported as a total loss
W.F.P. LT310 Lowestoft	Drifter/ Trawler MXYZ 187026	126 49	94 x 22 x 10 Wood	Diesel 1 x 3cyl 300hp AKD	1957 Summers Fraserburgh	Built for Lowestoft Motor Trawlers Ltd. 1968 Transferred to White Fish Authority 1969 Sold to Putford Enterprises Ltd. 1970 Sold to Brian Pearce, Poole 1971 Transferred to Brian Pearce and Hazel Adam Later Sold to A. C. R. Law Later Sold to L. Aspin and others
Wilronwood A546 Aberdeen	Trawler MEDF 303208	166 56	98 x 23 x 9 Steel	Diesel 1 x 5cyl 500hp AKD	1961 Brooke Marine Oulton Broad Yard No. 285	Refer to Oakleigh for history
Winkleigh LT422 Lowestoft	Trawler MEFW 302405	198 41	106 x 23 x 12 Steel	Diesel 1 x 6cyl 540hp Ruston	1961 Richards Lowestoft Yard No. 462	Built as LT422 Suffolk Craftsman for Small & Co. 1974 Sold to Putford Enterprises Ltd. 1974 Renamed Winkleigh 1981 Fishing registration cancelled 1981 Converted for use as a SSV 1993 Sold and left Lowestoft on 6th Aug. for Madagascar 2000 Vessel located at Capetown during September

Name Fishing Registration Port Registration	Vessel Type Call Sign RSS/ON	Gross Tonnage Net Tonnage	Dimensions (ft) Construction	Propulsion Unit(s) Make	Build Date Build Yard Build Location	History
Woodleigh LT240 Lowestoft	Trawler GGBA 301526	199 67	107 x 23 x 10 Steel	Diesel 1 x 6cyl 550hp Crossley	1960 Richards Lowestoft Yard No. 452	Built as LT240 for Putford Enterprises Ltd. 1975 Converted for use as a SSV 1975 Fishing registration cancelled 1982 Advertised for sale at £60,000 1985 Re-engined 1993 Sold for possible use as a restaurant 1993 Left Lowestoft on 13th July bound for Sheerness 1994 Advertised for sale at £50,000 1994 Detained off Cornwall after caught drug smuggling 1999 Laid up at Falmouth
Young Elizabeth Jersey	Drifter/ Trawler GQZC 183993	115 46	88 x 21 x 11 Steel	Diesel 1 x 5cyl 300hp Ruston	1953 Richards Lowestoft Yard No. 416	Built as LT375 for Small & Co. (Lowestoft) Ltd. 1968 Sold to Offshore Oil Rig Services Ltd. 1968 Fishing registration cancelled 1968 Port registration changed to Jersey 1976 Sold to Star Offshore Services Ltd., London 1977 Fully converted for use as a SSV 1983 Purchased by Putford Enterprises Ltd. 1987 Sold to Vivyan Rayner 2001 Reported as being at Amsterdam in use as a houseboat

The Putford trawler *Sedulous* hauling on the fishing grounds in the 1950s. From left to right the crew are Skipper Sid Cooper, Alfred Shreeve, unknown, Charlie Buckenham, "Frany" Martin, Harry Balls and Mate Alfred Meadows.

Mr. George Catchpole, a past director of Putford Enterprises, with the *Putford Achilles* at the North Quay, Lowestoft. George has provided substantial assistance in the preparation of this book. *Putford Achilles* works as a dual role cargo and standby vessel.

Built by Cochrane at Selby in 1928, the steam drifter/trawler *YH392 Hilda Cooper* was purchased by Putford Enterprises Ltd. from Bloomfields Ltd. of Gt. Yarmouth in 1956. She was then converted to diesel propulsion, and renamed *Specious*.

On the 13th October 1934, when this scene was recorded from the South Pier at Lowestoft, the *Hilda Cooper* had just been fitted with radio. A pile driver boiler is seen on the pierhead.

An earlier conversion to that of the *Hilda Cooper* was undertaken in 1953, when the Aberdeen built steam drifter *LT112 Homocea* was purchased, and after conversion became the diesel powered *Strenuous*.

She was sold for scrapping in 1964 and is seen here setting out from her homeport in the mid 1950s on another fishing trip.

Used as a drifter/trawler by her previous owners, *LT400 Arduous* was used initially for trawling by Putford, but ended her working days as a safety standby vessel. Her final role was as living accommodation on the banks of Lake Lothing.

Arduous was built in 1944 as the Admiralty *MFV 1509* at the Lowestoft shipyard of Richards Ironworks and was purchased by Putford Enterprises in 1956 as the *Eta*.

Former Admiralty *MFV1545* was another wooden fishing vessel to serve in the Putford fleet. She was acquired as *BM20 Iago* and in that guise we find her leaving Lowestoft in 1958. The following year the *Iago* became *LT170 Moreleigh,* and in 1965 she was sold and registered as *HL160*.

Two drifter/trawlers of somewhat different origins and designs on the Laundry Lane dual slipways in the early 1960s. On the left slipway is the Putford vessel *YH392 Specious* and on the right can be seen *LT231 Harold Cartwright,* owned by the Small & Co. subsidiary Pevensey Castle Ltd. The *Harold Cartwright* was built in 1950 at Richards shipyard in Lowestoft, and passed to South African owners in 1966.

As the Scottish drifter *LK497 Betty Leslie*, the *Boston Mosquito* was very well known at Lowestoft, since she visited the port for many consecutive years during the autumn herring season. Built as the Admiralty *MFV1504* at Lowestoft in 1944, *LT373 Boston Mosquito* was re-engined and extensively modernised in 1960. Jointly owned by Putford Enterprises and the Looker Fishing Co. Ltd., for a number of years, she was sold in 1972 and later renamed *April Diamond*. Here we see *Boston Mosquito* heading south off her homeport.

For many years up until the mid 1970s, and before becoming partners in the Boston Putford organisation, Putford Enterprises was a large fishing concern with many trawlers, for part of the time managed by Boston Deep Sea Fisheries. The first of two trawlers built for the Company, *LT240 Woodleigh*, is seen here on trials in 1960.

Below - The trawler *LT444 Bickleigh* was the second of two built in the early 1960s by Richards Ironworks at Lowestoft for Putford Enterprises.

Right - *Bickleigh* was sold in 1971 to Aberdeen, where she was re-registered *A201*.

The well-known Lowestoft trawler *LT313 Sheriffmuir*, seen here in the Waveney Dock, was in the fleet from 1968, and after conversion she undertook safety standby duties. Sold to Safetyships Ltd. in 1973, she became a total loss in 1976 after running aground near Aberdeen.

During the 1960s and early 1970s, the trawler fleet expanded rapidly with acquisitions from various sources. The Aberdeen trawler *A377 Dreadnought* was one such vessel, being used for trawling and later offshore support work. As with some other trawlers in the fleet, her trawl gear, in addition to being used for fishing, was also used for the recovery of crashed aircraft, a speciality for which Putford earned a much respected reputation.

Complete with her trawl gear, *Northleigh* approaches the pier heads at Lowestoft. In 1974, she had arrived as *A735 Emma Wood*, another purchase from the Aberdeen fleet. A long serving member of the Boston Putford fleet, as a safety standby vessel, *Northleigh* was passed to carry 100-150 survivors in the North Sea Trawler Class. As with many other vessels in the fleet, she was equipped with oil pollution treatment equipment. In 1987, *Northleigh* was sold and returned to fish in Scottish waters.

Destined to become the safety standby vessel *Dawn Cloud,* the Kirkcaldy great liner *KY194 Ardenlea* moved south to Lowestoft in 1986 after previously working out of Scottish ports as a standby vessel for other owners. A vessel with an intriguing history, she was built in 1963 at Peterhead as *GN75 Jarlshof* and became *A805 Ardenlea* in 1966.

Under Putford Enterprises ownership, *LT94 Boston Sea Dart* heads away from her homeport for the fishing grounds. One of a number of trawlers with "Boston" names that Putford became associated with, she was converted for standby duties in 1985 and renamed *Putford Dart*.

A selection of the now replaced 100 and 150 Survivor Class North Sea Trawler Type safety vessels of the Boston Putford Fleet

Top Left - *Dawn Gem, (Previously A200 Glenstruan)*

Top Right - *Paramount,* later renamed *Putford Eagle (A309 Paramount)*

Bottom Left – *Dawn Pearl, (A554 Eredene)*

Bottom Right - *Breydon Widgeon, (LT427 Boston Widgeon)*

Another Lowestoft built ship to serve in the Boston Putford fleet was purchased by Warbler Shipping as the *Researcher* in 1989. She had been built in 1966 by Brooke Marine as the supply ship *Lady Claudine* for P & O Offshore Services. Converted for safety standby duties, *Researcher* was renamed *Dawn Warbler*. Later this was changed to *Putford Warbler*. In addition to *Researcher*, she had other names under various owners, these being *Decca Navigator* and *Engineer*. *Putford Warbler* was sold in 1994, and she is seen here as built on trials off Lowestoft.

Above - After serving as a safety standby vessel within the Boston Putford fleet, the *Breydon Mallard* was sold in the spring of 1984 to Anglo Spanish interests, and converted back to a fishing vessel. This Lowestoft built trawler presented an unusual sight as she passed down the river at Great Yarmouth with her newly acquired fishing registration of *LT131*. *Breydon Mallard* was previously the Lowestoft trawler *LT445 Boston Beaver,* and was purchased from the Boston Deep Sea Fisheries subsidiary, Looker Fishing Co. Ltd., by Breydon Marine in 1978.
Top left - The wheelhouse of *Breydon Mallard*, whilst working as a safety standby vessel, showing the Breydon Marine houseflag.

One of the most unusual ships used by Warbler Shipping for survey and offshore support work was the 187ft. *Dawn Flight*. She was built in 1967 as the vehicle and cargo ferry *Rapillo*, but had been converted by her previous owners for diving/submersible support and standby work. Her six cylinder Atlas-MaK Maschinenbau main engine developed 800hp (588kW), and her auxiliaries included one 280kW and two 52kW 400 Volt AC alternator sets. Acquired in 1984, she was sold during 1991 to a Dutch company for further service.

A well-known and highly versatile vessel, the London registered Lowestoft based tug *Planter* is also the smallest vessel in the Boston Putford fleet. She is used for moving ships of the fleet in port and, when required, for manoeuvring vessels in and out of Lowestoft dry dock, general port towage and movement work.

An unusual view of the *Putford Guardian* carrying out boat drill, and before the ship was fitted with the now familiar Miranda davits which allow her to carry and launch various types of rescue craft, including larger and heavier Daughter craft. Miranda davits, seen painted yellow on various Putford ships in this book, were developed by the Royal Navy Fishery Protection Service during the Icelandic "Cod Wars" for launching fast rescue craft in the severe weather conditions experienced in the Arctic during the winter months, and are now common on ships of the Boston Putford fleet.

One of several Granton registered trawlers acquired by Putford and which later became units of the Boston Putford fleet, the *Chudleigh* arrived in Lowestoft as *GN77 Granton Harrier* in 1976. After successfully fishing the North Sea for ten years for Putford, her call for safety standby duties came in 1986. In 1993 she was sold to Holland for further service. The date when this scene was recorded was the 13th November 1976.

Jointly owned from 1979 by Boston Deep Sea Fisheries and Putford Enterprises, *LT454 Boston Whirlwind* was a typical example of the work of the Richards shipyard in Lowestoft, and the many trawlers they built for the Lowestoft fishing fleet in the 1950s and 1960s. This superb view of her leaving for the fishing grounds was recorded after the Christmas break on the 30th December 1974.

As a safety standby vessel, *Mincarlo* is featured elsewhere in this book. In this fine view, we see her leaving Lowestoft earlier in life on the 23rd July 1973, as the trawler *LT412,* and in the colours of Putford Enterprises. It is the intention of her present owners to restore *Mincarlo* to the condition she is seen in here, but in the colours of her original owners.

In addition to a great many near water trawlers in the Boston Putford fleet, a number of larger vessels could be found working as fishing and standby vessels. The Fleetwood trawler *FD42 Boston Seafoam* joined the Boston Deep Sea Fisheries Lowestoft fleet in 1970, and was renamed *Westleigh* after transferring to Putford Enterprises in 1974. She fished for several months before joining the growing number of redundant trawlers finding new work in a different harvest of the sea, that of supporting the offshore oil and gas industry.

The trawler *GN72 Granton Merlin* was one of many trawlers from other ports to join the Boston Putford fleet as safety standby vessels. Still essentially a trawler, but employed on standby duties, the *Granton Merlin* is seen passing the now demolished, but well known CWS canning factory at Lowestoft on the 6th February 1978. Later she was renamed *Umberleigh*, and at the end of her standby days, was sold and converted to a luxury yacht.

Previously with the Small & Co. (Lowestoft) Ltd. fleet as *LT395 Suffolk Punch*, the *Hatherleigh* was purchased by Putford Enterprises in 1974. She converted to safety standby work in 1981, and was sold to a Scarborough company in 1992.

Two drifter/trawlers were built for Small & Co. (Lowestoft) Ltd. in 1953 and named to commemorate the Coronation of that year. Later in life one of these two, *Young Duke,* became *KY377 Spes Aurea* after a change in ownership. Purchased by Putford Enterprises in 1973 she was renamed *Southleigh* and undertook safety standby work. *Southleigh* was sold in 1987 and initially used on salvage work, later she became a diving support vessel in Malta.

The other one of the pair was named *Young Elizabeth*, and with her fishing days over, she was purchased for use on offshore support and diving work. A unit of the Boston Putford fleet, *Young Elizabeth* is seen here being returned to the waters of Lake Lothing from the slip at the former George Overy's yard. The logo of Boston Putford is displayed on the wheelhouse.

A superb view of the Boston Putford safety standby vessel *Jacamar* off Corton in 1980. A former Aberdeen trawler, she was renamed *Dawn Monarch* in 1981 and employed for twelve years on standby work by Warbler Shipping.

Well known drifter and trawler owners Small & Co.(Lowestoft) Ltd. had a number of trawlers built in 1961at Richards Ironworks in Lowestoft. One of these, *Suffolk Craftsman*, later passed to Putford Enterprises and was renamed *Winkleigh*. After a number of years fishing for the Company, she was converted for use as a safety standby vessel.

Above - As a trawler, *Winkleigh* leaves Lowestoft.
Right - After conversion to a safety standby vessel.

Right - A scene recorded by rig worker Mr. Bob Lewis of Lowestoft, from the Shell AP platform in September 1969 with the supply ship *Suffolk Shore* in attendance at the drilling rig *Transocean II.* This rig was a six leg jack up, constructed in 1966 by Smith's Dock and could work in a depth of water up to 160ft., with a drilling capacity of 20,000ft. Her hull was 225ft. x 140ft., with accommodation for 50 persons. The derrick was 142ft. high, and towing requirements for the rig were at least 10,000hp.

Below - The same ship several years later, but with a different identity. As the *Putford Skua,* she is working adjacent to the 48/29A platform in the North Sea, as a diving support vessel.

Built to a high specification by Cochrane at Selby in 1961 as the Government research ship *Clione*, the *Putford Petrel* joined the fleet in 1988 and until 1999, when she was sold, worked as a safety standby vessel.

Quality built trawlers were readily available in the 1970s and 80s for other duties due to the rapid decline of the once great British fishing industry. The Aberdeen trawler *A417 Clova* was just one of many such vessels to join the Boston Putford fleet. Here we see her as the *Dawn Saviour* heading north off Lowestoft.

Within the Boston Putford organisation, the distinctive *Putford Puffin* initially had a different identity, that of *Dawn Patrol*. She started life as a Dutch owned salvage vessel, and in this 1991 view is in the process of being converted at Lowestoft for her new duties as a safety standby vessel. Some of her previous owners markings are still visible.

With the conversion complete, the *Putford Puffin* as the *Dawn Patrol* undergoing trials off Lowestoft in June 1991.

A fine view from an offshore platform of the *Putford Tern* on station with her Daughter craft deployed. Built in 1967 by the Cochrane shipyard at Selby as the *Kent Shore*, the *Putford Tern* was in the Boston Putford fleet from 1985 until 2000, when she was sold for further service.

An addition to the Warbler Shipping fleet in 1983, *LT767 Corella*, was built as a research vessel with stern trawling capabilities. In the Warbler fleet, she became the survey vessel *Dawn Sky*. Built for the Ministry of Agriculture, Fisheries and Food in 1967 by Brooke Marine, *Dawn Sky* was later converted for use as a safety standby vessel, and eventually renamed *Putford Sky*.

The *Granton Osprey* was another trawler to move south for work as a standby vessel. As the *Putford Osprey,* she was in the Boston Putford fleet from 1977 until 1993. In 1993, *Putford Osprey* was sold for further service, and left Lowestoft in July for Lisbon.

The safety standby vessel *Warbler,* built as the trawler *Carlton Queen,* on station at the Shell-Esso 49/26BT installation. Helicopters belonging to British Airways, one of which is seen here, were at one time used for ferrying personnel between shore and offshore installations. They had a convenient landing pad at the Shell base in Lowestoft, but later flights operated from Beccles Heliport. This base closed in 1995 when run by British International Helicopters, successors to British Airways Helicopters, after British International lost the contract to provide the services.

A 1982 scene showing the *Dawn Warbler* at sea with one of her smaller Putford/Dunlop southern North Sea rescue craft on sea trials. These rescue craft were developed during 1981 as a joint Putford/Dunlop venture, and were based on the Dunlop 10 man DOTI boat. Extensive modifications were carried out to the Dunlop boat, including redesign of the control console and the fitting of electric start for the Mercury 25hp engine. The *Dawn Warbler* was previously the *Warbler*.

The stern trawler *Sir Fred Parkes* was purchased in 1982 and became heavily involved in the English Channel cable guard project. By the late 1980s, she had been sold and was fishing in the South Atlantic.

The *Sir Fred Parkes* returned to fishing under Putford ownership and these two scenes were recorded on one of her fishing trips.

This stern trawler was completed in 1966 by Hall Russell & Co. Ltd. in Aberdeen. Her Mirrlees National 8 cylinder engine developed 2350hp(1792kW), and she had two auxiliary power units, one developing 350kW and the other 330kW, both at 220volts DC.

Like many distant water trawlers from Grimsby, Hull and Fleetwood, made surplus by rapidly declining fishing opportunities, and perhaps otherwise destined for the scrapyard, the *Sir Fred Parkes* was sold to Lowestoft owners and continued to serve for several years under the British flag, before eventually passing to Argentine owners.

On station undertaking a vital task, one of the chartered Britannia Marine standby vessels. These former Lowestoft stern trawlers have proved to be an ideal choice for this type of work. In 2003, four of this class, the *Britannia Conquest*, *Britannia Harvester*, *Britannia Monarch* and *Britannia Warrior* were working as part of the large Boston Putford fleet, and managed from Lowestoft. This superb image comes from the Ollington Collection.

The impressive *Putford Worker* was built in 1976, and after purchase in 1994, underwent an extensive refit before joining the Boston Putford fleet. She is one of the larger vessels in the fleet and works as a dual role safety and supply ship. Prior to becoming the *Putford Worker*, she was the *Maersk Worker*.

The tug/supply ship *Severn Mariner* was acquired in 1989 and after a refit and conversion work joined the fleet as the *Putford Athena*. She was built in 1975 in Holland, and this excellent photograph clearly demonstrates the capacity for dual role working with her cargo area, Daughter craft, and other recovery/rescue craft clearly visible.

Purchased as the *Nova Service* in 1988, the *Nova* is one of the single role ships in the fleet, and is jointly owned by Viking Standby and Putford Enterprises. *Nova* was built as the *Nova Service* for Offshore Marine Ltd. in 1969 at the Cochrane shipyard at Selby.

Typical of the larger ships in the fleet, the *Putford Rover,* seen here at Yarmouth, was an addition to the Boston Putford fleet in January 1997. She was built in 1982, and acquired as the *Al Mobil XXXIV* .

In contrast, the *Margaret Christina* represents an earlier generation of Boston Putford vessels. Well known for several major rescues, she was built in 1960 at Lowestoft and fished for Putford for four years, before becoming a safety standby vessel in 1975.
Margaret Christina sank in September 1983, but was raised and subsequently scrapped in Holland.

Ships of the Boston Putford fleet are a very common sight at Great Yarmouth. This May 1999 scene, shows the *Putford Worker* and *Putford Aries*.
During August 1999, the *Aries* was converted for dual role working by Richards shipyard at Yarmouth.

Previously the supply ship *Coral Sea 2* the *Putford Artemis*, built in 1975, serves as a dual role vessel in the fleet. Under tow, she arrives at Lowestoft, for conversion work to be carried out.

Work in progress in transforming the supply ship *Stirling Vega* into the *Putford Provider* at the North Quay in Lowestoft on the 27th January 2002.

A recent development has seen the introduction of larger stand alone Daughter craft, such as the *Putford Progress,* able to operate without the immediate close support of a mother ship.

PHOTOGRAPHIC INDEX

On the 9th December 1991, *Mincarlo*, as the *Putford Merlin*, was handed over for preservation to Mr. Cannell of the Lydia Eva Trust by Mr John Hashim, of Putford Enterprises at the former Brooke Marine shipyard, where the trawler was built.

Precedents in bankruptcy: containing forms of petitions in all cases which occur in the prosecution of commissions of bankruptcy; ... To which is added, an alphabetical abstract of the whole statute law relating to bankrupts

Thomas Moore

Eighteenth Century
Collections Online
Print Editions

Gale ECCO Print Editions

Relive history with *Eighteenth Century Collections Online*, now available in print for the independent historian and collector. This series includes the most significant English-language and foreign-language works printed in Great Britain during the eighteenth century, and is organized in seven different subject areas including literature and language; medicine, science, and technology; and religion and philosophy. The collection also includes thousands of important works from the Americas.

The eighteenth century has been called "The Age of Enlightenment." It was a period of rapid advance in print culture and publishing, in world exploration, and in the rapid growth of science and technology – all of which had a profound impact on the political and cultural landscape. At the end of the century the American Revolution, French Revolution and Industrial Revolution, perhaps three of the most significant events in modern history, set in motion developments that eventually dominated world political, economic, and social life.

In a groundbreaking effort, Gale initiated a revolution of its own: digitization of epic proportions to preserve these invaluable works in the largest online archive of its kind. Contributions from major world libraries constitute over 175,000 original printed works. Scanned images of the actual pages, rather than transcriptions, recreate the works *as they first appeared.*

Now for the first time, these high-quality digital scans of original works are available via print-on-demand, making them readily accessible to libraries, students, independent scholars, and readers of all ages.

For our initial release we have created seven robust collections to form one the world's most comprehensive catalogs of 18th century works.

Initial Gale ECCO Print Editions collections include:

History and Geography
Rich in titles on English life and social history, this collection spans the world as it was known to eighteenth-century historians and explorers. Titles include a wealth of travel accounts and diaries, histories of nations from throughout the world, and maps and charts of a world that was still being discovered. Students of the War of American Independence will find fascinating accounts from the British side of conflict.

Social Science

Delve into what it was like to live during the eighteenth century by reading the first-hand accounts of everyday people, including city dwellers and farmers, businessmen and bankers, artisans and merchants, artists and their patrons, politicians and their constituents. Original texts make the American, French, and Industrial revolutions vividly contemporary.

Medicine, Science and Technology

Medical theory and practice of the 1700s developed rapidly, as is evidenced by the extensive collection, which includes descriptions of diseases, their conditions, and treatments. Books on science and technology, agriculture, military technology, natural philosophy, even cookbooks, are all contained here.

Literature and Language

Western literary study flows out of eighteenth-century works by Alexander Pope, Daniel Defoe, Henry Fielding, Frances Burney, Denis Diderot, Johann Gottfried Herder, Johann Wolfgang von Goethe, and others. Experience the birth of the modern novel, or compare the development of language using dictionaries and grammar discourses.

Religion and Philosophy

The Age of Enlightenment profoundly enriched religious and philosophical understanding and continues to influence present-day thinking. Works collected here include masterpieces by David Hume, Immanuel Kant, and Jean-Jacques Rousseau, as well as religious sermons and moral debates on the issues of the day, such as the slave trade. The Age of Reason saw conflict between Protestantism and Catholicism transformed into one between faith and logic -- a debate that continues in the twenty-first century.

Law and Reference

This collection reveals the history of English common law and Empire law in a vastly changing world of British expansion. Dominating the legal field is the *Commentaries of the Law of England* by Sir William Blackstone, which first appeared in 1765. Reference works such as almanacs and catalogues continue to educate us by revealing the day-to-day workings of society.

Fine Arts

The eighteenth-century fascination with Greek and Roman antiquity followed the systematic excavation of the ruins at Pompeii and Herculaneum in southern Italy; and after 1750 a neoclassical style dominated all artistic fields. The titles here trace developments in mostly English-language works on painting, sculpture, architecture, music, theater, and other disciplines. Instructional works on musical instruments, catalogs of art objects, comic operas, and more are also included.

The BiblioLife Network

This project was made possible in part by the BiblioLife Network (BLN), a project aimed at addressing some of the huge challenges facing book preservationists around the world. The BLN includes libraries, library networks, archives, subject matter experts, online communities and library service providers. We believe every book ever published should be available as a high-quality print reproduction; printed on-demand anywhere in the world. This insures the ongoing accessibility of the content and helps generate sustainable revenue for the libraries and organizations that work to preserve these important materials.

The following book is in the "public domain" and represents an authentic reproduction of the text as printed by the original publisher. While we have attempted to accurately maintain the integrity of the original work, there are sometimes problems with the original work or the micro-film from which the books were digitized. This can result in minor errors in reproduction. Possible imperfections include missing and blurred pages, poor pictures, markings and other reproduction issues beyond our control. Because this work is culturally important, we have made it available as part of our commitment to protecting, preserving, and promoting the world's literature.

GUIDE TO FOLD-OUTS MAPS and OVERSIZED IMAGES

The book you are reading was digitized from microfilm captured over the past thirty to forty years. Years after the creation of the original microfilm, the book was converted to digital files and made available in an online database.

In an online database, page images do not need to conform to the size restrictions found in a printed book. When converting these images back into a printed bound book, the page sizes are standardized in ways that maintain the detail of the original. For large images, such as fold-out maps, the original page image is split into two or more pages

Guidelines used to determine how to split the page image follows:

• Some images are split vertically; large images require vertical and horizontal splits.
• For horizontal splits, the content is split left to right.
• For vertical splits, the content is split from top to bottom.
• For both vertical and horizontal splits, the image is processed from top left to bottom right.

PRECEDENTS

IN

BANKRUPTCY:

CONTAINING

FORMS of PETITIONS

In all CASES which occur in the PROSECUTION

OF

COMMISSIONS of BANKRUPTCY;

WITH

The PRACTICE of ftriking DOCQUETS—fuing out COMMISSIONS
—prefenting PETITIONS—obtaining ORDERS, CERTIFICATES,
&c—with the FEES to be paid for the fame—COMMISSIONERS'
PROCEEDINGS, &c

TO WHICH IS ADDED,

An ALPHABETICAL ABSTRACT of the whole STATUTE
LAW relating to BANKRUPTS

CALCULATED

As an ufeful OFFICE BOOK, for SOLICITORS, ATTORNIES,
CLERKS, &c

By THOMAS MOORE,

(Late of the BANKRUPT's OFFICE)

LONDON

PRINTED FOR THE AUTHOR,

AND SOLD BY P. URIEL, INNER TEMPLE LANE, AND
T. FLEXNEY, OPPOSITE GRAY'S INN, HOLBORN.

M.DCC LXXXVIII.

[*Entered at Stationers' Hall*]

Table of Contents,

L I S T

OF

S U B S C R I B E R S.

A.

MESS. Atkinson and Farrers, Chancery Lane
Meff. Abbot, Jenkins and James, New Inn
Meff Allen, Clifford's Inn
Mr. Allen, Poultry
Mr Auftin, Clement's Inn
Mr George Andree, Staple's Inn
Mr Edward Athawes, Cordwainer's Hall
Meff Annefley and Willet, Friday Street
Mr. John Afhe, Arundel Street, Strand
Mr. Thomas Ayrton, Prince's Street, Red Lion Square

B.

J Brimage, Efq Gray's Inn
Mr Frederick Booth, Craven Street
Mr John Berry, Meard's Court, Soho
Mr. Bridges, Serle Street
Mr John Barber, Pallgrave Place
Mr. W Browne Kirby Street
Mr Charles Bicknell, Chancery Lane
Meff Bull and Dyneley, Gray's Inn
Mr. Nathaniel Batten, Temple
Mr Thomas Bolton, Temple
Mr James Brindle, Temple
Mr H Brace, Temple
Mr John Bewls, New Inn
Mr. J B Bolton, Gray's Inn
Mr A Brown, Gray's Inn
Mr Barnett, Henrietta Street

Mr. William

Mr William Burdon, Copthall Court
Mr Buckland, Gray's Inn
Mess Bogle and Murphy, Doctors Commons
Mr Thomas Bunn, Clement's Inn
Mr Frederick Browne, Temple
Mr John Berry Southwark.
Mr. Bail , Bristol

C.

Mr Robert Crispin, Chancery Lane
Mess. Cudel and Smith, Gray's Inn
Mess Collett and Wimburn, Chancery Lane
Mr John Claudge, Crown Street
Mr Oliver Cromwell, Fll Street
Mr. William Corbett, Barker's Buildings, Holborn
Mr John Robert Cocker Gerard Street
Mr Joseph Cutting, Castle Street, Holborn
Mess Carter and Simpson, Boulogne Street
Mr. James Cook, Northumberland Street, Strand
Mr C C Cornwollers, Took's Court, Chancery Lane
Mr George Citter, Temple
Mr R W Clukson, Clement's Inn
Mr. William Clarke, Staple's Inn
Mr Clunnell Staple's Inn
Mr H Chester, Castle Street, Holborn
Mr. Thomas Champinte, John Street, Crutched Friars
Mr Thomas Cory, Dean Street, Soho
Mr. William Clulow, Chancery Lane
Mr James Chambers, Furnival's Inn

D.

Mess Dyneley and Bell, Gray's Inn
Mr William De Yongh, Cutlers Hall
Mr Jon Denner, Henrietta Street
Mr C B Darlington, Clifford's Inn
Mr. Edward Dawes, Angel Court, Throgmorton Street
Mess Dyne and Webb, Fall Street, Chatham Place
Mess Douce and Rivington, Fenchurch Buildings
Mess Dent and Green, Gray's Inn
Mr Edward Day, Temple

E.

Mr. John Ellis, Gough Square, Fleet Street
Mr R Edmunds, Exchequer Office of Pleas
Mr. Edwards, Staple's Inn
Mr John Edwards, Lothbury
Mr. James Edge, Temple

F.

Mess. Farrers and Atkinson, Chancery Lane
Mr. E. Foulkes, Covent Garden
Mr. F. Fairbank, Ely Place, Holborn
Mr. Edward S. Foss, Gough Square

Mr Fox,

Mr Fox, Parliament Street
Mr Peter Fox right, Ingram Court, Fenchurch Street
Mr Fox, Barnard's Inn
Mr Richard Foster, Dean Street, Soho
Mr William Fraser, Temple
Mr Peter Fry, Great Russel Street
Mr Walter Fletcher, Bryce Street
Mr Franco, Lincoln's Inn Lane

G

Mr Robert Genninghim, Gray's Inn
Mr Thomas Gee, Philpot Lane
Mr George Giles, Gray's Inn
Dr Thomas Gregor, Clifford's Inn
Mr George and Pen, Gray's Inn
Mr Robert George, Quality Court
Mr J. Gotolel, Temple

H

H. Baker, Esq. Gray's Inn
Messrs. Edmund William Herne, Paternoster Row
Mr Henry Halton, Adelphi
Mr Samuel Harmon, Jermyn Street
Mr George Hodgson, Charles Street, St James's
Mr James Houghton, Chancery Lane
Mr W Hayden, Clifford's Inn
Mr Fox, Gray's Inn
Mr William Houthup, Doctors Commons
Mr James Howe, Temple
Mr Thomas Holloway, Beam's Buildings, Chancery Lane
Mr Henry, Temple
Mr W Hibbs, Chancery Lane
Mr Charles Harmon, Wine Office Court, Fleet Street
Mr William Harry
Mr D Howard, George Street, Minories
Mr J Hague, Barlet's Buildings, Holborn
Mr Walter Hill, Gray's Inn
Mr Thomas Hine, Bolt Court
Mr H Havey, Clement's Inn
Mr Charles Hays, Manchester Buildings
Mr Thomas Hington, Carey Street
Mr S A Hoff, Plevse's Buildings
Mr Charles Harrison, Brunswick Street, Soho
Mr Philip, Great Marlborough Street
Mr Richard Hannom, Portland Street

I

J Jones, Esq. Gray's Inn
Messrs. James and Abbott, New Inn
Mr Harding, Temple

A 2

Mr Johnson,

Mr. l'Anson, Cannon-Row
Mr J W. Ivison, Mount Street
Mr. Gilbert Jones, Salisbury Court, Fleet Street
Mr. Jennings, Shire Lane
Mr. W. Johnston, Temple
Meff Johnson and Kelham, Hatton Garden
Mr. Thomas Johnson, Ely Place

K

Meff. Kettle, Pearson, and Loggen, Basinghall Street
Meff. Kelham and Johnson, Hatton Garden

L.

Mr Benjamin Lloyd, Chancery Lane
Meff Loggen, Pearson, and Kettle, Basinghall Street
Mr William Loveridge, Austin Friars
Mr T Lewis, Gray's Inn
Mr Joseph Lowten, Gray's Inn
Mr. Robert Long, Clement's Inn

M.

J. Manley, Esq, Temple
Mr Meggison, Hatton Garden
Mr. Thomas Muffendine, Barnard's Inn
Mr. John Marshall, Gray's Inn
Mr. Henry Mitchell, Cook's Court
Mr George Miller, Barnard's Inn
Mr. John Mills, Great Queen Street, Westminster
Mr. Charles Millett, Terrace, Gray's Inn Lane
Meff. Mitton and Young, Doctors Commons
Mr. Jame Mainstone, Effex Street, Strand
Mr. F. Matthews, Castle Street, Holborn
Mr. Joseph Morris, Temple
Mr. William Morton, Furnival's Inn
Mr. H. Mounfort, Gough Square
Mr. Charles Mayhew, New Inn

N.

Mr Samuel Naylor, Great Newport Street
Mr E Nash
Mr J. Neeld, Brydges Street

O.

Arthur Onflow, Esq. Temple

P.

J Perry, Esq Clement's Inn
Meff Pitches and Luard, Swithin's Lane
Mr. John Philpot, Bartlet's Buildings, Holborn
Meff. Pearson, Kettle, and Loggen, Basinghall Street
Mr. Benjamin Price, Chancery Lane

Mr. William

Mr. William Pittman, Exchequer Office of Pleas
Mr R. Patten, Barnard's Inn
Mr Samuel Plaſted, Barnard's Inn
Meſſ Palmer and Grover, Gray's Inn
Mr Charles Pryce, Temple
Mr. J Parry, Gray's Inn
Mr J Pearſon, Cook's Court, Serle Street
Mr Thomas Phillipſon, Ely Place, Holborn
Mr. F. C Peoy, Gray's Inn

R.

Mr. Daniel Robinſon, Gray's Inn
Mr. Rittſon, Southampton Buildings
Meſſ. Rivington and Douce, Fenchurch Buildings
Mr. Thomas Reed, Ely Place
Mr Robert Rider, Fetter Lane
Mr. John Redit, Serle Street
Mr Rorke, Gray's Inn
Mr J W Rogers, Mancheſter Buildings
Mr. John Raine, Fly Place
Mr Henry Roſſer, Kirby Street
Mr Peter Rich, Brownlow Street
Mr Richard Rudd, Great Queen Street
Mr John Robert, Great Ruſſel Street

S.

Mr. Willwyn Shepheid, Boſwell Court
Mr. Richard Shawe, New Bridge Street
Meſſ Smith and Cardel, Gray's Inn
Mr J Sim, Mark Lane
Mr Charles Smart, Lamb's Conduit Street
Meſſ Simpſon and Carter, Biſhopſgate Street
Mr Charles Shephard, Carey Street
Mr. A. Stevenſon, Ely Place, Holborn
Mr. John Santer, New Inn
Mr. John Stride, Carey Street
Mr J Stapleton, Clement's Inn
Mr James Seton, York Buildings
Mr. W Saunders, Crown Office, Temple
Mr Edward Sykes, New Inn
Mr Thomas Pitt Smith, Staple's Inn
Mr. Henry Sharpleſs, Curſitor Street
Mr John Stanley Smart, Exchequer Office of Pleas
Mr. John Scott, Thaives Inn
Mr. John Smith, Thaives Inn
Mr John Smith, Furnival's Inn
Mr T Skam, Barnard's Inn
Mr George Stubbs, Suffolk Street

Mr. Richard

T

Mr. Richard Troward, Norfolk Street
Mr Samuel Toulmin, Walbrook
Mr Mov Thomas, Walbrook
Mr J Thomas, Walbrook
Mr John Turner, Ely Place, Holborn
Mr John Tirrant, Thaves Inn
Mr James Taylor, Furnival's Inn

V

Meff Winburn and Collet, Chancery Lane
Meff A and J Wefton, Fenchurch Street
Mr Edmund Walker, Excnequer Office of Pleas
Meff Webb and Dyne, Earl Street, Chatham Place
Mr J Wilton, Castle Street Holborn
Men Wailet and Annefly, Friday Street
Mr John Watton, Walbrook
Mr John Williams, Sion College Gardens
Mr John Winter, Tooks Court
Mr William Wire, Ifcngall Street
Mr James White, Chancery Lane
Mr Benjamin Wilby, Soho Square
Mr William Waldington tor, Red Lion Court, Fleet Street
Mr W M Whitaker, Clifford's Inn
Mr James Worknam, Castle Street, Holborn

U

Mr Francis Vincent, Lant Street, Southwark

Y

Meff Young and Mitten, Doctor Commons
Mr. Thomas Younge, Clifford's Inn

PREFACE.

PREFACE.

THE Books that have been already written on the Subject of Bankruptcy, having been very learnedly filled with Explanations of the Law relating thereto, and many interesting and important Cases, decided by the Courts, very fully stated, some Precedents have also been inserted, and the Practice observed upon,—but a more enlarged and authenticated Collection of Precedents being wanted, and the whole of the Practice necessary to be explained—the Author of the following Sheets having had frequent Applications to compose such a Work, during the Time he was Chief Clerk in the Bankrupt's Office, presuming on the Experience of many Years in that Situation, and emboldened by the flattering Encouragement given him by a Number of the

most

moſt eminent Profeſſors of the Law, who readily
favored him with their Names, as Subſcribers to
this Undertaking—he humbly offers this Book
as a complete Compilation of Precedents, and
as a full Explanation of every Part of Practice,
the Whole of which, he flatters himſelf, will be
conſidered as a Supplement to all that has been
written on the Subject.

PRECEDENTS

IN

BANKRUPTCY.

FORMS OF PETITIONS.

Petition for a new choice of Assignees, one having become Bankrupt, and his Assignees to account.

In the matter of J. T a Bankrupt.

To the Right Honourable the LORD HIGH
CHANCELLOR of GREAT BRITAIN,

The humble Petition of J. B of I.
in the county of S Builder, one of the
Assignees of the said Bankrupt.

SHEWETH,

THAT on or about the
day of June, which was in the year of our Lord one
thousand seven hundred a commission of
bankrupt was awarded and issued against J. T of
H in the county of E. builder, and at the second
meeting of the commissioners under the said commission, upon the day of one thousand
seven hundred , the major part in value of
the creditors then present, did direct, that when any

money

money, amounting to the sum of one hundred pounds, should from time to time be received by, or arise out of the said bankrupt's estate, the same should be paid to T. G of I. aforesaid, merchant, and remain in his hands until the same should be divided amongst all the creditors of the said bankrupt, and at the same meeting your petitioner, and the said T. G were duly chosen assignees of the estate and effects of the said bankrupt, and thereupon the major part of the commissioners in the said commission named and authorized, executed an assignment of the personal estate of the said bankrupt to your petitioner, and the said I. G.

THAT soon afterwards the real estates of the said bankrupt were sold, and the same were conveyed to the purchaser thereof, by the major part of the said commissioners, and your petitioner, and the said I. G and the purchase-money for the same was thereupon paid to the said I. G.

THAT sundry debts were fully proved under the said commission, and divers other debts were claimed by other creditors of the said bankrupt, and particularly T. S of I merchant, as one of the executors and residuary legatees of I T. deceased, father of the said bankrupt, on behalf of himself, and the other executors and residuary legatees of the said I T claimed a debt of
pounds   shillings and   pence,   as due from the said bankrupt to them.

THAT on or about the   day of one thousand seven hundred   , a dividend of shillings and   pence, in the pound, was ordered by the major part of the commissioners acting under the said commission, to be made amongst such of the said creditors as had then proved their debts, and the claimants, when they had substantiated their claims by due proof of their debts, and under the said order several of the creditors who had proved their debts have been paid their dividends, and others have not yet received the same, and the said claims still remain undetermined

THAT

THAT on or about the   day
of   one thousand seven hundred   a commission
of bankrupt was awarded and issued forth against the
said T G and he was thereupon duly declared a bankrupt, and his estate and effects have since been duly
assigned unto I K. of I. aforesaid, gentleman, and W I.
of I aforesaid, draper.

THAT at the time of the date
and issuing of the said commission against the said I G
he had in his hands the sum of   thousand   hundred and   pounds   shillings and   pence,
belonging to the estate of the said J. I out of which the
dividend of   shillings and   pence in the pound,
so declared under the said commission against the said
J I ought to have been paid, some of the creditors who
had so proved their debts have been paid their dividends,
but many of them neglected to receive their said dividends before the said T G became bankrupt, and the
said claimants have not yet established their debts.

Your Petitioner therefore most humbly prays your Lordship, That
the said I. G. may be discharged
from being one of the assignees of
the estate and effects of the said J.
I and also from being banker under the said commission, and that
the major part of the commissioners
named in the said commission
against the said J I may cause
due notice to be given in the London Gazette, appointing a time
and place for the creditors of the
said J I who have proved their
debts, to meet, in order to proceed to the choice of one or more
person or persons to be assignee or
assignees of the estate and effects
of the said J I jointy with your
petitioner,

petitioner, in the room of the said T. G. and that the creditors of the said J T. who shall be present at such meeting, may proceed to such choice accordingly, and that after such choice shall be made, the said commissioners, jointly with your petitioner, may make a new assignment of the estate and effects of the said J. T remaining unreceived or undisposed of to your petitioner, and such person or persons as shall be so chosen in the room of the said T. G. and that the said T. G and the assignees of his estate and effects under the said commission against him, may join in such assignment, and that the assignees of the estate and effects of the said T. G. may come to an account before the said commissioners, for the estate and effects of the said J T come to their hands, or to the hands of any other person or persons, by their or any of their order, or for their or any of their use, as assignees under the said commission against the said T. G. with the usual directions for taking such account, and for production of deeds, papers, and writings, and that your Petitioner, and such new assignee or assignees, so to be chosen as aforesaid, may be admitted a creditor or creditors under the said commission against the said T G. and that the said T. G. and his assignees may forthwith deliver

deliver over to your petitioner, and such new affignee or affignees of the faid J. T all deeds, books, papers, and writings in their or any of their cuftody or power, relating to the eftate and effects of the faid J. T. and that fuch of the creditors of the faid J T. as had proved their debts before the faid dividend was declared, and who neglected to receive their dividends from the faid T. G. before he became bankrupt, and alfo the faid T. S and others, the creditors of the faid J. T. who had fo entered claims, but had neglected to complete the proof of their debts before the faid T. G. became bankrupt, may be paid in refpect of the faid dividend of   fhillings and   pence in the pound, rateably, and in proportion only to fuch dividend or dividends as your petitioner, and fuch new afsignee or afsignees fhall receive from the eftate of the faid T. G. Or that your Lordfhip will be pleafed to make fuch other order in the premifes, as to your Lordfhip fhall feem meet.

And your Petitioner fhall ever pray, &c.

Petition for choice of new Assignees, Assignees being dead, and representative of last Assignees to account to new Assignees.

In the matter of **C. B.** a Bankrupt.

> *To the Right Honourable the* LORD
> HIGH CHANCELLOR *of* GREAT
> BRITAIN.

> *The humble Petition of* N H---
> S. C. *and* J H *merchants and
> copartners, and* R. M. *Creditors of
> the said Bankrupt.*

SHEWETH,

THAT a commission of bankrupt, bearing date at Westminster the   day of   17 , was duly awarded and issued against C B on the petition of your petitioners, the said N H.--S. C. and J H. which commission was directed to certain Commissioners therein named, the major part of whom found and declared the said C. B. bankrupt.

THAT T. T. and G. A were duly chosen assignees of the estate and effects of the said bankrupt; and an assignment and bargain and sale of the personal and real estates and effects of the said bankrupt were executed to the said T. T. and G. A. by the major part of the Commissioners, in and by the said commission named and authorised, and the said T. T departed this life in the month of   now last past, but as yet no will of the said T. T. hath been proved, or administration from the proper Ecclesiastical Court taken out to his estates and effects.

THAT the said G. A who survived the said T T. and thereby became the surviving assignee of the said C B. the bankrupt, departed this life on the   day of   now last past, having first duly made and published his last will and testament in
writing.

writing, and thereof appointed his wife E. A. his brother H. A. and J I. of C. gentleman, joint executors thereof.

That the said E. A. H. A. and J I duly proved the said will of the said G. A. the surviving assignee of the said C. B. the bankrupt, in the proper ecclesiastical court, and took upon themselves the burthen and execution thereof.

Your petitioners therefore most humbly pray, your Lordship will be pleased to order the major part of the commissioners in and by the said commission of bankruptcy, named and authorised, to cause due notice to be given, of the time and place, for the creditors of the said bankrupt who have already, or shall hereafter in due time, come in and duly prove their respective debts under the said commission, to meet in order to their proceeding to the choice of one or more assignee or assignees of the said bankrupt's estate and effects, in the room of the said G A. deceased, the late surviving assignee thereof, and that the said E A. H. A and J I may be ordered, after such choice shall be had, to join with the major part of the said commissioners, in making and executing a new assignment and conveyance of the personal and real estate and effects of the said bankrupt, remaining unreceived, and not disposed of to such person or persons, who at such meeting shall be chosen to be such new assignee or assignees, and that the said

faid E A. H. A. and J. I. the executors of the faid G. A. may account to fuch new affignee or affignees, as fhall be duly chofen,
of the eftate and effects of the faid
bankrupt, upon their oath, for
fuch part thereof as came to the
hands of the faid G A. deceafed,
in his life-time, or of them the
faid E. A H. A. and J. I. fince
his deceafe, and that the faid E. A.
H. A. and J. I. as executors as
aforefaid, may be ordered to pay
the ballance of fuch account, if
the fame happen to be in favour
of the faid bankrupt's eftate and
effects (they being firft made all
juft allowances out of the fame)
to fuch new chofen affignee or affignees, and that they the faid
E. A H. A. and J. I. as executors
as aforefaid, may be alfo ordered
to deliver up, upon oath, to fuch
new affignee or affignees, all books,
papers, and writings, touching or
anyways concerning the eftate or
effects of the faid bankrupt.

And your Petitioner fhall ever pray, &c.

Petition to remove an Affignee, being infol.ent.

In the matter of W C. a Bankrupt.

To the Right Hon. the LORD HIGH
CHANCELLOR of GREAT LRITAIN.

The humble Petition of T K of C in the county of
M. chemiſt, and E. P of H C A-ſtreet,
London, Eſq two of the Affignees f the eſtate
and effects of W C. late of ι-ſtreet, London,
druggiſt, a bankrupt, and G W. of B. London,
merchant, on behalf of himſelf, and all other
creditors of the ſaid W C who have proved
their debts under the ſaid comn ſſion,

SHEWETH,

THAT a commiſſion of bankrupt, bearing
date the   day of   one thouſand ſeven hundred and
       was awarded and iſſued againſt the ſaid W C and
he was thereupon duly found and declared a bankrupt,
by the major part of the commiſſioners acting under the
ſaid commiſſion

THAT your petitioners T K and E P. together with W B. of 1-ſtreet, London, druggiſt,
were choſen affignees of the ſaid bankrupt's eſtate and
effects, and an affignment thereof was, on the   day
of   17 duly made and executed to them, by the
major part of the commiſſioners named in the ſaid commiſſion.

THAT on the   day of   17 a bargain
and ſale of the ſaid bankrupt's real eſtate was duly made
and executed by the major part of the commiſſioners,
named in the ſaid commiſſion, to your petitioners T K.
and E P. and the ſaid W. B the affignees of the eſtate
and effects of the ſaid bankrupt.

THAT the greateſt part of the ſaid bank-
rupt's eſtate and effects has been collected and got in,
and on the   day of   17 a dividend of 7s 6d in
pound was made, and on the   day of   17 a
farther dividend of 2s. 6d in the pound was made to,
and amongſt the creditors of the ſaid bankrupt

C   1 i 1

THAT your petitioner G W has proved
£   under the said commission.

THAT an advertisement was inserted in
the London Gazette, of the   day of   last, purporting, that the commissioners in the said commission
intended to meet on the   day of   then next, at six
o'clock in the afternoon, at Guildhall, London, to make
a final dividend of the estate and effects of the said bankrupt

THAT the major part of the commissioners,
in and by the said commission named and authorised,
met pursuant to the said advertisement, in order to make
a final dividend of the estate and effects of the said bankrupt, and your petitioner T. K and E P attended the
said meeting, to pass their respective accounts; but the
said W. B did not attend such meeting, to pass his account, or send any excuse for his non-attendance, although your petitioners apprehend and believe that the
said W B. has a considerable sum of money in his hands,
belonging to the estate of the said bankrupt, whereby
a final dividend could not then be made of the estate and
effects of the said bankrupt

THAT the said W. B is become insolvent,
and has had a meeting of his creditors, for the purpose
of compounding with them for their respective debts,
and at such meeting the said W. B or some person or
persons on his behalf, made an offer to his, the said
W B's creditors, of 6s. 8d in the pound, for their respective debts, whereby your petitioners conceive, that
the said W B. is no longer a proper person to be an assignee of the estate and effects of the said bankrupt.

YOUR petitioners therefore most humbly pray, that your Lordship will
be pleased to order, that the said
W. B be discharged from being
one of the assignees of the said
bankrupt's estate and effects, and
that another assignee may be chosen in his room or stead, and that
the

the said W B. may join with your petitioners T K and E P in an assignment of the said bankrupt's estate and effects, and also in a bargain and sale of the said bankrupt's estate; and the said W B may account before the commissioners, or the major part of them, in and by the said commission named and authorised, for the estate and effects of the said bankrupt, come to the hands of him the said W B or to the hands of any other person or persons for his use, and may pay or deliver the same to your petitioners T K and E P and such new assignee, that the costs of this application may be paid by the said W B

And your petitioners shall ever pray, &c

Petition of a sole Assignee to be removed, and for new choice, he undertaking to account and pay over to the Assignee or Assignees to be chosen

In the matter of M S M a bankrupt,

To the Right Hon the LORD HIGH CHANCELLOR *of* GREAT BRITAIN.

The humble Petition of C M of A in the City of London, merchant ,

SHEWETH,

THAT a commission of bankrupt under the great seal of Great Britain, bearing date the day of 17 was awarded and issued against the said M S M by the name and description of M S M. of street, London, grocer dealer and chapman, empowering the commissioners, or any three of them, to execute the same

THAT

THAT the faid M S M was, by the major part of the faid commiffioners, duly found and declared a bankrupt

THAT on the　　day of　　17　at a meeting of the faid commiffioners, at Guildhall, London, in purfuance of notice given in the London Gazette, for the choice of an affignee or affignees of the faid bankrupt's eftate and effects, your petitioner was, by the major part in value of the creditors of the faid M S M at fuch meeting chofen and appointed the fole affignee of the eftate and effects of the faid M S. M and an affignment of fuch eftate and effects was, by the faid major part of the faid commiffioners, made thereupon to your petitioner accordingly.

THAT your petitioner hath recovered and obtained a part of the efiate and effects of the faid M S M and there are other parts of the eftate and effects of the faid bankrupt, yet to be recovered and got in

THAT your petitioner hath for fome time paft been in a very bad ftate of health, and his health has been by illnefs fo much impaired, as to render him unable to carry on his trade and bufinefs, or to give that attention to the affairs of the faid bankruptcy which they require, there being feveral debts remaining due to the eftate of the faid bankrupt, for the recovery of which it will be neceffary to inftitute one or more fuit or fuits, as your petitioner apprehends and verily believes.

THEREFORE your petitioner humbly prays, that your Lordfhip will pleafe to order the commiffioners, in and by the faid commiffion named and authorifed, to advertife in the London Gazette for a meeting of the creditors of the faid M S. M to be holden at Guildhall, London, and then and there to proceed to the choice of another affignee or affignees of the eftate and effects of the faid M. S. M.

in the room and ftead of your petitioner, and to take your petitioner's accounts, your petitioner hereby offering to pay fuch fum
of money as, on the taking of the
faid account, fhall, after all juft
allowances, be found to be juftly
due and owing from your petitioner, to the eftate of the faid bankrupt, and to deliver over all fuch
books, papers, writings, bonds,
notes, and other fecurities, and all
other the eftate and effects of the
faid bankrupt, in the hands, cuftody, or power of your petitioner,
and join in an affignment thereof
to fuch new affignee or affignees,
as fhall be chofen in the room and
ftead of your petitioner, and that
the cofts of this application may
be paid out of the eftate of the faid
bankrupt.

And your petitioner fhall ever pray, &c.

---

*Petition to remove Affignees, for not acting and making a
dividend.*

In the matter of T. B. a bankrupt.

To the Right Hon. the LORD HIGH CHANCELLOR
of GREAT BRITAIN

*The humble Petition of J. G. P G. T S W B.
W G. and S P creditors of T B late of
Briftol, a bankrupt, on behalf of themfelves, and
the reft of the faid bankrupt's creditors.*

SHEWETH,

THAT in one thoufand feven hundred
a commiffion of bankrupt was awarded and
iffued againft the faid T B and he was found and declared bankrupt thereunder, and J. F. of in the
county of yeoman (which place adjoins to the city

of

of Briſtol,) and W. F. of Briſtol aforeſaid, diſtiller, were choſen aſſignees of the ſaid bankrupt's eſtate thereunder, and the ſame was aſſigned to them, and in about eight months afterwards, they, or one of them, poſſeſſed themſelves or himſelf of a conſiderable ſum of money, by ſale of the ſaid bankrupt's effects, and receipt of ſome put of his debts.

THAT the ſaid bankrupt, by his laſt examination, having charged the committee of a late conteſted election at Briſtol, with being indebted to him at his failure in upwards of   a meeting of the creditors of ſaid bankrupt was had on the   of   one thouſand ſeven hundred   purſuant to an advertiſement in the London Gazette, and the ſeveral Briſtol papers, and at ſuch meeting a memorandum was ſigned by all the creditors preſent, authoriſing the ſaid aſſignees to bring an action or actions, for recovery of the ſaid election debt, but the ſame was wholly omitted to be done by them and on the   of   one thouſand ſeven hundred   another meeting was had by ſuch creditors, in purſuance of the like advertiſements, whereat a memorandum was alſo ſigned by all the creditors preſent, authoriſing the ſaid aſſignees to treat for the ſettling or compounding ſuch election-debt, and to receive a compoſition therefore, and in caſe the ſame ſhould not be then forthwith ſettled and paid, to bring actions or an action for recovery thereof without delay, and both the ſaid aſſignees either attended at each of the ſaid meetings, or were immediately then afterwards made acquainted with ſuch reſolutions of the creditors, and memorandums for their ſafety in the premiſes as aforeſaid.

THAT the ſum of   was afterwards offered to be paid to the ſaid aſſignees, as a compoſition for ſuch election–debt, and the ſaid aſſignees having for ſo long a time neglected or omitted to bring ſuch action or actions as aforeſaid, for recovery of the whole of the ſaid election-debt, the creditors of the ſaid bankrupt agreed to the ſaid   being received in full, and directed

rected the said assignees to receive the same accordingly, yet nothing further hath been done therein by the said assignees, but why or for what reason, your petitioners cannot learn

THAT upon application to the said assignees, to appoint a meeting and divide the monies in their hands, the said Mr F. who hath about eighty pounds in his hands, submitted to do therein as the said Mr. F. should think proper to do on his part, and the said Mr. F. declines making any dividend under the said commission, until the said   shall be received; yet the said assignees do not take any steps whatsoever for receipt thereof, and your petitioners now apprehend and believe, that the said   is not intended to be paid, and that the said election debt will be wholly lost, unless steps are forthwith taken for recovery thereof.

THAT the creditors of the said bankrupt, who have proved their debts under the said commission, caused an advertisement to be inserted in the   Gazette of the   past, ‘ That they intended to meet on   the
" instant, and requested the attendance of the other
" creditors of the said bankrupt, in order to agree on
" some plan for bringing the affairs of the said bank-
" rupt to a conclusion,” and your petitioners well hoped the said assignees would have attended such meeting, and concurred in proper measures for the above purposes, but neither of the said assignees attended at such meeting and your petitioners cannot get the said assignees to make a dividend of the monies in their hands, or to take any steps whatsoever for recovery of the said election-debt, and other debts due to the said bankrupt's estate, notwithstanding the said creditors of the said bankrupt have authorised them so to do as aforesaid, and have always been ready to assist the said assignees in any measure whatsoever, proper to be done in the said bankrupt's affairs, for the benefit of his creditors, and the said W F is only a creditor of about twenty pounds, and hath not proved his debt under the said commission.

YOUR

Your petitioners therefore moſt humbly pray your Lordſhip, that the ſaid W F and J F. may be removed from being aſſignees under the ſaid commiſſion of bankrupt againſt the ſaid T. B and that the commiſſioners acting under the ſaid commiſſion may forthwith appoint, adveitiſe, and hold another meeting under the ſaid commiſſion, for the choice of a aſſignee, or new aſſignees thereunder, and that the ſaid W. F and J F may aſſign to ſuch new aſſignee, or new aſſignees, the eſtate and effects of the ſaid bankrupt now veſting in them, and the ſaid commiſſioners join in ſuch new aſſignment; and that the ſaid W F. and J. F. may alſo thereupon deliver to ſuch new aſſignee or new aſſignees, all books, papers, and writings, in their or either of their hands, of or belonging to the ſaid bankrupt's eſtate, and alſo forthwith, after ſuch choice, account with and pay and deliver over to ſuch new aſſignee or aſſignees, all monies or other effects in their hands, of or belonging to the ſaid bankrupt's eſtate, and the ſaid aſſignees having for ſuch a length of time been in poſſeſſion of money of and belonging to the ſaid bankrupt's eſtate, and refuſing or declining to divide ſame, or to act in the truſt as aſſented to, and directed as aforeſaid; that they the ſaid aſſignees may pay to your petitioners,

petitioners, or their folicitor herein, the cofts of this application,
or pay intereft for the monies received or poffeffed by them, fince
the fame hath or have been fo
poffeffed or received, and that
your petitioners may have fuch
further and other relief as the nature of their cafe may require,
and to your Lordfhip may feem
meet.

Petition for a new choice of Affignee, fole Affignee being dead.
In the matter of J M a bankrupt.

To the Right Honourable the LORD HIGH
CHANCELLOR of GREAT BRITAIN.

*The humble Petition of R S one of the creditors
of the faid Bankrupt,*

SHEWETH,

THAT a commiffion of bank-
rupt, bearing date at Weftminfter the   day of   17 ,
is duly awarded and iffued againft J. M. late of
in the county of   fhopkeeper, on the petition of
the faid R. S. which commiffion was directed to certain
commiffioners therein named, the major part of whom
found and declared the faid J. M. bankrupt.

THAT J P. of   in the faid county of
maltfter (fince deceafed) was duly chofen fole
affignee of the faid bankrupt, and an affignment of the
perfonal eftate and effects of the faid bankrupt was
executed to the faid J. P. by the major part of the commiffioners, in and by the faid commiffion named and
authorifed, and the faid J. P. departed this life on or
about the   day of   now laft paft, having duly
made and publifhed his laft will and teftament in writing,
and thereof appointed his fon J P and his daughters
C H. (the wife of I .H.) M P and I P. joint executor
and executrixes of the faid will.

D   T   r

THAT the faid C. H. M. P. and L. P. duly proved the faid will in the proper ecclefiaftical court, and took upon themfelves the burthen and execution thereof.

THAT the faid J. P. the fon, the other executor named in the fud will, did not join with the faid executrixes in proving the faid will, nor hath he yet proved the fame, but a power is referved for him to prove the fame, when he fhall apply for that purpofe.

YOUR petitioner therefore moft humbly prays, your Lordfhip will be pleafed to order the major part of the commiffioners in and by the faid commiffion of bankruptcy, named and authorifed, to caufe due notice to be given, of the time and place, for the creditors of the faid bankrupt who have already, or fhall hereafter in due time, come in and duly prove their refpective debts under the faid commiffion, to meet in order to their proceeding to the choice of one or more affignee or affignees of the faid bankrupt's eftate and effects, in the place of the faid J. P. deceafed, the late fole affignee thereof; and that the faid C H. M. P. and L P. may be ordered, after fuch choice fhall be had, to join with the major part of the faid commiffioners, in making and executing a new affignment of the perfonal eftate and effects of the faid bankrupt, remaining unreceived, and not difpofed of to fuch perfon or perfons, who at fuch meeting fhall be chofen to be fuch new affignee or affignees, and that the

faid

said C, H, M. P. and L. P, may account to such new assignee or assignees, as shall be duly chosen, of the estate and effects of the said bankrupt, upon their oath, for such part thereof as came to the hands of the said J. P. deceased, in his life-time, or of them the said C. H. M. P. and L. P. or either of them, since his decease, and that the said C. H. M. P. and L. P, and each of them, may be ordered to pay the ballance of such account, if the same happen to be in favour of the said bankrupt's estate and effects (they being first made all just allowances out of the same) to such new chosen assignee or assignees, and that the said C. H M P and L P and each of them, may be also ordered to deliver up, upon their oaths, to such new assignee or assignees, all books, papers, and writings, touching or anyways concerning the estate or effects of the said bankrupt.

To compel an Assignee to account and pay a dividend.

In the matter of F D. a bankrupt.

To the Right Honourable the LORD HIGH CHANCELLOR *of* GREAT BRITAIN.

The humble Petition of S S and F K Esqrs, Executors of J N Esq, deceased, W N T B and H P Creditors of the said bankrupt,

Sheweth,

THAT about the   17   a commission of bankrupt, under the great seal of Great Britain, was

awarded

awarded and iffued a amft E. D late of L. London, cheefemonger, dealer and chapman, and he was thereupon found and declared to be a bankrupt, within one or more of the ftatutes made concerning bankrupts, by the major part of the commiffioners acting under the faid commiffion.

THAT at a meeting of the creditors of the faid bankrupt, on or about the Sept 17 purfuant to notice in the Gazette, the faid J N and E W of L -ftreet, cheefemonger, who had formerly been in partnerfhip with the faid E D the bankrupt were chofen affignees of the faid bankrupt's eftate and effects and an affignment of the faid bankrupt's real and perfonal eftate was executed to them

THAT the faid J N one of the affignees of the faid bankrupt died fometime in or about th month of 17 having before his death duly made and publifhed his laft will and teftament, and thereof appointed your petition is S S and F K his executors, who have duly proved the fame in the prerogative court of the archbifhop of Canterbury

THAT the faid E W having become the furviving affignee of the faid bankrupt, by the death of the faid J N and having thereby got a confiderable fum of money into his hands to make a further dividend amongft your petitioners and the other creditors of the faid bankrupt who have proved their debts under the faid commiffion has neglected fo to do

THAT the faid E. W ftood indebted to the joint ftock of himfelf and the bankrupt previous to his the faid E D's bankruptcy, by a promiffory note of hand, in the words and figures following—"London, " June 17 I promife to pay the joint ftock of E D " and felf when accounts are fettled E W "

THAT the faid E W refufes to account for or pay the faid fum of fecured by his faid promiffory note, or to make any dividend thereof amongft the bankrupt's creditors, but on the contrary infifts upon a much larger fum being fet off againft another promiffory note, entered into by the faid bankrupt, previous to his

bankruptcy,

bankruptcy, and which is in the words and figures following.—"London, June 17 I promise to pay to the "joint stock of self and E W. pounds. E D."

THAT your petitioners are advised and most humbly submit that the said sum of by the said promissory note from the said E W was a debt due to the bankrupt's estate, and constituted a part thereof, and ought to be paid or accounted for, and divided amongst the bankrupt's creditors, inasmuch as the bankrupt thereby gained a credit amongst his several creditors, and the said E. W ought not to be permitted to set off his promissory note, but prove the same as a debt under the commission, and receive a dividend equal with the bankrupt's other creditors. Forasmuch as the said E W the assignee of the bankrupt's estate and effects has had a considerable sum of money in his hands, to the amount of belonging to the creditors of the said bankrupt for two years or thereabouts, without charging himself with any interest for the same

Your petitioner therefore most humbly prays your Lordship, that the said E W the assignee, may be directed to account for the sum of secured by his said note of hand, and may be directed to account for interest on balances that have from time to time remained in his hands, and may make a dividend amongst the creditors of the said bankrupt who have proved their debts, and that your petitioners may be paid their costs of this application

And your petitioners shall ever pray, &c.

Form

Form of a Petition to compel the Assignees of a bankrupt to bring in accounts before the Master.

In the matter of A M a bankrupt.

> To the Right Honourable the LORD HIGH CHANCELLOR *of* GREAT BRITAIN.

> *The humble Petition of* T. D. T W. E. H. J S. H. *and* R. A. *of the City of Bristol, bankers and copartners,* T T I. E B. G. *and* J. E *of the same city, bankers and copartners,* J. G H. *of the same city, merchant,* W P L. *of the same city, merchant,* C F S. *of the same city, merchant,* S. E. *and* W E. *of the same city, linen-drapers and copartners,* M. H. *of the same city, merchant,* W F *the younger, of the same city, distiller and* F. W *of the same city, linen-draper, on behalf of themselves, and all other the like creditors of* J. S *and* J. B. *late of Cheapside, London, goldsmiths, partners, and bankrupts, and of* A. M *of Tokenhouse-yard, in the city of London, merchant, also a bankrupt,*

SHEWETH,

THAT your petitioners, on the ⸻ day of ⸻ last, preferred their petition unto your Lordship, in the matter of the said A M stating as therein particularly mentioned, and praying, that they might be at liberty to bring an action or actions against the said J S. and J B. and the said A M upon one or more of the bills in question, and therein particularly mentioned, and that the assignees of the said A M might be bound and concluded by the event of such action or actions, and in the mean time, that the certificate of the said A M might be stayed, and that in case the petitioners should succeed in proving a partnership between the said J S J B and the said A M that the commissioners under the commission awarded and issued against the said A M might be directed to keep separate and distinct accounts of the said J. S A M and J B's joint and

and separate effects, and that the petitioners might prove their respective debts under the separate commission awarded and issued against the said A. M. and assent to or dissent from the signing his certificate, and in case the joint effects of the said J. S. A. M. and J. B. should fall short in paying the petitioners their respective debts, that then the petitioners might be at liberty to take a dividend with the rest of the separate creditors of the said A. M. for such respective sums as the joint effects shall fall short in paying, and in the mean time, the assignees of the said A. M. might be restrained from making a dividend of the separate effects; or that your Lordship would be pleased to make such other order therein, as to your Lordship should seem meet.

THAT the said petition came on to be heard before your Lordship on the   day of   last, in the presence of counsel for the petitioners, for the assignees of the estate and effects of J. S. and J. B bankrupts, and for the assignees of the estate and effects of A. M. a bankrupt, when your Lordship, upon hearing the said petition read, and what was alledged by all parties, was pleased to order (among other things) that it should be referred to Mr.   one of the Masters of the Court of Chancery, to enquire whether the said A. M. or J. M. his son, or either or which of them, was at any time, and when in partnership with the said J. S. and J. B. in any and what transaction, and for better making the said inquiry, the said bankrupts, the assignees of their respective estates and effects, and all proper parties, were to be examined before the said master, upon interrogatories or otherwise, as the said master should think fit, and produce before the said master, upon oath, all books, papers, and writings, in their respective custody or power, under both the said commissions, as the said master should direct.

THAT your petitioners have taken out the usual number of warrants for the said assignees of the estate and effects of the said J. S. and J. B. bringing in before the said master all books, papers, and writings, in

their

their refpective cuftody, or power, under the faid commiffion, againft the faid J S and J B in obedience to
your Lordfhip's faid order, but that the faid afsignees
have not complied therewith, as by the certificate of the
faid mafter, bearing date the　　day of　　appears

Your petitioners therefore humbly
pray your Lordfhip, that your
Lordfhip will be pleafed to order,
that N M J W and F B the affignees of the eftate and effects of
faid J S and J B may, within
feven days, peremptorily produce
before the faid mafter, upon oath,
all books, papers, and writings in
their refpective cuftody or power
under the faid commiffion againft
the faid J S and J B Or that
your Lordfhip will be pleafed to
make fuch other order in the premifes, as to your Lordfhip fhall
feem meet.

And your petitioners fhall ever pray, &c.

*Petition to prove a debt, and for Affignees to make a dividend,
and pay intereft on the money kept in their hands.*

In the matter of G. I. a bankrupt.

To the Right Hon. the LORD HIGH CHANCELLOR
of GREAT BRITAIN

*The humble Petition of F M. and M C on be-
half of themfelves and all others the creditors of
the faid bankrupt,*

SHEWETH,

THAT R K being, in May 17　indebt-
ed to your petitioners in the fum of　　upon the balance of account for money advanced by your petitioners
for the ufe of the faid R K. he the faid R K together
with the faid bankrupt G. I. as his furety, by their joint
and

and feveral bond or obligation, bearing date the   day
of   17   became jointly and feverally bound to your
petitioners in the penal fum of   conditioned for the
payment of the fum of   with intereft for the fame,
at the rate of 5 per cent. per annum, on or before the
      day of   then next.

THAT on or about the   day of   17
a commiffion was awarded and iffued againft the faid
R K upon which he was found and declared a bankrupt, and his eftate and effects were affigned to W. I. and
R W. the affignees chofen under that commiffion, and
the faid R. K afterwards obtained his certificate of conformity under the fame.

THAT the faid R. K. was then the furgeon
of the   Eaft Indiaman, and in   17   was about to
fail to the Eaft Indies on board the faid fhip, and your
petitioners have lately difcovered, that before the faid
R K left England, the faid G J applied to the faid
R K and obtained from him a certain bill of exchange,
dated the   day of   17   drawn by the faid G J.
upon and accepted by the faid R. K. payable at
      days after fight, for the fum of   gold ftar pago-
das, at 6s fterling the pagoda, amounting to   fterling, which bill the faid G I afterwards indorfed, and
by fuch indorfement directed the contents thereof to be
paid to Meffrs M C P and F of Madrafs aforefaid, and
fuch bill was tranfmitted by the faid G I fo indorfed, to
Meffrs. M C. P and I. who received and prefented fuch
bill to the faid R. K at Madrafs, for payment, and he,
on the   of   17   duly paid the amount thereof to
the faid M C P and F. who wrote a receipt thereon,
and delivered up the fame to the faid R K

THAT although the pagodas mentioned in
the faid bill of exchange, were therein drawn for at the
price of, or exchange of   fterling for each pagoda, yet
that fuch pagodas were then at the exchange of, or equal
in value to   fterling the pagoda; and fuch bill was
paid by the faid R K at the rate of   the pagoda, and
amounted in the whole to   fterling.

E   THAT

THAT on or about the   day of   17
a commiffion of bankrupt was awarded and iffued againft
the faid G. I. upon the petition of J. F. whereupon he
was found and declared a bankrupt, and his eftate and
effects were affigned to the faid J. F. and A. P, the affignees chofen under that commiffion

THAT by an anfwer lately put in by the faid
G. I. together with J F and A. P. his affignees, to a bill
filed againft them by the faid R. K. in the court of exchequer, they admit that your petitioners' faid bond is
yet outftanding and unfatisfied; that your petitioners
have a right to come in and prove the fame, under the
commiffion of bankrupt iffued againft the faid G I. that
the faid bill of exchange was fo given by the faid R. K.
to the faid G I for the purpofe of enabling him to fatisfy
and pay to your petitioners the aforefaid bond, in which
the faid G. I. had joined, as furety for the faid R K. but
which neverthelefs he had not done.

THAT the faid G. I. not only fraudulently
concealed the receipt and payment of the faid bill, for the
purpofes aforefaid, from your petitioners, but after the
faid G. I. had obtained fuch bill of exchange from, and
the faid R. K. had failed for the Eaft Indies, upon your
petitioners' application to the faid G. I. for payment of
the faid bond, previous to his bankruptcy, he requefted
your petitioners not to compel or infift upon the faid G. I's
paying the fame, alledging to your petitioners as an in-
ducement therefore, that the faid R. K. was gone to the
Eaft Indies, and had taken with him a confiderable in-
veftment, and upon his return home would be able to,
and would pay off and difcharge the whole monies due to
your petitioners upon the faid bond.

THAT your petitioners were entirely igno-
rant of of the faid G. I's having received fuch bill of exchange from the faid R. K. for fuch purpofe as aforefaid,
prior to the faid R K's return from the Eaft Indies, in
or about November laft, when the faid R, K caufed an
application to be made your petitioners, to know if the
faid G, I, had paid to your petitioners the monies due
upon

upon the said bond, he having received of the said R. K. the monies for that purpose.

THAT the said R K. is since dead, and your petitioners have no other remedy to obtain payment of their said debt, otherwise than by proving the same under each of the commissions of bankrupt against the said G I. and R. K. which they have not yet done

THAT your petitioners have been informed, and verily believe, that the said J. F. and A P the said G I's assignees, either have, or long since might have received money sufficient from and out of the household goods, debts, stock in trade, and other effects of the said bankrupt G I sufficient for a dividend among the creditors seeking relief under that commission

THAT the said G I ever since his said bankruptcy, hath continued in the possession of the dwelling-house he then lived in, and of the household goods and furniture thereof, and the said G I hath obtained his certificate under his said commission

THAT the said J F and A P might and ought before now to have proceeded to a dividend of the said G I's estate and effects, come to their hands or possession, and if such dividend had been advertised to be made, your petitioners might and would have proved their said bond debt, at the meeting of the commissioners to declare such dividend, without being at any extra expence for that purpose.

THAT your petitioners not having, for the reasons aforesaid, proved their debt under the said commission against the said G I and conceiving that the said J F and A P ought long since to have made such dividend as aforesaid, your petitioners' solicitor, on their behalf, on or about the   day of   last, caused the said J F and A P to be served with a notice in writing, to the purport and effect following that is to say, in the matter of G I a bankrupt—" Mr J F and Mr A P the said bankrupt's assignees, I do hereby give you notice, that unless you do, within   days from the date hereof, cause a dividend of the said bankrupt's estate and

effects

effects to be duly advertised, to be declared by the commissioners under the said commission, I shall, on behalf of Messrs F M and M C. alone, or jointly with others, prefer a petition to the Lord Chancellor, in order that the said F M and M C may prove their debt under the said commission, and for such dividend to be declared, dated the   day   17   J W "

no dividend of the estate and effects of the said G I under the said commission, hath yet been declared or advertised, and your petitioners have not been paid or satisfied any part of their said debt.

YOUR petitioners therefore most humbly pray your Lordship, that your petitioners may be at liberty to go before the major part of the commissioners named in the said commission of bankrupt against the said G. I. and prove their said debt under the commission, and that the said J F and A P may be directed to advertise and proceed to a dividend of the said G I's estate and effects, with liberty for your petitioners to make such proof of their said debt, at declaring such dividend, and that your petitioners may be paid a dividend, in respect of their said debt, rateably with the rest of the said bankrupt's creditors seeking relief under that commission and in case it shall appear that a sufficient sum of money hath come to the hands of the said J F and A. P. or either of them, whereby a dividend might have been made among the creditors of the said G.I. then that interest may be computed ed thereon, from the time that such dividend ought to have been made and paid by the said J F. and A P. for the benefit of the creditors at large of the said G I seeking relief under his commission, and that the proceedings had and taken under that commission may be produced before your Lordship, on the hearing of this petition. or that your Lordship will be pleased to make such further or other order in the premises, as to your Lordship shall seem meet

And your Petitioner shall ever pray, &c.

Petition to prove a debt under more than one commission, after receiving a dividend of 15s in the pound.

In the matter of I D. a Bankrupt.

To the Right Hon the LORD HIGH CHANCELLOR of GREAT BRITAIN.

The humble Petition of H P of D. miller, J. F. of the same place, grazier, J P of the same place, salesman, R. F. of the same place, merchant, T. B and R L. of the same place, salesmen and co-partners, T G of the same place, draper, T S. of the same place, draper, J L. of the same place, sailmaker, S N. of E in the county of K smith, J. P of P-street, London, dryfalter; R F of the city of C victualler, and Mary his wife, and G. B. of D in the said county of K. cordwainer.

Sheweth,

THAT W. P. and J A late of R near D. in the county of K. paper-makers and copartners, were accustomed to draw bills of exchange on J. D of in the parish of S. in the county of S. stationer, and which bills the said J. D. accepted.

THAT on the　　　day of　　1 78 a commission of bankrupt was awarded and issued against the said J. D. and on the　　day of　　17 a commission of bankrupt was also awarded and issued against the said W. P. and J A and the several parties were accordingly and respectively declared bankrupts

THAT previous to either of the said commissions issuing, all the said bankrupts were indebted unto your petitioner H. P. in the sum of　　on account of one bill of exchange, bearing date the　day of 1 7　and which was indorsed to your said petitioner in consideration of money lent and advanced by your said petitioner unto the said P. and A.

THAT the said bankrupts were also indebted unto your petitioner J. F. in the sum of　on two other of the like bills of exchange, bearing date respectively the　of　1 7　, and the　of　1 7 , for　each, and which were indorsed to your said petitioner, in consideration of　lent and advanced by your petitioner unto the said P. and A.

THAT the said bankrupts were also indebted unto your petitioner J. P in the sum of　on another of the like bills of exchange, bearing date the　of　1 7 for the sum of　and which was indorsed to your said petitioner, in consideration of　lent and advanced by your petitioner unto the said P and A.

THAT the said bankrupts were also indebted unto your petitioner R F. in the sum of　on another of the like bills of exchange, bearing date the　of　·7 and which was indorsed to your petitioner in consideration of goods sold and delivered, and money lent and advanced by your petitioner unto the said P. and A

THAT the said bankrupts were also indebted unto your petitioner T B and R. L in the sum of on three other of the like bills of exchange, bearing date respectively the　　of　1 7 the first for　the second and third for　each, and which were also indorsed dorfed to your petitioner, in confideration of   for monies lent and advanced by your petitioner unto the faid P. and A.

THAT the faid bankrupts were alfo indebted unto your petitioner T. G. in the fum of   on another of the like bills of exchange, bearing date the   day of   17 payable to   or order, and who indorfed the fame to your petitioner in confideration of goods fold and delivered by your petitioner to the faid

THAT the faid bankrupts were alfo indebted unto your petitioner T. S. in the fum of   on two other of the like bills of exchange, bearing date refpectively the   of   17 for   each, and which were indorfed to your petitioner in confideration of goods fold and delivered, and monies lent and advanced by your petitioner unto the faid P. and A.

THAT the faid bankrupts were alfo indebted unto your petitioner J. L. in the fum of   on four other of the like bills of exchange, bearing date refpectively the   of   17 the firft for   the fecond and third for   each, and the fourth for   and which were indorfed to your petitioner in confideration of money lent and advanced by your petitioner unto the faid P. and A.

THAT the faid bankrupts were alfo indebted unto your petitioner S. N. in the fum of   on another of the like bills of exchange, bearing date the   of   17 which was indorfed to your petitioner in confideration of work and labour done and performed by your petitioner for the faid P. and A.

THAT the faid bankrupts were alfo indebted unto your petitioner J. P. in the fum of   on two other of the like bills of exchange, bearing date refpectively the   of   17 the one for   and the other for and which were indorfed to your petitioner in confideration of monies lent and advanced, and goods fold and delivered by your petitioner to the faid bankrupts P. and A.

THAT the faid bankrupts were alfo indebted to your petitioner R. F. and Mary his wife (late M. R. widow)

widow) in the fum of   on four other of the like bills
of exchange, two of which bear date the   day   of
17 for   each, and the others bearing date the
day of   17 for   each, and were indorfed to your
petitioner M. F. before her intermarriage with the faid
R. F. by the faid P. and A. in confideration of monies
before that time lent and advanced to them by your petitioner.

THAT the faid bankrupts were alfo indebted
to your petitioner G. B. in the fum of   on another of
the like bills of exchange, bearing date the   of
17 for that fum, and was indorfed to your petitioner
in confideration of monies lent and advanced to the faid
P. and A.

THAT all the above-mentioned feveral bills
of exchange were accepted by the faid J D the bankrupt.

THAT your petitioners have feverally proved
their refpective debts, under the commiffion againft the
faid P and A and at which time the faid bills were exhibited to the commiffioners, and indorfed by them
according to the ufual practice

THAT your petitioner J P who is refident
in town, and T B who happened to be in London, attended at the third meeting under the faid J D's commiffion being the   day of   17 and at which time
they had not received any thing under P. and A 's commiffion, and then offered to prove their refpective debts,
but the folicitor refufed them for the reafon then alledged
by him, which was, that your petitioners did not produce
the accounts current between them and the faid Meff.
P. and A and for no other caufe whatfoever, And your
faid petitioners placing too much confidence in the re-
prefentation of the faid folicitor at that time, were per-
fuaded by him they could not, without the production
of fuch account, prove their faid debts under that commiffion, and therefore have fince and before any other
meeting was had under D's commiffion, received fifteen
fhillings in the pound from the eftate of P and A and
therefore at this time cannot make the ufual affidavits of
the

the whole amount of their original debts, but your petitioners are advised, and humbly hope, that such stratagem of the solicitor under D.'s commission, will, in equity, have no effect on your petitioners' claim.

THAT previous to any dividend being declared under the said commission, against the said P. and A. all your petitioners (except the said J. P.) made affidavits or affirmations of their respective debts, with an intent to exhibit the same at the next meeting to be had under the commission against the said J. D. and at which time your petitioners as stated and sworn to by them in their respective affidavits, had received no security or satisfaction whatsoever, save and except the said bills.

THAT on the   day of   last, a meeting was held at Guildhall, London, under D.'s commission, for the purpose of declaring a dividend, at which time, being the first meeting of creditors under that commission after your petitioners had proved their debts under P. and A.'s commission, your petitioners' solicitor attended and tendered the said several affidavits, when the solicitor under that commission objected to your petitioners being admitted creditors, upon the suggestion that your petitioners had since the making of their affidavits, received a dividend of 15s. in the pound from the estate of P. and A.

Your petitioners therefore most humbly pray your Lordship, that they may severally be admitted creditors under the said J. D.'s commission, for the amount of their respective bills in their respective hands, on the affidavits and affirmations made by your petitioners, and receive a proportionable dividend with the other creditors of the said J. D. your petitioners hereby undertaking, that in case the dividends arising under the said J. D.'s

J

commiffion, and P. and A 's commiffion, amount to a greater fum
than twenty fhillings in the pound,
to refund the overplus for the benefit of the other creditors, and that
your petitioners may be paid the
cofts of this application, and that
in the mean time the affignees of the
faid J D may be reftrained from
making any dividend of his eftate
and effects, and that your Lordfhip
will make fuch further order in the
premifes as to your Lordfhip may
feem meet.

And your petitioners fhall ever pray, &c.

----

*Petition to prove a debt, and receive a dividend, after claim
made, and a dividend of 5s. in the pound*

In the matter of J P a bankrupt

To the Right Hon the Lord High Chancellor
of Great Britain

*The humble Petition of W D of the parifh of
in the county of   dyer.*

Sheweth,

THAT a commiffion of bankrupt under
the great feal of Great Britain, bearing date the
day of   17   was awarded and iffued againft the
faid J P. by the name and defcription of J. P of the
parifh of   in the county of   merchant, dealer
and chapman, carrying on the bufinefs of a merchant,
dealer and chapman, under the ftile and firm of J P
and company, and he was thereupon found and declared
a bankrupt, and J A. of   in the county of   merchant, and J. S. of   ftreet, in the city of London,
merchant, were chofen affignees of his eftate and effects,

and

and an aſſignment thereof was duly made to them accordingly.

THAT the ſaid J P was, at and before the date and ſuing forth of the ſaid commiſſion, and ſtill is juſtly and truly indebted to your petitioner in the ſum of pounds ſhillings and pence, upon balance of account for money lent and advanced to the ſaid bankrupt, and for work and labour done and performed, and materials found and provided, in dying ſundry goods for the ſaid bankrupt, for which ſaid ſum of pounds ſhillings and pence, or any part thereof, your petitioner hath not received any ſecurity or ſatisfaction whatſoever, ſave and except a promiſſory note for the ſum of pounds ſhillings, bearing date the day of 17 drawn by the ſaid bankrupt, under the firm of J P and company, payable to your petitioner or order, two months after the date thereof.

THAT a meeting of the major part of the commiſſioners named and authoriſed in and by the ſaid commiſſion, was held at Guildhall, London, on the day of 17 for the purpoſe of making a dividend of the eſtate and effects of the ſaid bankrupts, when your petitioner being unable, on account of illneſs, to attend the ſaid meeting to prove his debt; your petitioner cauſed a claim to be entered amongſt the proceedings under the ſaid commiſſion, and not any meeting of the ſaid commiſſioners, for proof of debts, hath been ſince had under the ſaid commiſſion.

THAT the ſaid aſſignees at the ſaid meeting, admitting they had ſufficient money in their hands to pay h c ſhillings in the pound, on the debts proved and claimed under the ſaid commiſſion, the major part of the ſaid commiſſioners then ordered a dividend of five ſhillings in the pound to be made to the ſeveral creditors who had proved their debts under the ſaid commiſſion, and to the claimants, when they had made out their reſpective claims.

Your petitioner therefore most humbly prays your Lordship, that he may be at liberty to prove his said debt of   pounds   shillings and   pence, under the commission against the said J. P. and be let into and receive the said dividend of five shillings in the pound, with the rest of the creditors of the said bankrupt who have already proved their debts, and receive the same under the said commission, and that your petitioner may have and receive such further or other dividends in respect of his said debt, as the other creditors shall or may have or receive out of the said bankrupt's estate, and that the proceedings under the said commission may be produced before your Lordship, at the hearing of this petition or that your Lordship will make such other order in the premises, as to your Lordship shall seem meet.

And your petitioners shall ever pray, &c.

Petition to prove a debt, upon a bond given by the bankrupt to petitioner, in lieu of a former bond to another, refused by the commissioners

In the matter of J V a bankrupt

To the Right Hon th LORD HIGH CHANCELLOR *of* GREAT BRITAIN.

The humble Petition of C S of the parish of in the county of bierii, and W H of the parish of in the faid county, fmith,

Sheweth,

THAT J V now or late of the parish of in the county of innholder, in or about the year of our Lord 17 having occasion for the sum of applied to M M late of the parish of in the county of widow, deceased, to advance and lend him the same, which she accordingly did, and for securing the repayment thereof, the said J V by his certain bond or writing obligatory bearing date the day of in the said year of our Lord 17 acknowledged himself to be held and firmly bound to the said M M in the penal sum of conditioned for the payment by him the said J V to her the said M M of the said sum of pounds, with interest for the same after the rate of 5 per cent per annum, at a day therein mentioned, are long since past

That in and by a certain indenture, bearing date the day of and made between her the said M M of the one part and your petitioners of the other part, reciting, that the said M M then had lawful issue of her body three sons (to wit, J S C S. and W A for whom she was willing and desirous of making some provision after her decease, and further reciting, that the several persons named in the schedule thereunto annexed, or therein otherwise then were and stood justly and truly indebted to the said M M in the several sums of moneys respective ...

h

which she the said M M had agreed to assign unto your petitioners, and also to raise and pay them the sum of   making together the sum of   at the time, in the manner, and upon the trusts therein after mentioned it is by the said indenture witnessed, that for and in consideration of the natural love and affection which she the said M M had for and towards her said children, and also for and in consideration of the sum of ten shillings, to her paid by your petitioners, the receipt whereof is thereby acknowledged, she the said M. M did bargain, sell, assign, transfer, and set over to your petitioners, all and singular the debts and monies in the said schedule particularly mentioned, and did covenant within twelve calendar months then next ensuing, to pay, or cause to be paid to your petitioners, the said sum of making, together with the amount of the debts therein before mentioned, the said sum of   which said sum of   was thereby declared, by and between the said parties thereto, to be so vested in your petitioners, upon trust to call in the said several sums of money, in the said schedule mentioned, and invest the same, together with the said sum of   on such government, or other security or securities, as your petitioners should from time to time think fit, and pay, apply, and dispose of the interest, dividends and produce of the said sum of   unto the said M. M and her assigns, for her life, to and for her own sole and separate use, and after her death, upon trust, to pay and assign the sum of part of the said sum of   to the said J S. on his attaining 21, to and for his own use and benefit, and upon further trust, to pay and assign the further sum of further part of the said sum of   unto the said C S. on his attaining 21, to and for his own use and benefit; and upon further trust, to pay and assign the further sum of   residue of the said sum of   to the said W A. on his attaining 21 to and   his own use and benefit as by the said indenture now in your petitioners' custody, relation being thereunto had, may and will more fully and at large appear.

Thar

THAT the said sum of   so due and owing from the said J V to the said M M was one of the debts assigned by the said indenture, and comprized in the said schedule thereto annexed or under written, and the said bond or writing obligatory, for securing the repayment thereof, was by her the said M M delivered to your petitioners, and the said M M who afterwards intermarried with one W P, in or about the month of 17   departed this life intestate, leaving the said W P. her surviving, who procured letters of administration to be granted to him, of the estate and effects of the said M M out of the prerogative court of the Archbishop of Canterbury, and thereby became her personal representative.

THAT your petitioners at various times caused application to be made to the said J V for payment of th said sum of   and the interest due thereon, and the said J V at length professing his then inability to discharge the said principal sum of   and your petitioners thinking it for the advantage of the said trust estate, and for the more speedy recovery in either of the said sum of   that the said J V should execute a new bond to your petitioners for the sum, agreed to give the said J V further time to raise and pay the said sum of   upon his giving your petitioners a new bond for the same in their own names, and paying up the interest due on the said former bond, and which he the said J V promised to do.

THAT accordingly the said J V in and by his certain writing obligatory, bearing date the   day of   17   acknowledged himself to be held and firmly bound to your petitioner, in the penal sum of   conditioned for payment to your petitioners of the said sum pr   with interest for the same after the rate of 5 per cent per annum, on the   day of   then next ensuing, and the said J V further promised to discharge the arrear of interest due on the said former bond, upon receipt whereof your petitioners were ready and willing to deliver up the same to be cancelled.

THAT

THAT the said J V never paid your petitioners the said arrear of interest, so is aforesaid due and owing to your petitioners on the said first mentioned bond, and also neglected to pay the principal and interest due on the said last mentioned bond, and your petitioners, from some intimations they had received, being apprehensive that the said J V. was in bad circumstances, your petitioners, in or about the latter end of the said year   caused the said J V. to be held to bail for the sum of   and upwards, due to your petitioners, for principal and interest on the said last mentioned bond

THAT the said J V in consequence of such arrest, applied to your petitioners, and requested them to accept a part of the said debt, on account of which your petitioners accordingly agreed to do, and did not proceed further in the said action

THAT in or about the month of   17 a commission of bankrupt, under the great seal of Great Britain was awarded and issued forth against the said J V directed to   commissioners therein named, on which he was soon afterwards found and declared to be a bankrupt

THAT there is now justly due and owing to your petitioners, from the said J V, upon principal and interest remaining due on the said last mentioned bond, the sum of   and a meeting for a dividend of the said bankrupt's estate and effects being advertised in the London Gazette, to be held on Thursday the   day of   last past, your petitioner C S made an affidavit of such debt, and carried the same to be forwarded, together with the said bond, to Mr F, the solicitor under the said commission, to be proved at the said meeting

THAT shortly after, your petitioner C S. received a letter from the said Mr F of which the following is a copy, viz —" V a bankrupt   Sir, By the commissioners direction I send you the above memorandum and by their order return you the inclosed " and which said memorandum is as follows, viz — ' Memo-
' randum

" randum, C S of the parish of   in the county of
"   brewer, attempted to prove before us, by affi-
" davit, a debt of   pounds   shillings and
" pence, due from the said bankrupt to the said C. S.
" and W. H. of the parish of   in the county of
" smith, for principal and interest said to be remaining
" due on the said bankrupt's bond to the said C. S. and
" W H, bearing date the   day of   17 but it
" appearing to us, that the said bond was given in lieu
" of a certain other bond, entered into by the said bank-
" rupt, to one Mrs. M deceased, and it not appear-
" ing to us how the said C. S. and W H have become
" entitled to the same, and it also appearing to us, by
" the account of the said bankrupt, that the said Mr.
" M was, upon the ballance of accounts, including
" the said money due on the said bond, indebted to
' the said bankrupt the sum of   pounds and   shil-
" lings, the said proof of the said C. S is rejected "

         THAT your petitioners are not aware that
the said M. M was indebted to the said J V in any manner whatsoever, but in case she was, your petitioners
conceive, that the said J V is not entitled to set such
demand, if any he has, against the said bond debt, so
due and owing to your petitioners, as aforesaid, but
ought to apply to the said W. P the personal representative of the said M M for the same, and the said
W A being still an infant, of the age of   years, or
thereabouts, your petitioners do not think themselves at
liberty to allow such demand, if any, to be set off against
the said bond debt

                    YOUR petitioners therefore most
                    humbly pray your Lordship, that
                    the commissioners named and au-
                    thorised in and by the said com-
                    mission of bankrupt, so as afore-
                    said issued against the said J V
                    may be directed to admit your
                    petitioners to prove the said debt
                    of   so due and owing to them
         G

as aforefaid, and that in the mean time they may be ftayed from making a dividend of the faid bankrupt's eftate and effects, and that the coft of this application may be paid your petitioners, out of the faid bankrupt's eftate and effects, or that your Lordfhip will be pleafed to make fuch other order in the premifes, as to your Lordfhip fhall feem meet.

And your petitioners fhall ever pray, &c.

Petition for an Executor to prove a debt, after a dividend being made.

In the matter of J. B. a bankrupt.

To the Right Hon. the LORD HIGH CHANCELLOR of GREAT BRITAIN.

The humble Petition of T S. of   in the county of   grocer, furviving Executor named and appointed in and by the laft will and teftament of R. S late of   aforefaid, gentleman, deceafed, a creditor of the faid bankrupt,

Sheweth,

THAT the faid bankrupt, on or about the day of   in the year of our Lord 17   borrowed of the faid R S. deceafed, the fum of   and which the faid R. S did then advance and lend to him, and for fecuring the repayment thereof, the faid bankrupt, in and by his certain bond or writing obligatory, bearing date on or about the fame   day of   17   became held and firmly bound unto the faid R. S deceafed, in the penal fum of   conditioned for payment by the faid bankrupt, his heirs, executors, or adminiftrators, unto the faid R S. deceafed, his executors, adminiftrators, or affigns, of the fum of   and intereft after the

rate

rate of   per cent. per annum, on the   day of next enfuing, the date thereof

THAT a commiffion of bankrupt under the great feal of Great Britain, bearing date at Weftminfter the   day of   17   directed to certain commiffioners therein named, hath been duly awarded and iffued forth againft the faid J B. and he has been thereupon declared and found bankrupt, and R. T. of   in the parifh of   in the county of   cutler, J A of   in the parifh of   aforefaid, and S S of   aforefaid, carpetmaker, have been fince duly chofen and appointed affignees of the faid bankrupt's eftate and effects, which faid R T. J A. and S S have accepted the faid affigneefhip, and acte therein.

THAT the meetings held in the faid commiffion were duly advertifed in the London Gazette, as your petitioner believes, and the faid affignees have proceeded to get in and receive the perfonal eftate and effects of the faid bankrupt, and divers proceedings have been had, and feveral debts proved under the faid commiffion, by divers perfons, creditors of the faid bankrupt, and the faid affignees have made one or more dividends of the faid bankrupt's eftate and effects, to and amongft the creditors of the faid bankrupt who have proved debts as aforefaid, to the amount or value in the whole of 12s 6d in the pound, on the feveral debts fo proved as aforefaid

THAT the faid R. S. died on or about the   day of   17   having firft duly made and publifhed his laft will and teftament in writing, bearing date on or about the   day of   17   and appointed your petitioner and G. S. executors thereof, and fuch will hath been fince proved by your petitioner in the prerogative court of   and the faid G S hath fince departed this life, whereby your petitioner is become the only furviving executor of the faid laft will and teftament of the faid R. S and entitled to have and receive a dividend equal with the other creditors of the faid bankrupt, for and in refpect of the debt fo as aforefaid due

G 2   and

and owing from the said bankrupt, upon his bond, to the said R. S deceased, as aforesaid.

THAT there was justly due and owing from the said bankrupt, upon his said bond, before the date and issuing forth of the said commission, the said principal sum of   and   for one year's interest thereof, the said bankrupt having duly and regularly paid the interest of the said principal sum of   except as aforesaid, as and when, or soon after the same from time to time became due, and the said principal sum of   and the interest thereof as aforesaid, still remains due and owing to your petitioner.

THAT your petitioner never saw or read, observed or was informed, of the several advertisements which have from time to time been inserted in the London Gazette, for holding the several meetings held under the said commission, or any of them, and hath not proved the debt so as aforesaid due and owing to him, as surviving executor as aforesaid, from the said bankrupt, upon his bond as aforesaid under the said commission, and the said R. T. J. A. and S. S now refuse to permit and suffer your petitioner to prove his said debt, notwithstanding they have a sufficient sum of money in their hands, part and parcel of the said bankrupt's estate and effects, to answer and pay the dividend which will be coming due to your petitioner, for and in respect of his said debt, at and after the same rate and in like manner as the other creditors of the said bankrupt have been paid and satisfied, as your petitioner has been informed and believes.

YOUR petitioner therefore most humbly prays your Lordship, that he may be at liberty to prove his debt, or sum of   and interest so as aforesaid due and owing to him, as executor as aforesaid, from the said bankrupt, under the said commission of bankrupt awarded

awarded and iſſued forth againſt
the ſaid J. B. and that the ſaid
R. T J. A. and S. S. may be
ordered and directed to pay unto
your petitioner, ſuch and the like
dividend or dividends, for and in
reſpect of his ſaid debt, as hath
been paid, or that ſhall or may
hereafter become due, owing, or
payable to the other creditors of
the ſaid bankrupt, who have
proved debts, and ſought relief
under the ſaid commiſſion as
aforeſaid, and that the ſaid commiſſion of bankrupt, and all the
proceedings under the ſame, may
be produced at the hearing of
this petition or that your Lordſhip will make ſuch other order
in the premiſes, as to your Lordſhip ſhall ſeem meet.

And your petitioner ſhall ever pray, &c.

———

Petition to prove a debt, on Policies of Inſurance.

In the matter of J. A. and T A. Bankrupts.

To the Right Honourable the LORD HIGH
CHANCELLOR *of* GREAT BRITAIN.

*The humble Petition of T B and D. B. of
ſtreet, London, merchants and copartners, at-
torneys and agents for J. M. of Calcutta, in
Bengal*

Sheweth,

THAT your petitioners did, on or about
the day of 17 preſent their petition unto your
Lordſhip, on behalf of the ſaid J M praying, that the
claim entered by your petitioners, on behalf of the
ſaid

said J. M. might be admitted as a proof of debt under the said commission; and that a rateable dividend might be retained thereon, until your petitioners should substantiate their debt under the same, to the satisfaction of this honourable court, or prove the same in manner as by law required, and that the said bankrupts, or their assignees, might be directed to deliver up unto your petitioners certain policies upon the ship and certain other papers and writings in the said petition described and set forth, and for other purposes in the said petition mentioned and expressed

THAT the said petition came on to be heard before your Lordship on the day of 17 whereupon your Lordship was pleased to order," that it should be referred to the major part of the commissioners named in the commission of bankrupt issued against the J A and T. A. to take an account of all dealings and transactions between the said bankrupts and J. M. in the said petition mentioned, and what was actually due from the said bankrupts to the said J M at the time of the issuing the commission of bankrupt against them; in the taking of which account the said commissioners were to make all just allowances, and for the better taking and clearing the said account, the parties were to be severally examined before the said commissioners, upon interrogatories or otherwise, as the said commissioners should think fit, and were to produce before the said commissioners, upon oath, all books of account, papers, and writings, in their respective custody or power, relating thereto, as the said commissioners should direct, that the petitioners should be at liberty, in the mean time, to inspect all the books of the said bankrupts, in the hands of the said assignees, and to take copies or extracts therefrom, and all further directions in the matter of the said petition were thereby reserved until after the said commissioners should have made their certificate, when any of the parties were to be at liberty to apply to your Lordship in relation thereto, as they should

should be advised, and such order should be made as should be just."

That the major part of the commissioners acting under the said commission, did, in pursuance of the said order of the said   day of   last, meet at   on the   day of   17 and by their report of that date did certify, that by virtue of the order of the said   of   last, they had been attended by the proper parties, for the purpose of taking the accounts between the said bankrupts and the said J. M. and that the account to the certificate annexed was admitted by the assignees, save as therein after mentioned and sworn to by the said J A one of the said bankrupts, and J D. the clerk to the said bankrupts, to be a true copy of the account current, existing between the said bankrupts and the said J. M. at the time of the date and issuing of the said commission, and that it appeared to them, that the ballance then due from the said bankrupts to the said J M. was   and that it appeared to them by the said accounts thereunto annexed, and admitted by all parties then present, that the said bankrupts had received, on account of the said J. M at the times mentioned in the said account, the sum of and that in the said account current, the said bankrupts had charged and been allowed a commission of   per cent on the sum of   which the said J A. declared upon his oath to be the whole of the commission he ever meant to have charged the said J N. for transacting his business in England, and that it appeared to them, that no commission whatsoever had been charged in the said account current, on the sum of   received by the said bankrupts, after the   of   17   the time of the ballancing the said account, whereupon it was contended by the assignees of the said bankrupts, that there ought to be charged the same commission of   per cent. on the said sum of   as had been, so as aforesaid, charged on the said sum of   the commission being claimed as a commission for receiving the money, but it appearing to them by the bankrupt's accounts

counts, and by his evidence given before them, that the
said commission of   per cent had theretofore been
charged by him, and (if he had continued folvent)
would have been by him charged as a commission, both
for receiving and paying; they were of opinion, that
the said commission of   per cent, ought not to be
charged on fo much of the faid fum of   as then remained due to the faid J M viz on the faid fum of
but that it ought to be charged on the fum of   to
which commiffion of   per cent. on the faid fum of
amounted to   and being deducted fiom the faid ballance of   would leave a ballance of   which they
certified to be the ballance juftly due to the faid J. M.
from the faid bankrupts.

TUAT on the   day of   your petition-
ers did, on the part and behalf of the faid J M prefent
a petition unto the then Lords commiffioners of the great
feal of Great Britain, praying, that they would order,
that the faid report of the faid commiffioners of the faid
    day of   laft, might in all things be ratified and
confirmed, and that the petitioners might, on behalf of
the faid J M. be admitted creditors under the faid
commiffion of bankrupt for the fum of   by the faid
certificate reported due to the faid J. M from the faid
bankrupts, at the time of the date and fuing forth of
the faid commiffion, might be directed to pay unto the
petitioners, in refpect of the faid debt of   fo reported due to the faid J. M. a rateable dividend, in proportion with the reft of the bankrup's' creditors feeking
relief under the faid commiffion, and that the faid affignees might be directed to deliver up to your petitioners,
as well the faid policies of affurance, fo effected by the
faid bankrupts, on account of the faid J. M on the
faid fhip   as aforefaid, as alfo f veral other papers
in the faid petition mentioned, and for other purpofes in
the faid petition prayed.

THAT the faid petition came on to be heard
on the   day of   17   when the faid Lords commiffioners of the great feal were pleafed to order, that
the

the petitioners on behalf of the said J. M be admitted creditors under the said commiffion for the sum of by the said commiffioners' certificate found to be due to the said J M from the said J A. and T A at the time of the iffuing the commiffion of bankrupt against them, and that the petitioners be paid a dividend or dividends, in refpect of the said fum of rateably and in equal proportion with the reft of the said bankrupts' creditors, feeking relief under the said commiffion; and by confent of the counfel for the said affignees, they did order, that the said affignees fhould deliver up to the petitioners the feveral policies of affurance on the fhip the refpondentia, bond, and letter of attorney of the said G H in the said petition mentioned, and alfo all other bills, bonds, notes, policies of affurance, and other fecurities, papers, and writings in their refpective cuftody or power, which have at any time or times been remitted by the said J M or any other perfon or perfons on his behalf, or on his account, to the said bankrupts, or which fhould or might at any time or times thereafter come to the hands, cuftody, or power of the said affignees, for or on account of the said J M

THAT the said bankrupts and their affignees, in purfuance of the above in part recited order of the day of 17 delivered up unto your petitioners certain policies on the said fhip to the amount of

THAT the said J M. in the said account with the said bankrupts, is charged with as and for the premium and policies, on two policies said to be effected at Briftol and Exeter, for the fum of and for the commiffion of per cent for effecting the fame

THAT the said bankrupts, or their affignees, have not delivered up to your petitioners the said two policies, fo charged to be effected at Briftol and Exeter, for the said fum of as aforfaid, in as much as the fame are retained by the perfons effecting the fame, for the premiums paid thereon.

H

THAT

THAT a return of premium for ſhort intereſt is due upon the ſaid policies, and which has been paid and returned by the ſolvent underwriters, on the ſaid other policies, to the amount of

THAT it has been diſcovered by your petitioners, and the ſaid bankrupt, and their aſſignees, that the ſaid J. M. in the account taken before the ſaid commiſſioners, has been over-credited the ſum of   on which ſum of   your petitioners have not received the dividend of 4s. in the pound, paid under the ſaid commiſſion.

THAT your petitioners are adviſed, and humbly inſiſt, that they are entitled to ſurcharge the ſaid bankrupts' eſtate with the ſaid ſum of   ariſing as aforeſaid, offering to allow unto them the ſaid ſum of   which will leave a ballance of   which your petitioners claim to be added to the debt already proved under the ſaid commiſſion.

YOUR petitioners therefore moſt humbly pray your Lordſhip, that they may, on the behalf of the ſaid J. M. be admitted creditors for the ſum of   over and above the debt already proved under the ſaid commiſſion; and that your petitioners may, on behalf of the ſaid J. M. be paid the full dividend of 4s. in the pound, already declared under the ſaid commiſſion, as well on the ſaid ſum of   as alſo upon the debt already proved under the ſaid commiſſion, or ſo much thereof as the ſame has not been received upon, together with ſuch further dividend or dividends as may hereafter be declared under the ſaid commiſſion, rateably and in proportion

portion with the reft of the creditors feeking relief under the faid
commiffion, and that the cofts of
this application may be paid to
your petitioners, out of the faid
bankrupts' eftate and effects.

And your petitioners fhall ever pray, &c.

---

*Petition to prove a debt, and receive a dividend, the bankrupt
fetting up a partnerfhip not known to the petitioner*

In the matter of J. B. a bankrupt.

To the *Right Hon.* the LORD HIGH CHANCELLOR
of GREAT BRITAIN.

The humble Petition of *J. R.* of   in the county
of   merchant.

Sheweth,

THAT your petitioner having received an
order from J. B. the faid bankrupt, to fupply him with
a quantity of   goods, did, in or about the month
of   17   fend the goods fo ordered by the faid
J B to him at his houfe at   in the county of
and which were duly received by the faid J B as the
faid J. B. foon afterwards by letter informed your petitioner, which faid goods amounted in price and value
to the fum of   pounds   fhillings.

THAT in or about the month of   in the
year of our Lord   17   a commiffion of bankruptcy iffued againft the faid J. B. and the faid J B was
declared bankrupt thereon; and not having paid or in
any manner fatisfied your petitioner, his faid debt of
or any part thereof, your petitioner made a proper affidavit of the amount thereof, and fent the fame
to a correfpondent at   aforefaid, in order to have the
fame duly proved as a debt under the faid commiffion.

THAT your petitioner's faid correfpondent
did accordingly attend at a public meeting of the com-

miffioners acting under the faid commiffion, and tender-ed and offered to prove your petitioner's faid demand as a d bt under the fame; but the faid J. B oppofed fuch proof, alledging, that two perfons, of the names of C and G were jointly concerned with him the faid J B in the faid goods, fo furnifhed by your petitioner to the faid J B as aforefaid, and therefore, that your petitioner was only entitled to prove one third part of the amount of his faid debt under the faid commiffion againft the faid J B and muft take his remedy for the other two third parts thereof, againft the faid C and G. and the commiffioners accordingly refufed to per-mit your petitioner to prove more than the faid one third part of his faid demand, and therefore your petitioner did not prove any part thereof.

THAT at the time the faid J B ordered and received the faid goods from your petitioner as afore-faid, he the faid J. B acted as a feparate trader and dealer, nor did your petitioner know or had ever heard, that the faid J B. was connected in partnerfhip with any perfon or perfons whomfoever, nor did the faid J. B. then, or at any time, five as aforefaid, intimate to your petitioner, in any manner howfoever, that any other perfon or perfons, was or were concerned with him the faid J B either in the faid goods fo delivered by your petitioner to the faid J B as aforefaid, or in any other manner, but your petitioner received the order for the faid goods from the faid J. B. in the way of his the faid J. B.'s own feparate bufinefs, as a feparate dealer and merchant, and for his feparate account, and your peti-tioner accordingly delivered the faid goods to him on his own fole and feparate credit, without any fort of know-ledge or intimation whatever, either directly or indirectly of any other perfon or perfons being concerned or inte-refted therein. Nor did your petitioner ever hear of, or know that any fuch perfons exifted as the faid C and G. or either of them, fave as aforefaid. And your petitioner hath caufed enquiry to be made at P. aforefaid, and other places, after the faid C. and G. but could not learn where

they

they lived, or in what situation of life they were; but your petitioner hath lately been informed that they reside some where in North America.

THAT at the time your petitioner delivered the said goods to the said J B. as aforesaid, your petitioner was in partnership in his said house at B aforesaid, with W. R. and L. C. who had likewise a house of trade in London, in which your petitioner had no connection or interest whatever.

THAT in the month of   17   the said W. R. and L. C were declared bankrupts under a commission of bankrupt, awarded against them, and your petitioner thereby became the only solvent partner of his said house, and upon the settlement of accounts between your petitioner and his said partners, there appeared to be a ballance of several thousand pounds due from the said W R. and L. C to your petitioner, and your petitioner being obliged to satisfy all the debts due from the said partnership, is thereby intitled to receive all the outstanding debts due thereto, and is therefore intitled to the interest and benefit of the said demand of   pounds   shillings, upon the estate of the said J. B as aforesaid.

YOUR petitioner therefore most humbly prays, that your Lordship will be pleased to direct the acting commissioners named and authorized in and by the said commission of bankrupt, against the said J B. to permit your petitioner to prove his said debt of   under the said commission, and that a meeting of the said commissioners may be held for that purpose, at the expence of the said bankrupt's estate, and that your petitioner may be paid such dividend under the said commission as the rest of the creditors of the said J B. have already received, and also to receive a due

proportion

proportion of all future dividends to be made of the said bankrupt's estate, in common with the rest of the creditors, and that your petitioner may also be paid the costs of this application out of the said bankrupt's estate, or that your Lordship will be pleased to make such other order therein as to your Lordship shall seem meet.

And your petitioner shall ever pray, &c.

Petition for the Trustee of the Widow of a Bankrupt to be paid Dividends.

In the matter of W. C. and R. C. surviving Copartners of L. H. deceased, bankrupts.

To the Right Hon. th. LORD HIGH CHANCELLOR *of* GREAT BRITAIN.

The humble Petition of T. B. a Trustee for and on behalf of M. H. wife of J. H and M. S. wife of E. S formerly M. C. spinster, devisees and residuary legatees, named in the last will and testament of M. H. deceased,

Sheweth,

THAT your petitioner, and the above-named M. H. and M. S did on the   prefer their petition to your Lordship, stating that the said bankrupts W. C. and R. C. together with the said L. H deceased, were in the year 17   in partnership together as booksellers in London, and being greatly distressed for money, they applied to one S. B. to lend them the sum of pounds for the use of the joint trade, which he declined advancing, unless they would prevail on the said M H then the wife of the said L. H to mortgage a freehold estate of which she was seized in fee, situate at M. and L in the county of K. and which was then let at   pounds

per

per annum, as a fecurity for the repayment of the faid pounds and intereft.

THAT the faid M H. was prevailed upon to mortgage the faid eftate, on the faid L. H. W C. and R C agreeing to give and execute to your petitioner T. B. as truftee for the faid M. H. a bond in the penalty of   pounds, conditioned for the due payment to the faid S B. of the principal and intereft fo lent by him to the faid copartners, and to indemnify the faid M. H.'s eftate from the payment of the fame, or any part thereof.

THAT in confequence of the faid L H. W C. and R C entering into and executing fuch bond, bearing date the   the faid M. H. with her hufband L. H by indentures of leafe and releafe, dated the   and by a recovery fuffered in confequence thereof, conveyed the faid eftates to the faid S. B. his heirs and affigns, fubject to a provifo, that in cafe the faid L. H. W C. and R. C fhould pay the faid S. B. the faid pounds and intereft, on the   day of   then next enfuing, then the faid S. B and his heirs, fhould reconvey the faid premifes to the faid L. H. and M. his wife, their refpective heirs and affigns, as tenants in common, and not as joint tenants, and that until default fhould be made in payment of the principal and intereft, the faid L. H and M his wife, their heirs and affigns, fhould receive the rents, iffues, and profits, of the premifes

THAT the faid L H departed this life on or about the   of   inteftate, without having by himfelf or his partner paid the faid   pounds and intereft to the faid S B , and upon the death of the faid L. H the faid M his widow, took out adminiftration; but did not poffefs herfelf of any part of his effects (they being all joint property) except a few houfhold goods, which were not near fufficient to pay his private debts.

THAT in the month of   17   the faid M H. died, having firft duly made and publifhed her laft will and teftament in writing, whereby fhe devifed her freehold eftate at M. and J in the county of K. (being the fame eftate fo mortgaged to the faid S B as aforefaid) unto your petitioner M H. and the petitioner M S by her then maiden name of M. C. their heirs and affigns, and made your petitioners M. H. and M. S her refiduary legatees, and appointed J. W. her executor, who proved the faid will in the prerogative court of Canterbury.

THAT on or about the a commiffion of bankrupt was awarded and iffued againft the faid W. C. and R. C. as furviving partners with the faid L H. deceafed, and afterwards I. C. A H. and E. B. were duly chofen affignees of the faid bankrupts' eftate and effects, and an affignment thereof was made and executed to them by the major part of the commiffioners.

THAT the faid S. B. having received no part of his principal fum of pounds, fo lent as aforefaid, was permitted by the major part of the commiffioners, to prove a debt of under the faid commiffion, for principal and intereft due to him, and fecured by the faid mortgage, fo made to him by the faid L. H. and M. his wife

THAT foon after proving his faid debt, the faid S. B got into poffeffion of the rents and profits of the faid mortgaged premifes.

THAT the faid J. W. the executor of the faid M. H. being poffeffed of the faid bond fo given and executed by the faid L H. W. C and R. C to your petitioner T B. for payment of the faid pounds, and intereft to the faid T B. and to indemnify the faid M. H.'s eftate from the payment thereof, was permitted by the commiffioners to claim the faid fum of pounds, under the faid commiffion

THAT the faid affignees and S B the mortgagee, fometime afterwards put up the faid eftate at M. and L. the property of the faid M H to fale by public auction, and the fame was fold for the fum of

THAT your petitioners the faid M. H and M. S the heirs at law and devifees of the faid M H. from the perfuafions of the faid affignees, and at their particular defire and intreaty, and on their affurances that

your

your petitioners M H. and M S. should not be pre-
judiced, were prevailed upon to join in releasing the
equity of redemption of the said mortgaged premises to
the purchaser thereof, without receiving one shilling, your
petitioners M H. and M S not doubting but that the
claim of the said J W would be admitted to be proved,
your petitioners M H and M S having by the means
aforesaid been deprived of the said estate so devised to
them by the said M H That the said assignees on or
about the   day of   17   petitioned the then Lord
High Chancellor, that the said debt to proved by the said
H B and the said claim to made by the said J W might
be disallowed and struck out of the proceedings, but on
hearing the said petition, his lordship refused to make any
order thereon That the said assignees had caused two
dividends to be made under the said commission one of
two shillings and six pence in the pound, and one of five
shillings in the pound, making together seven shillings
and six pence in the pound, and had then advertised a
final dividend to be made That your petitioners M H.
and M S from the representations of the said assignee
at the time they prevailed on your petitioners M H and
M S to execute the release of the equity of redemption
of the said mortgaged premises, had no doubt but they
should be permitted, or the said J W would be permitted
to prove the said bond for   pounds, and receive
a dividend rateably with the other creditors, the said
assignees having admitted they had retained monies sufficient in their hands to pay same, yet to your petitioners'
very great surprize they have since refused to permit the
said J W to prove same, and your petitioners were thereby
precluded from receiving one shilling satisfaction out of
the said bankrupt's estate on account of the said bond
unless your lordship would permit the said bond to be
proved, and therefore praying that it might be referred
to the major part of the commissioners to take an account
of what had been received by the said S B by the sale
of the said estate at M and L and by receipt of the rents
and profits thereof, and that so much be struck off his

I   debt

debt fo proved under the faid commiffion, and that your petitioner the faid T B. or your petitioners M H and M S as devifees under the will of the faid M H. might be admitted to prove under the faid commiffion the faid bond for the fum of   pounds given by the faid bank-rupts, and the faid L. H. deceafed, to you petitioner T. B with intereft from the time of the death of the faid M. H. to the date and fuing forth of the faid commiffion, and that the petitioners might receive the two dividends of two fhillings and fixpence, and five fhillings in the pound, already declared, and all future dividends to be declared, the affignees admitting they had retained mo-nies in their hands to anfwer the claim made by the faid J. W and that the claim of the faid J W. might be dif-allowed and ftruck out of the proceedings under the faid commiffion, the debt being immediately owing from the faid bankrupts to your petitioner T. B on the faid bond in truft for your petitioners M. H and M. S and that your petitioners might have fuch further and other relief in the premifes as to your lordfhip fhould feem meet , whereupon your lordfhip ordered all parties con-cerned to attend your lordfhip on the matter of the faid petition on the then next day of petitions, when your lordfhip was pleafed to order that your petitioner T B as truftee named in the laft will and teftament of M H in the faid petition named, fhould ftand in the place of the faid S B in refpect of all future dividends which fhould accrue or be made under the faid commiffion, and receive fuch future dividends accordingly upon the trufts declared by the will of the faid M H. concerning the refidue of her perfonal eftate

    THAT in the faid order no notice is taken of the two dividends of two fhillings and fix pence in the pound, and five fhillings in the pound already made by the affignees under the faid commiffion, and retained by the faid affignees in their hands to be paid the faid S B. for his faid debt fo proved by him as aforefaid   That the faid S. B hath not demanded or received from the af-fignees of the faid W. C. and R. C. the faid two firft
                                                        dividends

dividends of two shillings and sixpence in the pound, and five shillings in the pound, so retained by the said assignees in their hands, on the debt so proved by him under the said commission, nor means to demand or receive the same, and is willing your petitioner should stand in his place and receive the same

Your petitioner therefore most humbly prays your Lordship to order, that the assignees of the said W. C. and R. C. pay to your petitioner, as trustee of the said M. H. as aforesaid, the said two dividends of two shillings and sixpence in the pound, and five shillings in the pound, on the said debt of so proved by the said S. B. under the said commission, and retained by the assignees in their hands, in like manner as is directed by your Lordship, respecting the future dividends to be made under the said commission

And your petitioner shall ever pray, &c.

Petition to prove a debt, upon an award.

In the matter of A. L. a Bankrupt.

To the Right Honourable the LORD HIGH CHANCELLOR *of* GREAT BRITAIN.

The humble Petition of J. L. *of the Island of Guernsey, merchant, surviving partner of R. L. widow, and E. L. both of the same place, deceased.*

Sheweth,

THAT in or about the year 17 the said A. L. the bankrupt, together with N. L. his brother, since deceased, were engaged and concerned as co-

I 2   partners,

partners in a very large and extensive mercantile business.

THAT some disputes and differences arising
between them, the said A. L brought his action at law
in his Majesty's Court of King's Bench, against the said
N L deceased, which came on to be tried before Lord
Mansfield, at Guildhall, the fittings after Trinity Term
17   when it was ordered by the Court, by and with
the consent of the said A. L. and N L then counsel
and attornies, that the Jury should find a verdict in the
said cause for the plaintiff A L the bankrupt's damages   and costs   subject to the order and award
to be made pursuant thereto.

THAT it was amongst other things agreed
to and ordered, that all matters in difference between the
parties should be referred to the award or arbitrament,
final end and determination, of W H of   London,
merchant, who was to make and publish his award in
writing, of and concerning the premises in question, between the said parties, on or before the   day of Mi-
chaelmas Term then next ensuing, and that the said
parties should and did perform, fulfil, and keep such
award so to be made by the said W H as arbitrator as
aforesaid

THAT it being found impossible for the said
W H the arbitrator, to make his award by the time
limited by the said in part recited order of *nisi prius*, the
said A L. the bankrupt, and N L deceased, and your
petitioner, together with the said R. L. widow, and
E L both since deceased, entered into an agreement
(and which said agreement was afterwards made a rule of
the said court of King's Bench) whereby they agreed to
enlarge the time for the said W. H to make his award,
until the   day of the then next Hilary Term.

THAT the said W H in and by a certain
deed or instrument of award in writing, under his hand
and feal, bearing date the   day of   17   after
reciting to the effect herein before recited, did amongst
other things state, that he had found out and discovered
that

that the ſaid A. L. the bankrupt, and N L deceaſed, in
their then late joint trade, were then jointly indebted unto
your petitioner, and his late partners deceaſed, in the
ſum of   of lawful money of Great Britain.

That the ſaid W H, did thereby, amongſt
other things, award and order, that the ſaid N L deceaſed, his executors, adminiſtrators, or aſsigns, ſhould,
on or before the   day of   then next enſuing, pay
and ſatisfy, or cauſe to be paid and ſatisfied unto your
petitioner, and his aforeſaid late partners deceaſed, their
executors, adminiſtrators, or aſsigns, the ſum of   of
like lawful money, in part ſatisfaction of the ſaid debt
or ſum of

That the ſaid W H did thereby further
award and order, that the ſaid A L. the bankrupt, and
the ſaid N. L. deceaſed, or the ſurvivor of them, his
executors, adminiſtrators, or aſsigns, ſhould, when thereunto requeſted by your petitioner, and his late partners,
the ſaid R and E L. deceaſed, or any or other of
them, and at their expence, in due form of law duly
execute an aſsignment unto your petitioner, and his ſaid
late partners deceaſed, their executors, adminiſtrators,
and aſsigns of debts, being part of the debts mentioned
in the ſecond ſchedule of the ſaid now reciting award.

That in order to reduce the ſaid ſum of
to the ſum of   the balance that would be due
to your petitioner, and his ſaid late partners deceaſed,
from the ſaid late joint trade, after they ſhould have received from the ſaid N L the ſum of   the ſaid W H.
did thereby further award and order, that your petitioner, and his ſaid late partners deceaſed, ſhould, at the
time of the execution of the ſaid aſsignment, pay to the
ſaid A L the bankrupt, the ſum of   and to the ſaid
N L. deceaſed, the like ſum of   of like lawful
money

That the ſaid W H did thereby further
award and order, that if any of the ſaid laſt mentioned
debts ſhould prove bad, or that the ſame, or any of
them, ſhould not be recovered or received by force, or

by

by virtue of the said assignment, without the wilful neglect or default of your petitioner, and his said late partners deceased, their executors, administrators, or assigns,
on or before the   day of   which would be in the
year of our Lord 17   that then and in such case so
much of the sum of   as should have been to recovered or received, should from that day be considered and
deemed as a debt due to your petitioner and his said
late partners deceased, from the said A. L the bankrupt,
and N. L. deceased, each of whom was immediately
thereafter to pay unto your petitioner, and his said late
partners deceased, their executors, administrators, or
assigns, one moiety or half part of the said last mentioned debt, with lawful interest for the same, to be computed from the   then last past, and that thereupon such
and so many of the said debts, so to be assigned as aforesaid, should, by your petitioner and his said late partners
deceased, their executors, and administrators, be reass-
signed at the expence of the said A L the bankrupt
and N L jointly, their executors, administrators, or
assigns.

THAT after the making and publishing the
said award, application was from time to time made by
your petitioner, and his said late partners deceased, to
the said A L. the bankrupt, to join in and execute the
said assignment of the said debts, in the said award ordered to be executed by him the said A. L and N L.
(the said N L. being at all times during his life ready
to have executed the same) but the said A L. the bankrupt wholly refused to comply therewith, and the full
assignment hath never been executed

THAT the said N L. departed this life insolvent, in or about the month of   17 That a commission of bankrupt under the great seal of Great Britain, bearing date on or about the   day of   17
was awarded and issued against the said A L who was
thereupon duly found and declared a bankrupt, and
P L Esq P P. T B and W B. were chosen assignees
of his estate and effects.

THAT

THAT your petitioner, being advised that he was entitled to prove the said sum of   under the said commission so awarded and issued against the said A L he has caused application to the assignees chosen under the said commission, to be admitted as a creditor to prove the same, who have refused to admit such proof without your Lordship's order for that purpose.

YOUR petitioner therefore most humbly prays your Lordship, that your petitioner may be admitted a creditor under the said commission, for the said sum of   and that he may be paid out of the said bankrupt's estate, now in, or which shall hereafter come to the hands of the said assignees under the said commission, a dividend or dividends in respect thereof, rateably and in equal proportion with the other creditors of the said bankrupt, seeking relief under the said commission or that your Lordship will be pleased to make such other order in the premises, as to your Lordship shall seem meet.

And your petitioners shall ever pray, &c.

Petition for a sum arising from the sale of an estate to be paid, and petitioner to prove remainder under the commission.

In the matter of W. F. a bankrupt.

To the Right Honourable the LORD HIGH
CHANCELLOR of GREAT BRITAIN

The humble Petition of J P. of   street, London, Tobacconist,

Sheweth,

THAT in or about the month of   17
your petitioner lent the said W F the bankrupt,
the sum of   pounds, and for securing the repayment
thereof with interest, the said W. F. together with W
N, then of   in the county of   as surety for the
said W. F. entered into and executed a joint bond to
your petitioner, and the said W. N having afterwards
departed this life, the said W.F requested your petitioner
to deliver up the said bond to be cancelled, it being as
the said W. F. alledged the earnest desire of the said W.
N 's executors to have the same so delivered up, and your
petitioner consented thereto, and did deliver up the same,
upon being assured by the said W F. that he would immediately replace the said bond with such other security
as your petitioner should approve of, and in the mean time
the said W F. gave his note of hand to your petitioner
for the said sum of

THAT the said W F. soon afterwards in-
formed your petitioner by letter that he could not obtain for your petitioner such sufficient security for the
said debt as he the said W F had expected, and that
therefore he had sent his own bond for the same to your
petitioner, and your petitioner at the same time received
a bond from the said W F dated the   day of   17
whereby the said W. F. became bound to your petitioner in the penal sum of   conditioned for the payment of the sum of   with lawful interest

THAT your petitioner not thinking the
bond of the said W F. alone, a sufficient security for the
said debt or sum of   and having informed the said
W F

W F of your petitioner's difapprobation of fuch fecurity, he thereupon fent your petitioner the title deeds of a certain eftate, fituate at   in the county of   of which he was feized and in poffeffion, and r quefted your petitioner to accept and keep the fame as a collateral fecurity for the faid debt, he the faid W F at the fame time informing your petitioner that it was the beft fecurity he could then give for fuch debt, and which faid title deeds have ever fince remained and now are in the poffeffion of your petitioner, and he hath no other fecurity for his faid debt, than the faid title deeds and the aforefaid bond from the faid W F. he your petitioner having long fince delivered the faid note

THAT in the year 17   the faid W F duly conveyed and affigned all his eftate and effects to P A I A. and G W all of   in the county of S in truft and for the benefit of his the faid W F's creditors, and in or about the month of   in the fame year they the faid truftees caufed the faid W F's faid eftate at   as aforefaid to be put up to fale by auction, and R. I of the city of   ironmonger was declared to be the higheft bidder and the purchafer thereof at the price or fum of

THAT the title deeds of the faid eftate having been depofited with your petitioner as a fecurity for the faid debt or fum of   as aforefaid, he on being applied to by the faid truftees P A. I A and G W to deliver up fuch deeds, refufed to deliver up the fame, unlefs the faid purchafe money was paid to your petitioner, and he was permitted to come in as a creditor upon the faid W F's eftate and effects for the refidue of his your petitioner's faid debt

THAT foon afterwards and before the faid truftees had executed the trufts of the faid deed, or difpofed of the faid W F.'s effects by virtue thereof, to wit on or about the   day of   17   a commiffion of bankrupt under the great feal of Great Britain was awarded and iffued againft the faid W F and he was thereupon duly found and declared a bankrupt by the major part of the commiffion as named in fuch commiffion, and S G

K   of

of   aforesaid, gentleman, and W I of the same place, gentleman, were duly chosen assignees of the said bankrupt's effects, and an assignment thereof hath been made to them by the major part of the commissioners named in the said commission, upon the usual interests, and bargain and sale of the said bankrupt's real estate hath been executed to them by the said commissioners duly enrolled.

THAT the whole of the said principal of for securing whereof the said bankrupt gave his said bond, and deposited with your petitioner the title deeds of the said estate as aforesaid, still remains due and owing to your petitioner, with an arrear of interest for the same, and the said R. L. who purchased such estate of the said trustees P. A I. A and G W. as aforesaid hath paid a considerable part of his said purchase money to them, which they have paid over or accounted for to the said assignees, who claim the remainder thereof.

THAT your said petitioner is advised and humbly insists that he hath a lieu in equity upon the said estate and the title deeds thereof, for his said debt, and the said sum of   for which the said estate was sold to the said R. L. as aforesaid, ought to be paid to your petitioner in part discharge of his said debt, and that he ought to be admitted a creditor under the said commission of bankruptcy for the remainder of such debt, and receive a dividend in respect thereof out of the said bankrupt's other estates and effects, and your petitioner hath accordingly applied to the said S. G. and W. T the assignees under the said commission of bankruptcy, to have the sale made of the said bankrupt's estate at   to the said R. L. as aforesaid, compleated and confirmed by them, and to be paid the said purchase money of   in part of your petitioner's said debt, and to be admitted a creditor under the said commission for the remainder of such debt, he your petitioner having offered on, being paid such purchase money, to deliver up the title deeds of the said estate, but the said assignees S G. and W. T have refused to

permit

permit any part of the said purchase money of   to be paid to your petitioner.

> Your petitioner therefore most humbly prays, that your Lordship will be pleased to order that the said sum of   for which the said estate was sold to the said R L, as aforesaid, be paid to your petitioner in part discharge of the debt due to him from the said bankrupt, and that your petitioner be admitted a creditor under the said commission of bankrupt for the remainder of such debt, and be paid a dividend in respect thereof out of the said bankrupt's said estate and effects, rateably and in proportion with his other creditors, or that your Lordship will be pleased to make such order in the premises as shall be just

And your petitioner shall ever pray, &c.

Petition to be paid a dividend on a debt after three dividends having been paid

In the matter of T W   a bankrupt.

> *To the Right Hon the* LORD HIGH CHANCELLOR *of* GREAT BRITAIN
>
> *The humble Petition of A. B,*

Sheweth,

THAT a commission of bankrupt under the great seal of Great Britain, having on or about the day of   17   been awarded and issued against T W   of London, merchant, he was therefore found and declared to be a bankrupt, and T W since has

T M

J. M and T E were duly chofen affignees of the eftate and effects of the faid bankrupt.

THAT three feveral dividends, amounting together to the fum of   fhillings in the pound, have been made of the eftate and effects of the faid bankrupt amongft the feveral creditors who had come in and fought r lief under the faid commiffion, previous to the making of fuch feveral dividends.

THAT fince the making of the laft of the three faid dividends, viz on or about the   day of 17   your petitioner proved a debt under the faid commiffion, amounting to the fum of   upon which no dividend has been hitherto paid to your petitioner

THAT the faid commiffion having abated by the death of the major part of the commiffioners therein named, the fame hath been fince renewed, and the renewed commiffion directed to   but the commiffioners have never acted under the faid renewed commiffion

THAT the faid J. M and T G the furviving affignees of the faid bankrupt, have fince making of the laft dividend under the faid commiffion received and got in upon account of the faid bankrupt's eftate, feveral confiderable fums of money, and there is now remaining in their hands, much more than fufficient to pay your petitioner the three feveral dividends which have been already made under the faid commiffion, upon the debt of   fo proved by him under the faid commiffion, without difturbing any dividend already made.

Your petitioner therefore moft humbly prays your Lordfhip that you would be pleafed to direct the commiffioners in the faid renewed commiffion, named, or the major part of them, to proceed under the faid commiffion, or to order the faid J M. and T E the furviving affignees of the faid bankrupt out of the monies now remaining in their

their hands, or which fhall hereafter come to their hands belonging to the faid bankrupt's eftate, to
pay to your petitioner the three
feveral dividends, amounting together to the fum of   fhillings
in the pound, upon the faid debt
of   fo proved by him as aforefaid, and alfo to pay to your petitioner all fuch future dividends
as fhall be made of the faid bankrupt's eftate upon his faid debt of
      rateably and in proportion
with fuch other of the faid bankrupt's creditors as already have or
hereafter fhall come in and feek relief under the faid commiffion.

And your petitioner fhall ever pray, &c.

---

*Petition to compel a folicitor to deliver up the proceedings
under a commiffion, &c.*

In the matter of E L. a bankrupt.

To the Right Honourable the LORD HIGH
CHANCELLOR *of* GREAT BRITAIN

*The humble Petition of T S of   in the county
of   merchant, on the behalf of himfelf, and
E his wife, adminiftrator and adminiftratrix of
C. G. deceafed*

Sheweth,
      THAT on or about the   day of   in the
year of our Lord   17   a commiffion of bankrupt
under the great feal of Great Britain, was awarded and
iffued againft E. L. of   in the county of   under
which he was found and declared a bankrupt, and C G
and R C both of   in the county of   merchants,
                                                    were

were duly chofen afsignees, to whom the eftate and effects of the faid E. L. were afsigned, by the major part of the commifsioners acting under the faid commifsion.

THAT the commifsioners named in the faid commifsion are all of them dead, and the faid R. C. the afsignee, died feveral years ago

THAT the faid C. G. furvived the faid R. C. but is lately dead inteftate, leaving E. his daughter, your petitioner's wife, his perfonal reprefentative

THAT your petitioner and his wife have taken out letters of adminiftration to the effects of the faid C. G.

THAT your petitioner, upon infpecting the books and accounts of the faid C. G. found, that there remained in his hands, at the time of his death, a fum of money arifing from the eftate of the faid E. L. and your petitioner, being defirous that the fame fhould be divided amongft the faid E. L.'s creditors, applied for and obtained a renewed commifsion of bankrupt, under the great feal of Great Britain, againft the faid E. L. bearing date the   day of   laft, directed to

THAT J. B. late of   aforefaid, but now of   in the city of London,   being the folicitor to the firft mentioned commifsion, and having all the proceedings under the fame in his cuftody, your petitioner caufed feveral applications to be made to him, to deliver fuch proceedings to your petitioner, and at length obtained from him the faid firft mentioned commifsion, the counterparts of the bargain and fale and afsignment of the eftate and effects of the faid bankrupt, but the commifsioners named in the faid renewed commifsion, finding that they could not with propriety act under the fame, without having all the other proceedings under the faid firft mentioned commifsion before them, your petitioner applied again to the faid J. B. to deliver the fame to your petitioner, but he refufed fo to do, pretending, that his bill on the afsignees for foliciting the faid firft mentioned commifsion, had not been paid

That

THAT your petitioner found, amongst the papers of the said C G deceased, the said J B's bill of fees for soliciting the said first mentioned commission, with the said J. B's receipt for the amount, which is now in the possession of your petitioner, and also the said J B's promissory note to the said C G and R C for the sum of   pounds   shillings, and it appears by the accounts of the said C. G. that the said J B. is now considerably indebted to the estate of the said bankrupt.

THAT your petitioner, on or about the   day of   17   caused a notice in writing to be served on the said J B. purporting, that if he did not deliver the proceedings under the said first mentioned commission to your petitioner, an application would be made to your Lordship, for an order upon him to deliver the same, and that he might pay the costs of such applicaton, and your petitioner in such notice informed the said J B that your petitioner was willing to pay any just demand he had upon the said late assignees, after giving credit for what the said J B. should be found indebted to the said bankrupt's estate.

THAT your petitioner hath, since the said   of   last, caused repeated applications to be made to the said J. B. for the said proceedings, and the said J B. hath promised to deliver the same, but hath hitherto neglected so to do, and he now alledges that such proceedings are mislaid.

THAT the commissioners named in the renewed commission cannot act under the same, not having the proceedings under the said former commission, and having no account of the debts proved under such former commission.

THAT your petitioner is desirous that the said renewed commission should be proceeded in, and that the money so appearing to be in the hands of the said C G as assignee under the said first mentioned commission, be divided amongst the creditors of the said B J but in as much as the commissioners named in the said renewed commission cannot divide the same, thout without having the proceedings taken under the former commifsion.

> Your petitioner therefore moft humbly prays, that your Lordfhip will be pleafed to order, that the faid J. B. do deliver to your petitioner, upon oath, all the proceedings under the faid firft mentioned commifsion, now in his cuftody, poffefsion, or power, your petitioner hereby offering to pay what if any thing fhall appear to be due to the faid J. B. for his fees and difburfements on account of the faid commifsion, and that the faid J. B. may be ordered to pay your petitioner the cofts of this application, or that your Lordfhip will be pleafed to make fuch other order for the direction of the commifsioners named in the faid renewed commifsion, and your petitioner, as to your Lordfhip fhall feem meet

And your petitioner fhall ever pray, &c.

Petition for folicitor to deliver up proceedings under a commiffion.

In the matter of J. W. a bankrupt.

To the Right Hon the LORD HIGH CHANCELLOR *of* GREAT BRITAIN

The humble Petition of R P *the furviving affignee of the eftate and effects of* J W. *late of a bankrupt,*

Sheweth,

THAT on or about the month of
17   a commiffion of bankrupt under the great feal of Great Britain, was awarded and iffued againft the faid J W. who was thereupon, by the major part of the commiffioners named in fuch commiffion, found and declared to be bankrupt, within the intent and meaning of the feveral ftatutes made and in force concerning bankrupts, and H. B. and J N (both fince deceafed) together with your petitioner, were duly chofen and appointed affignees of the faid bankrupt's eftate and effects

THAT the faid H. B and J. N being both fince deceafed, your petitioner is become the furviving and only affignee of the faid bankrupt's eftate and effects.

THAT your petitioner employed J. R of   ftreet, gentleman, to act as the folicitor under the faid commiffion; but your petitioner is become defirous of changing his folicitor, and to employ another perfon to act as the folicitor under the fame

Your petitioner therefore humbly prays your Lordfhip, that the faid J R may be directed to deliver unto your petitioner, within fuch time as your Lordfhip fhall be pleafed to order, the bill of fees and difburfements claimed to be due to him the faid J. R as folicitor for or on account of his bu-

ing acted under the said commiſſion, to be ſigned by him, and that ſuch bill, when delivered, may be referred to one of the maſters of this hon. court, to be taxed, your petitioner hereby offering and ſubmitting to pay unto the ſaid J R whatever ſhall appear to be due or coming to him on the taxation of ſuch his bill, and that the ſaid J R. may account before the maſter, upon oath, for all ſums of money received by him from your petitioner, or any other perſon, on account of the ſaid bankrupt's eſtate, or otherwiſe in relation thereto, and be directed to pay unto your petitioner what ſhall appear to be coming from him the ſaid J. R. on the ballance of his account, and that upon payment to him the ſaid J. R. of what ſhall appear to be due to him on the taxation of his ſaid bill as aforeſaid, he may be directed to deliver up unto your petitioner, or to the ſolicitor to be appointed by your petitioner, the ſaid commiſſion of bankrupt, the proceedings under the ſame, and all deeds, books, papers, and writings whatever, relating thereto, and to the ſaid bankrupt's eſtate, in the cuſtody or power of him the ſaid J R.

And your petitioner ſhall ever pray, &c.

Petitior

*Petition by the clerk to a commission, for the assignees to pay
the bill to the choice of assignees; and also the subsequent
costs taxed by the master.*

In the matter of W. W. a bankrupt.

To the Right Hon. the LORD HIGH CHANCELLOR
of GREAT BRITAIN,

  The humble Petition of S. B. clerk or solicitor to
  the commission of bankrupt awarded and issued
  forth against the said H. W.

Sheweth,

  THAT a commission of bankrupt under the
great seal of Great Britain, bearing date at Westminster
the day of 17 and directed to J C and L B.
Esqrs. and A B and E. B. gentlemen, was duly awarded and issued forth against the said W. W. by the name
and description of W. W. of in the parish of in
the county of paper-maker, upon the petition of
R. S of stree , in the city of London, merchant,
whereupon the said W. W. was duly declared a bankrupt, and the said R S and C M of in the county of aforesaid, anchor smith, were duly chosen
assignees of the estate and effects of the said W W and
an assignment thereof was made to them accordingly

  THAT your petitioner's bill of fees and
disbursements, up to the execution of the assignment,
was taxed and allowed by the major part of the commissioners, at the sum of pounds shillings and
  pence, and the said R S. and C. M were directed
by the said commissioners, to pay your petitioner the
said sum of money, out of the first effects of the said
bankrupt, that should come to their hands , and that the
bill of fees and disbursements due to your petitioner, for
business done by him respectively the said commission,
subsequent to the execution of the said assignment, hath
been also taxed by H Esq. one of the masters
of this hon. court, and allowed at the sum of pounds
  shillings and pence, which sums together amount

to the fum of   pounds   fhillings and   pence, and which now remains juftly due and owing from the faid afsignees to your petitioner.

THAT the faid R. S and C M are poffef-fed of more effects belonging to the faid bankrupt's eftate, than will be fufficient to pay and fatisfy your pe-titioner's faid demands, but although your petitioner hath frequently called upon and requefted them fo to do, they both have hitherto wholly refufed to fatisfy your petitioner the fame, or any part thereof

YOUR petitioner therefore moft humbly prays your Lordfhip, that your Lordfhip will be pleafed to order, the faid R S. and C. M. affignees of the eftate and effects of the faid W W. as aforefaid, forthwith to pay and difcharge your petition-er's faid bills of fees and difburfe-ments, fo taxed, and allowed at the faid fum of   pounds fhillings and   pence, as afore-faid, together with the cofts of this application to your Lordfhip: or that your Lordfhip will make fuch other order in the premifes, as to your Lordfhip fhall feem meet

And your petitioner fhall ever pray, &c.

Petition

Petition to tax solicitor's bill of fees.

In the matter of T. C. late of L. in the
county of   merchant, a bankrupt.

> *To the* Right Honourable *the* LORD HIGH
> CHANCELLOR *of* GREAT BRITAIN

> *The humble Petition of T. S. and J. B. the younger,
> who with J C. are the trustees named in a
> settlement made on the marriage of the said
> bankrupt, with his now wife A C.*

Sheweth,

THAT several disputes having arisen between the assignees of the said T C. and your petitioner, as trustee under the said settlement, respecting a
claim made by your petitioners, as such trustees, to be
admitted creditors under the said commission against the
said bankrupt, and your petitioners being under the necessity of applying to your Lordship, for an order to
prove the sum so claimed by them, your petitioners employed the said J C and his partner H B. solicitors, in
     to obtain such order, and to solicit and transact
other business for your petitioners, as trustees is aforesaid

THAT the said Messrs C and B have lately
delivered in a bill of their fees and disbursements, for
the soliciting and transacting such business, amounting
to the sum of   pounds   shillings

THAT your petitioners are advised, that
they, as trustees, will not be warranted in paying such
bill, without the same is taxed and settled by one of the
masters of this hon court.

> YOUR petitioners therefore humbly
> pray, that the said bill of fees and
> disbursements, so delivered as is
> foresaid, may be referred to one
> of the masters of this hon court,
> to tax and settle the same, your
> petitioners

petitioners hereby undertaking to
pay what the said master shall report to be due on the said taxation,

And your petitioners shall ever pray, &c.

Petition of a bankrupt, to have his certificate allowed.

In the matter of P. G. M. a bankrupt.

To the Right Honourable the Lord High
Chancellor *of* Great Britain.

The humble Petition of the said bankrupt,

Sheweth,

THAT on the   day of   17   a commission of bankrupt under the great seal of Great Britain, was awarded and issued against your petitioner and
he was, by the major part of the commissioners under
the said commission, duly found and declared a bankrupt.

THAT the said commissioners, on the
day of   last, duly certified to your Lordship, that
your petitioner had in all things conformed himself
thereto, and that a requisite number of creditors had
signed the certificate.

THAT on the   day of   last, T A. late
of the East Indies, but then of   street   square, a
creditor of your said petitioner, preferred a petition
to your Lordship, praying to be admitted to prove his
debt under the commission against your petitioner

THAT the said T A accordingly proved
his debt under the said commission, which prevented
your petitioner from obtaining his certificate

THAT in order to counteract the said petition of the said T A several other creditors of your
said petitioner, on the   day of   last, preferred a
petition to your Lordship, praying to be admitted to
prove their debts, and to assent to or dissent from the
allowance

allowance of your petitioner's said certificate; which your Lordship was pleased to order, and thereby referred the same back to the commissioners to be reviewed.

THAT in pursuance thereof, the said last mentioned creditors did accordingly prove their respective debts, and signed the certificate.

THAT the said commissioners have reviewed their said certificate, and added a supplemental one thereto, wherein they have certified, that the creditors of your petitioner who petitioned your Lordship to come in and prove their debts, had so done, and had signed the said certificate, who, with those who had already signed, constituted 4-fifths in number and value of the creditors of your petitioner, whose debts were not less than

THAT another petition remains against the allowance of the said certificate, presented even since the month of   last, by A. M

THAT your Lordship ordered the matter of the said petition to be referred to the said commissioners, and for them to report the same

THAT on the month of   last, the said A M became a bankrupt, without having once called a meeting of the said commissioners, and the assignees since his bankruptcy never having done so, your petitioner having deposited securities in the hands of the said A M before his bankruptcy, sufficient to discharge his debt due from your petitioner

> Your petitioner therefore humbly your Lordship, that the said certificate may be allowed, your petitioner having conformed in all things to his bankruptcy.

And your petitioner shall ever pray, &c.

Another Petition of a bankrupt to have his certificate allowed.

In the matter of C. R. a bankrupt.

To the Right Hon. the LORD HIGH CHANCELLOR
of GREAT BRITAIN.

The humble petition of C. R. the bankrupt,

Sheweth,

THAT your petitioner confidering him-
felf as entitled to the reverfion in fee (after the death of
his mother L. R. who was at that time living) of five
clofes of land called   fituate in the parifh of   in the
county of   and alfo that, at the deceafe of the faid
L. R he would be poffeffed of or well intitled unto a
certain leafchold meffuage and land called   containing by eftimation   acres, and fituate in the faid parifh
of   under and by virtue of a leafe thereof, for the
term of two thoufand years, commencing from the feaft
of St. Michael the Archangel, in the forty-firft year of
the reign of her late Majefty, Queen Elizabeth, and being at that time in great want of money, did fometime in
the year 17   apply to J I. for the loan of   and
that the faid J. I. advanced the faid fum of   to your
petitioner on the fecurity of his faid reverfionary intereft
in the faid freehold and leafehold premifes, after the death
of the faid L. R. and that in confideration of fuch fecurity, the faid fum of   was lent and advanced by the
faid J. I. to your petitioner.

THAT fometime in the month of March
     your petitioner being again diftreffed for money,
and confidering himfelf (the faid L R being then dead)
as feized in fee of the faid freehold, and well intitled unto
the faid leafehold premifes, applied to J T for the loan
of   and agreed to fecure the repayment of the faid
fum of   with intereft, by a mortgage of the faid freehold and leafehold premifes, to the faid J. I and that
the faid premifes were accordingly demifed by indenture, bearing date on or about the   day of the faid
month of March 17   by your petitioner to the faid

J. T

J T. his executors, administrators and assignes, for the term of one thousand years, subject to a proviso for redemption, on the payment of the said sum of   with interest, after the rate of five per cent, per annum, upon the   then next ensuing

THAT your petitioner at the time of making the aforesaid second mortgage, was perfectly unconscious of any impropriety or misconduct on his part in the said transaction, as he then verily believed that the said premises were fully sufficient and adequate to pay and discharge both the said principal sums, there being at that time (as your petitioner was advised) some hundred pounds worth of timber growing thereon.

THAT on or about the   day of   17 (the said two principal sums of   and   being then respectively undischarged, and some arrears of interest having also accrued and become due thereon) a commission of bankrupt issued against your petitioner, who was accordingly found and declared a bankrupt

THAT your petitioner having passed his final examination, and the certificate of his conformity having been accordingly signed by four-fifths in number and value of the creditors who had proved their debts under the said commission, and by the major part of the commissioners named therein, the same was advertised for your Lordship's allowance in the London Gazette, on the fifth day of October in the same year

THAT the said J. T. (not having proved the said debt of   with certain arrears of interest accruing thereon, under the said commission) on or about the   day of the said month, presented a petition to your Lordship, and therein prayed that he the said J. T might be at liberty to go before the major part of the commissioners named in the said commission, and prove the said sum of   and the interest thereof as a debt under the said commission, against the said C. R. for the purpose of his assenting to or dissenting from the allowance of the said bankrupt's certificate, and that such proof might be without prejudice to his said mortgage, and to his right

to

to be paid a dividend, or dividends out of the said bankrupt's estate, in respect of the said debt, in case he should lose the benefit of his said mortgage by means of the said prior mortgage to the said J. I. and that in the mean time the allowance of your petitioner's certificate might be stayed.

THAT immediately after presenting the said petition to your Lordship, the said J. T filed his bill in chancery against the said J. I for the purpose of impeaching his said mortgage, to which bill your petitioner together with T S W. A. and G. V who had been duly chosen assignees of the estate and effects of your petitioner, and in whom also the fee simple of such part of the said mortgaged premises as were freehold, also vested, were made parties.

THAT on or about the day of your Lordship was pleased to order and direct, on hearing counsel on both sides, that the said J T. should be allowed to prove the said debt in the manner, for the purposes, with the savings as aforesaid, and your Lordship was also pleased to order and direct, that the allowance of your petitioner's certificate should be stayed.

THAT your petitioner being advised that he was very materially interested, in the speedy determination of the said suit so instituted in the said court by the said J T. against the said J I. together with the said T. S. W. A. G. V. and your petitioner put in an immediate full, and sufficient answer to the said bill, and that the said T. S. W. A. and G. V. also fully and sufficiently answered the same; but that no measures have been since taken by the plaintiff, the said J. T. to bring the said suit to a speedy issue, although four terms have elapsed since the commencement thereof, by which delay your petitioner is much aggrieved and injured

YOUR petitioner therefore most humbly prays your Lordship that his certificate, the allowance of which was stayed by your Lordship's order made the day of 17 be now allowed.

And your petitioner shall ever pray, &c.

Petition

Petition to stay the allowance of a bankrupt's certificate.

In the matter of T. F. a bankrupt,

To the Right Hon, the LORD HIGH CHANCELLOR
of GREAT BRITAIN,

The humble Petition of H. A.

Sheweth,

THAT your petitioner many years ago, from a with of serving the said T. F. in his setting out in life, and establishing himself in trade, became security for him in several bonds for sums of money borrowed of various persons,

THAT some of those persons some time afterwards requiring payment of their money, called upon your petitioner for the same, whereupon your petitioner did in the months of   17   pay them and the other persons to whom he had become security as aforesaid, their respective demands to the amount of

THAT the said T. F. also became indebted to your petitioner in the sum of   upon bond.

THAT for the indemnifying your petitioner against the debts for which he had become security, the said T. F. gave your petitioner a bond in the penalty of

for the purpose of indemnifying your petitioner against the said bonds so executed by your petitioner on behalf of the said bankrupt, and also gave your petitioner a warrant of attorney to enter up judgment on the said bond, upon which a judgment was accordingly entered in his majesty's court of King's Bench.

THAT your petitioner after payment by him of the aforesaid   applied to the said T. F. for repayment thereof, as well as of the said sum of   so due to your petitioner as aforesaid; whereupon he shewed and gave your petitioner a state of his affairs, by which it was made to appear that he had more than sufficient to pay all his creditors, but your petitioner suspecting that the same was not a genuine state of his affairs, insisted on payment of his money, and the said T. F. not paying

the

the fame after repeated promifes by him fo to do, your petitioner fued out execution on the faid judgment, on or about the 17 and by virtue thereof, the fheriff on the fame day took the faid T F's goods in execution.

THAT on the 17 a commiffion of bankrupt iffued againft the faid T. F. and the meffenger under the faid commiffion, entered and claimed poffeffion of all the faid T F.'s effects.

THAT your petitioner fufpecting the faid commiffion fo obtained was fraudulent, applied to the faid fheriff to fell the effects fo taken under the faid execution, and the fheriff on being indemnified by your petitioner, proceeded to a fale thereof, and paid the produce thereof to your petitioner.

THAT the affignees under the faid commiffion brought an action againft the faid fheriff for a recovery of the value of the faid effects, alledging that the faid T F. had fome time previous to the iffuing of the faid commiffion, and the faid execution, committed one or more acts of bankruptcy

THAT the faid action came on to be tried at the fitting after laft Eafter Term in the court of King's Bench, when a verdict was given for the faid affignees, by which they recovered the whole amount of the faid effects fo fold by the faid fheriff.

THAT your petitioner relying on the validity of his faid execution, did not prove his debt under the faid commiffion during any of the fittings appointed in the London Gazette, and that fince the faid verdict was fo given, no meeting has been had to prove debts under the faid commiffion.

THAT there is due to your petitioner and upwards, from the faid T. F , that your petitioner is the principal creditor of the faid T. F. all his other debts not amounting, as your petitioner is informed and believes, to fo much as your petitioner's debt.

THAT the commiffioners under the faid commiffion, have as your petitioner is informed, figned
the

the certificate of the said bankrupt's conformity, and the same has been advertised in the London Gazette to be allowed, unless cause shall be shewn against the same on or before the   day of 17

THAT a dividend of the said bankrupt's estate is advertised to be made on the   day of   next.

THAT your petitioner proposes to prove his debt under the said commission on the said   day of   or on such other day, whereon a meeting of the commissioners under the same shall be held.

YOUR petitioner therefore most humbly prays your Lordship, that the allowance of the said bankrupt's certificate may be stayed until your petitioner shall have proved his said debt, and that your petitioner may then have liberty to assent to, or dissent from the same, or that your Lordship will be pleased to make such other order therein as to your Lordship shall seem meet.

And your petitioner will ever pray, &c.

Petition of a separate Creditor to stay the Certificate of one of the Bankrupts, under a joint Commission.

In the matter of J. T. and J. R. bankrupts.

To the Right Hon the LORD HIGH CHANCELLOR of GREAT BRITAIN

The humble Petition of H. B. of C -street, London, merchant,

Sheweth,

THAT a joint commission of bankrupt, under the great seal of Great Britain, hath been awarded and issued against the said J. T. and J. R. by the names and description of J. T. and J. R. or   in the county of of merchants and partners, and they have been thereupon found and declared bankrupts.

THAT previous to the iſſuing of the ſaid joint commiſſion of bankrupt againſt the ſaid J. I and J. R. the ſaid J. T. was on his own ſeparate account indebted to your petitioner in the ſum of   pounds ſhillings   and   pence

THAT the ſaid J. T. hath, with the conſent of four-fifths in number and value of the creditors under the ſaid joint commiſſion ſo iſſued againſt him and the ſaid J. R. as aforeſaid, procured his certificate to be ſigned by the commiſſioners acting under the ſaid commiſſion, which now lays for your Lordſhip's allowance thereof, and in regard that your petitioner hath not been able to prove his debt due from the ſaid J. T. on his own ſeparate account, under the joint commiſſion againſt the ſaid J. I and J. R ſo as to enable him to aſſent to, or diſſent from the allowance of the ſaid certificate, although the ſaid J. T. is poſſeſſed on his own ſeparate account, of divers effects, independent of the partnerſhip with the ſaid J.R.

YOUR petitioner therefore moſt humbly prays your Lordſhip, that he may be at liberty to prove his ſaid debt of   due to your petitioner from the ſeparate eſtate of the ſaid J T. under the joint commiſſion of bankrupt againſt the ſaid J T. and J R. and that your petitioner may be paid his dividends thereon out of the ſeparate eſtate of the ſaid J I. ſo far as the ſame will extend, and for that purpoſe, that the aſſignees under the ſaid commiſſion may be directed to keep ſeparate accounts of the joint eſtate of the ſaid J. T and J R. and of the ſeparate eſtate of the ſaid J. T and that your petitioner may be at liberty to aſſent to, or
diſſent

diffent from, the certificate of the said J. T. under the said commisfion, and that your Lordfhip in the meantime would be pleafed to ftay your allowance thereof, and that the cofts of this application may be paid your petitioner out of the feparate eftate of the faid J T. and that your Lordfhip will be pleafed to make fuch further or other order in the premifes as to your Lordfhip fhall feem meet.

And your petitioner fhall ever pray, &c.

Petition for Affignees under a joint Commiffion to take feparate Accounts.

In the matter of H R. and W. M. bankrupts.

To the Right Honourable the LORD HIGH CHANCELLOR of GREAT BRITAIN

The humble Petition of C Y of   in the county of M merchant, on behalf of himfelf and the reft of the feparate creditors of the faid H R one of the faid bankrupts,

Sheweth,

THAT on or about the   day of   a joint commiffion of bankrupt, under the great feal of Great Britain, was awarded and iffued againft them the faid H R. and W M and on the fame day a feparate commiffion of bankrupt was alfo iffued againft the faid W M. and the faid H. R. and W M. jointly, and the faid W.M. alone, has thereupon refpectively been declared bankrupts accordingly, by means whereof as well the joint eftate and effects of the faid H. R. and W M as the feparate eftate and effects of the faid H R. have been feized and taken under the faid joint commiffion, and upon the affignment thereof to the affignees to be chofen under the faid joint commiffion, fuch affignees will take the fame without diftinguifhing or dividing the joint from the feparate effects of the faid H. R. to your petitioner's great detriment and oppreffion,

THAT

THAT the said H R. was before the date and suing forth of the said commission, and still is justly and truly separately indebted unto your petitioner, and sundry other persons, in divers sums of money, on his own separate account, as well for goods sold and delivered by them respectively to the said H. R. as on several other accounts, and that the said H R was at the time of the issuing of the said commission, possessed of, or otherwise intitled unto a very considerable personal estate in his own right, and your petitioner is advised that such separate estate is first liable to the payment of the several and respective separate debts of the said H R

THAT assignees of the estate and effects of the said H R and W. M have not yet been chosen under the said joint commission.

THAT under the several circumstances of this case, your petitioner and other the separate creditors of the said H. R. cannot be admitted to prove their respective separate debts under the said joint commission, so as to bind the separate estate of the said H. R for the benefit of your petitioner, and the rest of the separate creditors of the said H R. without your Lordships order for that purpose.

YOUR petitioner humbly prays That your Lordship will be pleased to order that your Petitioner and the rest of the separate creditors of the said H. R may be at liberty to go before the major part of the commissioners named in the said joint commission against the said H. R and W. M and prove their separate debts under the said joint commission, and that the said commissioners may appoint a meeting for that purpose, and due notice thereof given in the London Gazette, and that after proving the same, they may be

be permitted to vote in the choice
of one or more afsignee or afsignees of the faid bankrupt's eftate
and effects; and that the afsignee
or afsignees when chofen, may
take diftinct accounts of the joint
eftate of the faid H.R. and W.M
and alfo of the feparate eftate of
the faid H. R. that fhall come to
their hands, under the faid joint
commifsion, or to the hands of
any other perfon or perfons by his,
their, or either of their order, or
for his, their, or either of their
ufe, diftinguifhing the faid feparate eftate and the faid joint eftate
of the faid H. R and W. M from
each other, and that what on the
taking fuch accounts fhall be
found to belong to the joint eftate of the faid H R. and W. M.
may be applied by the faid affignee or afsignees in the firft
place towards fatisfaction of their
joint creditors, and that, what
upon the taking of the faid account fhall be found to belong to
the feparate eftate of the faid
H. R. may be applied by the faid
affignee or afsignees in the firft
place towards fatisfaction of his
feparate creditors, and in cafe
there fhall happen to be a furplus
of the feparate eftate of the faid
H R after all his feparate creditors fhall be fully paid and fatisfied their whole demand, then
that fuch furplus may be carried
to the account of the joint eftate

of the said H R and W M. and be applied in satisfaction of their joint creditors, and in case there shall happen to be a surplus of the joint estate of the said H R and W. M. after all their joint creditors shall be fully paid and satisfied their whole demand, then that such surplus may be divided into moieties, and that one moiety thereof be carried to the account of the separate estate of the said H R and be applied in satisfaction of his separate creditors, and that your petitioner and other the separate creditors of the said H R may be at liberty to assent to, or dissent from the allowance of the separate certificate of the said H R and that the costs of this application may be paid to your petitioner by the assignee or assignees, when chosen under the said joint commission out of the separate estate of the said H. R or that your Lordship will be pleased to make such further or other order in the premises as to your Lordship shall seem meet.

And your petitioner shall ever pray, &c.

Petition for creditors to prove their separate debts, under a joint commission.

In the matter of M. S and J. S bankrupts.

To the Right Hon, the LORD HIGH CHANCELLOR *of* GREAT BRITAIN.

*The humble Petition of E. T. and W T of
street, London, wine merchants on behalf of
themselves, and the rest of the separate creditors
of the said J. S.*

Sheweth,

THAT on or about the   day of   inst
a joint commission of bankrupt, under the great seal of
Great Britain, was awarded and issued against the said
M S and J S by the name and description of M S
and J S. of   street, London, pewterers and copartners, and they were thereupon found and declared bankrupts, and their estate and effects, as well joint as separate, have been assigned by the major part of the commissioners acting under the said commission, to D C
of   street, London, gentleman, as the provisional assignee thereof, who hath possessed himself as well of the
separate estates of the said bankrupts, as of their joint
estate, without distinguishing or dividing the joint effects
from the separate estates of the said bankrupts.

THAT the second meeting of the commissioners under the said commission, for the choice of
assignees of the said bankrupt's estate and effects, is appointed to be held at Guildhall, London, on the   day
of   inst.

THAT the said J S. was, at and before the
date and suing forth of the said commission, and still is
justly and truly indebted unto your petitioner, in the
sum of   for goods sold and delivered by your petitioners to the said J. S.

THAT the said J S. was, at the time of issuing
the said commission, seised and possessed of, or otherwise
well entitled unto, a very considerable personal estate, in

N 2   his

his own right, which, as your petitioners are advifed, is in the firft place, fubject and liable to the payment and difcharge of the feparate debts of the faid J. S.

THAT your petitioners, and the other feparate creditors of the faid J. S. cannot be admitted to prove their feveral and refpective feparate debts under the faid commiffion, fo as to bind the feparate eftate of the faid J. S. for the benefit of your petitioners, and the reft of the feparate creditors of the faid J S. without your Lordfhip's order in that behalf.

YOUR petitioners therefore moft humbly pray, that your Lordfhip will be pleafed to order, that your petitioners, and the reft of the feparate creditors of the faid J S may be at liberty to prove their feveral and refpective debts under the faid joint commiffion, and that they may be at liberty to affent to, or diffent from, the allowance of the certificate of the faid J. S. and that it may be referred to the major part of the commiffioners named in and authorifed by the faid commiffion, to take a diftinct account of the feparate eftate of the faid J. S. for the benefit of your petitioners, and the reft of his feparate creditors, and that the cofts of this application, and of taking fuch account, may be paid out of the faid feparate eftate, or that your Lordfhip will be pleafed to make fuch other order in the premifes, for the relief of your petitioners, and the reft of the feparate creditors of the faid J. S. as to your Lordfhip fhall feem meet.

And your petitioners fhall ever pray, &c.

Petition

Petition for separate creditors to prove their several and respective debts, under a joint commission

In the matter of W. D. and H. B. bankrupts

To the Right Hon the LORD HIGH CHANCELLOR *of* GREAT BRITAIN.

The humble Petition of J. L and J F assignees of the said bankrupts, on behalf of themselves and the rest of the separate creditors of the said W. D. and H B. respectively ,

Sheweth,

THAT on or about the   day of   17
a joint commission of bankrupt, under the great seal of Great Britain, was awarded and issued against the said W D and H B. late of   in the city of London, printsellers, and partners, dealers and chapmen, and they were thereupon declared bankrupts accordingly, and their estates and effects, as well joint as separate, have been assigned to your petitioners, as assignees duly chosen under the said commission, without distinguishing or dividing the joint effects, from the respective separate estates and effects of the said bankrupts

THAT the said W D and H. B against whom the said joint commission was so awarded and issued, were, before the date and suing forth of the said commission, and still are, justly and truly indebted to your petitioners respectively, and others, (as your petitioners are informed and believe) on the said bankrupts' respective separate accounts, in large sums of money, as well for monies lent and advanced to the said W D and H. B respectively, by your petitioners as on other accounts.

THAT the said bankrupts, at the time of issuing the said commission, were respectively possess'd of, or otherwise entitled unto, personal property in their own right; and your petitioners are advised, that such respective separate estates are first liable to the payment of the several and respective separate debts of the said bankrupts, respectively.

Tit f

THAT on or about the   day of inst. the said joint commission was renewed, upon the petition of your petitioners, as assignees as aforesaid, for the reasons in the said petition mentioned.

THAT your petitioners, as assignees as aforesaid, have possessed themselves, not only of the respective separate estates and effects of the said bankrupts, but also of the joint and partnership estate and effects of the said bankrupts

THAT your petitioners, as assignees as aforesaid, being willing and desirous to make a fair and equal distribution, as well of the said joint effects, as of the said separate effects of the said bankrupts respectively, and as your petitioners, and the other separate creditors of the said bankrupts, under the circumstances of this case, cannot be admitted to prove their several and respective separate debts, under the joint commission, so as to bind the respective separate estates of the said bankrupts, for the benefit of your petitioners, and the rest of the separate creditors of the said bankrupts, nor can your petitioners, as assignees as aforesaid, safely and legally marshall the said respective separate estates, without your Lordship's order for that purpose.

Your petitioners therefore most humbly pray your Lordship would be pleased to order, that your petitioners, and the rest of the respective creditors of the said bankrupts, may be at liberty to prove their several and respective separate debts, under the said joint commission against the said bankrupts respectively, and that it may be referred to the major part of the commissioners named and authorised in and by the said joint renewed commission, to take your petitioners' distinct accounts of the joint and separate estates of the

said

said bankrupts respectively, for
the benefit of then said joint and
several and respective separate creditors; and that the joint estate
of the said bankrupts may be applied amongst the joint creditors
in a rateable manner, and the respective separate estates of the said
bankrupts, amongst the respective
separate creditors in like manner,
agreeable to the usual order made
in such cases; and that your petitioners may be at liberty to retain in their hands, as well the
costs of this application, as of
taking the said respective separate
accounts, out of the respective
separate estates of the said bankrupts · or that your Lordship
would be pleased to make such
other order in the premises,
for the relief of your petitioners,
as to your Lordship shall seem
meet.

And your petitioners shall ever pray, &c.

Petition with exceptions to a master's report.

In the matter of S B a bankrupt

> *To the Right Hon the* Lord High Chan-
> cellor *of* Great Britain.

> *The humble petition of D N of the Borough of S
> in the County of S lighterman,*

Sheweth,

THAT your petitioner hath lately filed exceptions to the report of W G Esq one of the masters of
this honorable court made in the above matter, bearing
date

date the   day of   and S. M the petitioner in this matter having preferred a petition to your Lordſhip to confirm ſuch report,

ouR petitioner therefore moſt humbly prays your Lordſhip to order the ſaid exceptions to be ſet down to be argued before your Lordſhip on the next day of petitions, and at the time of the hearing of the ſaid petition of the ſaid S M to confirm the ſaid report as aforeſaid,

And your petitioner ſhall ever pray, &c.

In the matter of S. B a bankrupt

EXCEPTIONS *taken by D N to the report of W G. Eſq one of the maſters of the high court of Chancery, bearing date the   day of   17   to whom this matter was referred by virtue of an order of the ſaid court bearing date the   day of   17   on the hearing of the petition of S M in this matter,*

FIRST, for that the ſaid maſter hath in and by his report, certified that he does not find any ſum of money to have been bona fide due to the ſaid D N. from the ſaid S. B the bankrupt, at the time of the date and ſuing forth the commiſſion of bankrupt againſt the ſaid S. B.---*Whereas* the ſaid maſter ought to have found that the ſum of   was bona fide due to the ſaid D N. from the ſaid S B. at the time of the date and ſuing forth the ſaid commiſſion of bankrupt againſt the ſaid S. B

In all which particulars the ſaid D. N excepts of the ſaid maſter's report, and prays that he may review and alter the ſame.

Another

Another Petition with exceptions to a Master's report.
In the matter of P. and R. bankrupts.

To the Right Hon. the LORD HIGH CHANCELLOR.

The humble Petition of *P. M. W. B. M P* and
T S the *surviving assignees of the estate and
effects of E R. a bankrupt*,

Sheweth,

THAT by a certain order made in this
matter by   the late lords commissioners for the custody
of the great seal of Great Britain, bearing date the   day
of   17   it was referred to Mr   one of the masters of the high court of Chancery, to take an account of all dealings and transactions between the said
P and R and the said E R and of all money really and
bona fide, lent, paid and advanced by the said P and R.
to and for the use of the said E R and also, of all money,
securities for money and goods had and received by the
said P and R or by any other person or persons by them,
or either of them order, or for their, or either of their
use from the said E R.

THAT in pursuance of the said order the
said master hath been attended by the solicitor, for the
assignees of the estate and effects of the said P and R and
also by the solicitor for your petitioners, and has proceeded to take the accounts by the said order of reference
directed to be taken, and did prepare a draft of his report, to which your petitioner did object.

FOR THAT the said master hath in his said
report, allowed several sums therein mentioned to have
been paid by the said P. and R to W J M, and M B
in the said report also mentioned, amounting together to
the sum of   to be set off against a certain judgment
entered up by your petitioners against the assignees of
the said P and R. for the sum of

THAT the said master notwithstanding such
objections so made and laid before him, on the behalf of
your petitioners as aforesaid, hath signed his report,
bearing date the   day of   17   without paying
any regard thereto.

THAT your petitioners are advised and humbly submit it to your Lordship's judgment, that the said master ought not to have allowed the said several sums above mentioned, or either of them to be set off in such manner as he hath set off the same, in the schedule to his report thereof, your petitioners except to the said master's report, in the particulars above mentioned, and pray that the same may in that respect be let aside or rectified.

> YOUR petitioners therefore humbly pray that the above exceptions taken to the said report by them, may come on to be argued before your Lordship, and that your Lordship will be pleased to appoint a day for that purpose, or that your Lordship will be pleased to make such other order in the premises as to your Lordship shall seem meet.

> And your petitioner shall ever pray, &c.

Petition for money to be placed in the Bank, in trust.

In the matter of A. S. the elder, a bankrupt.

> *To the Right Hon. the* LORD HIGH CHANCELLOR *of* GREAT BRITAIN.

> *The humble Petition of A S the younger, the only surviving son of the said bankrupt, an infant, under the age of 21 years, that is to say, of the age of 17 years, or thereabouts, by J O. his next friend,*

Sheweth,

THAT your petitioner, by his next friend, did, on the   day of   17   prefer his petition to your Lordship, thereby shewing, that C. O. late of

in

In the county of   gentleman, deceafed, did, by his laft will and teftament in writing, bearing date the day of   17 difpofe of his perfonal eftate and effects, which amounted to a confiderable fum, after payment of all his juft debts, legacies, and funeral expences, and he did, by his faid will, give and bequeath, in the words and to the purport and effect following (that is to fay,)

' I leave to C. and J. and A S--s, jun. the fons of A S of
" ftreet,   pounds each, the intereft to be added
" to the principal yearly, till they fhall refpectively at-
" tain the age of 21 years; and in cafe one fhould die
" before that age, to the furvivor I give and bequeath
" unto my brother J. O and A. S fenior, and the fur-
' vivor of them, his heirs, executors, and adminiftra-
" tors, upon the feveral trufts herein after mentioned,
' viz. upon truft, that they the faid truftees, or the fur-
" vivor of them, his heirs, executors, or adminiftrators,
" do, and fhall, as foon as conveniently may be after my
" deceafe, put and place out at intereft, in fome of the
" public funds, or government, or other good and fuf-
' ficient fecurities all thofe legacies that are not yet
" become due; and I do hereby nominate, conftitute,
" and appoint the faid J O. and A S. joint executors
' and refiduary legatees of this my will "

THAT the faid petitioner did alfo fhew, that the faid teftator departed this life on or about the   day of   17 without altering or revoking his faid will, and that the faid executors therein named did, foon after the deceafe of the faid teftator, duly prove the faid will, in the prerogative court of the archbifhop of Canterbury, and by virtue of the probate of the faid will or the faid A S poffeffed himfelf of affetts of the faid teftator, more than fufficient to pay and fatisfy all his juft debts legacies, and funeral expences, and alfo, that th faid C S. and J S. your petitioner's brothers, were both of them living at the time of the death of the faid teftator but the faid C. S departed this life on or about the   day of   17 an infant under the age of 21 years, that is to fay, of the age of   years, or thereabouts,

O 2

abouts, and that the faid J S. departed this life on or about the day of 17 an infant, under the age of 21 years, that is to fay, of the age of years, or thereabouts, whereby your petitioner, as furviving his faid two brothers, who died under the age of 21 did become well entitled to the faid legacies of pounds and pounds, given to them in manner aforefaid, together with intereft thereon, and alfo to the faid fum of

pounds, fo given to your petitioner as aforefaid, together with intereft thereon, to be computed from one year after the death of the faid teftator.

THAT the faid petition did alfo fhew, that no part of the faid legacies, or either of them, was by the executors of the faid teftator, vefted in any government or other fecurities, in fuch manner as is directed by the will of the faid teftator, and alfo, that a commiffion of bankrupt was awarded and iffued againft the faid A S. the elder, on or about the day of 17 directed to certain commiffioners therein named, the major part of whom duly found and declared the faid A. S a bankrupt, and that the faid bankrupt did, on or about the day of 17 at the firft fitting under the faid commiffion, furrender himfelf to the major part of the commiffioners in the faid commiffion named, and being examined by the faid commiffioners, he did admit and acknowledge, that he had then before received affetts of the faid teftator, more than fufficient to pay and fatisfy his juft debts, legacies, and funeral expences, and particularly, that he had received of the faid J O. his co-executor, the whole of the faid fum of

pounds, for the purpofe of invefting the fame in fuch manner as was directed by the faid teftator's will, for fecuring the legacies given thereby, to which your petitioner, by furvivorfhip, was then become entitled, and that application was made to the faid commiffioners, that proof fhould be made of the amount of the faid principal fum, and intereft, under the faid commiffion, for the benefit of your petitioner, and that the faid commiffioners refufed admitting fuch proof, without your Lordfhip's order being firft obtained for that purpofe

THAT

THAT your petitioner therefore prayed, that your Lordship would be pleased to order and direct, that the said J O. might be at liberty, as trustee for your petitioner, to prove the said sum of   pounds, together with interest thereon, at and after the rate of   pounds per cent. per ann. to be computed from one year after the death of the said testator, until the date of the said commission, and that he might vote in the choice of assignees in respect thereof, and receive a dividend thereon rateably and in proportion with the rest of the creditors of the said bankrupt, who should come in and seek relief under the said commission, such proof to be made without prejudice to any claim or demand which your petitioner might have on the said J O touching the premises, and that such sums of money as should be received of the dividend or dividends, on the sums so proved by the said J O might be paid into the bank, in the name and with the privity of the accountant general of the court of chancery, to be placed to the credit of your petitioners' account, subject to your Lordship's further order, and for general relief

THAT the said petition coming on to be heard before your Lordship, on or about the   day of   17   your Lordship was pleased to order, that your petitioner, or J O his guardian, should be at liberty to go before the major part of the commissioners, named in the commission of bankrupt issued against the said A S the elder, to prove the debt and interest due thereon, in the said petition mentioned, and should be admitted a creditor under the said commission, for what he should so prove, and be paid a dividend or dividends in respect thereof, rateably and in equal proportion with the rest of the said bankrupt's creditors, seeking relief under the said commission, but such proof was to be made without prejudice to any demand the said A S the younger, might have on the said J O and without prejudice to any claim the assignee of A S the elder, might have on the estate of C O the testator, and your Lordship also ordered that the said J O should pay

into

into the bank, in the name and with the privity of the accountant general of the court of chancery, to be placed to the credit of your petitioner, all and every dividend and dividends which should from time to time accrue due, and be received by the said J. O. in respect of the said debt, subject to your Lordship's further order.

THAT the affignees of the estate and effects of the said A S. the elder, did, on the   day of 17   prefer their petition to your Lordship, thereby shewing, that being advised that upon the death of the said C S under the age of   years, the said legacy of   pounds, so given by the will of the said testator C. O. became deviseable between the said J S. and A. S. his brothers, equally between them, but that upon the death of the said J S who also died an infant, under the age of   years the said petitioners were also advised, that his interest in the sum of   pounds, the moiety of the said   pounds, legacy given to his brother C S to which he was entitled as having survived him, did not survive to the said A S. the younger, the only surviving brother, but that the same became well vested in the said A S. the father, as the administrator of his said son, J. S.

THAT the said petition therefore prayed, that your Lordship would order and direct, that so much of the dividends as should be paid into the bank, by virtue of your Lordship's order made on the petition of your petitioner as aforesaid, as should arise or become due or payable, in respect of the sum of   pounds, the moiety of the said legacy of   pounds, which was given to the said C S by the will of the said testator, be paid to the said affignees, of the estate and effects of said A S the bankrupt, for the benefit of themselves, and the rest of the creditors of the said bankrupt, who already have or should in due time come in and seek relief under the said commission or that your Lordship would be pleased to make such other order in the premises, as to your Lordship should seem meet

THAT

THAT the said petition coming on to be heard before your Lordship, on or about the   day of   17   your Lordship was pleased to order, that the said assignees should pay the dividends which already have or should become due on the sum of   pounds, in the said petition mentioned, into the bank, in the name and with the privity of the accountant general of the court of chancery, to be placed to the credit of this matter, subject to your Lordship's further order, instead of the payment thereof to the said J O. is directed by your Lordship's order made in this matter on the   day of   17

THAT in pursuance of your Lordship's order of the   day of   17   the said assignees paid into the bank the sum of   pounds   shillings and   pence, which said last sum was in pursuance of your Lordship's order of the   of May last, laid out in purchase of   pounds   shillings, and   pence, 3 per cent. consol. bank annuities

THAT in pursuance of your Lordship's said order of   17   the said assignees paid into the bank the further sum of   pounds   shillings and   pence, and as it will be for the benefit of all parties to have the said sum of   pounds   shillings and   pence, cash in the bank, laid out in the purchase of bank 3 per cent. consol annuities, as also all such further and other sum or sums of money as shall or may be paid into the bank, in pursuance of your Lordship's last mentioned order

YOUR petitioner therefore most humbly prays, That your Lordship would be pleased to order and direct, that the said sum of   pounds   shillings and   pence, cash, in the bank, standing in the said accountant general's name, placed to the credit of this matter, and also all such further and other sum or sums of money as shall or

may

may be paid into the bank, in purfuance of your Lordship's order of
17 may be laid out in the purchafe of bank 3 per cent annuities, in the name and with the
privity of the faid accountant general, in truft in this matter, and
that the faid accountant general
may declare the truft thereof accordingly, fubject to your Lordship's further order, and that the
faid accountant general may draw
on the bank according to the form
prefcribed by the act of parliament for the relief of the fuitors
of this honourable court, and the
general rules and orders in that
cafe made and provided.

And your petitioner will ever pray, &c.

---

*Petition of a bankrupt to finish his laft examination after the
time appointed, the commiffioners not having attended to
take the examination.*

In the matter of T. W. bankrupt,

To the Right Honourable the LORD HIGH
CHANCELLOR of GREAT BRITAIN.

The humble Petition of the faid T. W. bankrupt,

Sheweth,

THAT a commiffion of bankrupt under
the great feal of Great Britain, bearing date at Westmin-
fter, the   day of   laft, upon the petition of J P
of   in the county of   yeoman, was awarded and
iffued againft your petitioner, by the name and defcription of T W of   in the county of   money fcri-
vener, dealer and chapman, which commiffion was hitherto

rected to E. G. and G P. H Efqrs. and T. K. W. L. and J M. K. gentlemen, commiffioners to execute the fame

THAT your petitioner hath been duly declared bankrupt by the major part of the fud commiffioners in and by the faid commiffion, named and authorifed, and by fummons under their hand, and alfo by notice in the London Gazette, of Saturday the day of 17 was required to furrender himfelf to the faid commiffioners, or the maj r part of them at the Dolphin Inn, in in the faid county of to be examined by them on the da, of the faid month of and the day of the month of laft refpectively, at ten of the clock in the forenoon, on each of the fud days, touching the difclofure and difcovery of his eftate and effects, and on the day of laft, your petitioner was by fuch fummons and notice required to finish his examination under the faid commiffion

THAT your petitioner did furrender himfelf to the faid commiffioners, on the faid day of laft, and fubmitted to be examined, touching the difclofure and difcovery of his eftate and effects, and to conform himfelf to the feveral acts of parliament, made and now in force concerning bankrupts.

THAT your petitioner did attend at the Dolphin Inn, in aforefaid, on the faid day of inftant to furrender, and was ready to furrender himfelf to the major part of the commiffioners in the faid commiffion, named and authorifed, to make a full difclofure and difcovery of his eftate and effects, but one of the fud commiffioners in the faid commiffion named, being a creditor of your petitioner, fo that he cannot, and did or does not chufe to act as a commiffioner, and two others of the fud commiffioners (that is to fay) the faid E G and J K being on a journey and could not be had in due time to take fuch examination which was unknown to your petitioner until the faid day of inftant, it becomes neceffary for your petitioner to

P have

have another meeting fixed and appointed for that purpofe.

Your petitioner therefore moft humbly
prays your Lordfhip, that you
would be pleafed forthwith to appoint another meeting at the Dolphin Inn, in   aforefaid, for
your petitioner to appear and fur
render himfelf before the faid
commiffioners in the faid commiffion named, or the major part of
them, to make a full difclofure
and difcovery of his eftate and
effects, and alfo to finifh his laft
examination under the faid commiffion; and to order the faid
commiffioners to caufe due notice
of fuch meeting to be given in the
London Gazette, that fuch of your
petitioner's creditors as fhall think
proper, may be prefent at your
petitioner's laft examination, or
that your Lordfhip will be pleafed
to make fuch order in this matter
for your petitioner's relief as to
your Lordfhip fhall feem meet.

And your petitioner (as in duty bound)
fhall ever pray, dated the   day of   in the year of
our Lord 17

Bankrupt's examination after time, being in the Fleet Prifon.
In the matter of R. C. a bankrupt.

To the Right Honourable the LORD HIGH
CHANCELLOR of GREAT BRITAIN.

The humble Petition of the faid bankrupt,
Sheweth,

THAT a commiffion of bankrupt, bearing
date at Weftminfter the 3d day of May 17   was awarded

ed and iffued againft your petitioner, by the name and defcription of K. C. late of   in the county of ta'low-chandler, foap boiler, dealer and chapman, on the application of T P of the city of   gentleman, one of your petitioner's creditors, directed to   commiſsioners therein named, the major-part of whom having met together in the city of   foon after the iſsuing of the faid commiſsion, declared your petitioner a bankrupt, and R S gentleman, is the fole afsignee under the faid commiſsion.

THAT by the commiſsioners' fummons, and alfo by a notice inferted in the London Gazette of Tuef-day the   day of   17   your petitioner finds he was required to furrender himfelf before the major part of the commiſsioners acting under the faid commiſsion on the twenty-fifth and twenty-fixth days of the faid month of May, at the houfe of Eleanor Morris, widow, being the Pheafant Inn in Silver-ftreet, in the city of   in order to be examined, touching the difclofure and dif-covery of his eftate and effects, and on the twenty-firft day of June then next following, your petitioner was by fuch fummons and notice to attend the faid commiſsioners, at the fame place, to finifh his examination under the faid commiſsion.

THAT fuch commiſsion of bankrupt was fo taken out againft your petitioner without his knowledge or privity, and that in the month of   laft, your pe-titioner was arrefted in the court of common pleas, at the fuit of S K, a creditor of your petitioner, for   pounds or there-abouts, to which action fpecial bail, was filed.

THAT on the   day of   laft, your pe-titioner was committed to the Fleet-prifon, in difcharge of his bail in the faid action, by the honourable Mr. Juftice   and your petitioner has ever fince remained and ftill is a prifoner in the faid prifon, charged with the faid action.

THAT about a week or ten days after your petitioner's faid imprifonment, he received a letter from his wife, informing him of the faid commiſsion of bank-

rupt,

rupt, and which was the first information he received of the said commission having issued, but your petitioner could not come out of the said prison to attend the commissioners on the said commission at either of their said meetings; nor did the said commissioners or any person concerned under the said commission, send any warrant or order to the warden of the Fleet, requiring your petitioner's attendance, although your petitioner has been, and is willing, and desirous to surrender himself, and to be examined, and to make a full and true discovery of his estate and effects under the said commission.

YOUR petitioner therefore most humbly prays your Lordship to order the major part of the commissioners named in the said commission, forthwith to appoint one or more meetings for your petitioner to appear and surrender himself before them, and to make a full disclosure and discovery of his estate and effects, and to finish his examination under the said commission, and that your Lordship will also be pleased to order that the said commissioners may cause your petition to be brought before them, for that purpose, and that your Lordship would be pleased to direct the commissioners to enter among their proceedings an account of the cause which prevented your petitioner from surrendering himself and finishing his examination within the time aforesaid, or that such other order may be made in this matter for your petitioner's relief, as to your Lordship shall seem meet

And your petitioner will ever pray, &c.

Peti.

Petition for bankrupt's examination to be taken after the time limited, on account of his being abroad, at the time of the issuing the commission.

In the matter of J W a bankrupt.

To the Right Hon. the LORD HIGH CHAN-
CELLOR *of* GREAT BRITAIN.

The humble petition of the said J W.

Sheweth,

THAT a commission of bankrupt under the great seal of Great Britain, bearing date at Westminster the   day of   last, upon the petition of T. L of   in the city of L warehouse-keeper, was awarded and issued against your petitioner, which commission was directed to Ld K.--- S ---E B ---W. P.---Esquires,-- and D K. gentleman, as commissioners to execute the same

THAT your petitioner hath been declared a bankrupt by the major part of the said commissioners, acting under the said commission, and by summons under their hands, and also by notice in the London Gazette, on Saturday the   day of   last, was required to surrender himself to the said commissioners, or the major part of them, at Guildhall, London, to be examined by them on the   and   days of   and   day of   last respectively, at   of the clock in the forenoon, on each of the said days, touching the disclosure and dis-covery of his estate and effects, and on the said   day of   last, your petitioner, was by such summons required, to finish his examination under the said com-mission.

THAT your petitioner being at the time of the issuing of the said commission upon his passage to New-York, in North America, to which place he was going for the purpose of collecting in various large sums of money due to him from persons resident there, he was totally ignorant of the said commission having issued against him, and therefore could not finish his examination in the time limited for that purpose and the said T. L. and

and J D. the younger, C. M and J S having been duly chosen assignees of your petitioner's estate, they on the   day of   last, preferred their petition to your Lordship, and obtained an order thereon for forty-nine days to be computed from the   day of   for your petitioner to surrender himself, and finish his examination.

THAT your petitioner never heard of any commission of bankrupt having issued against him, till the   day of   last, being the time of the arrival of the packet which sailed from the port of Falmouth, in   last, when he received notice of the said commission having issued, and for your petitioner to surrender himself within the time aforesaid, but the said notice not having reached your petitioner till the said   day of   it hath not been in his power to compleat his examination within the time limitted by the said order.

THAT your petitioner, during the time he was at New-York used his best endeavours for collecting in his debts, for the benefit and advantage of his creditors, and set out on his return from New-York, aforesaid, to L. two days after he received notice of the said commission having issued against him, having first assigned to a trustee who acted as attorney or agent for several of your petitioner's creditors in America, all his outstanding claims in America, for the benefit of all his creditors, and is now arrived in England for the purpose of compleating his examination.

YOUR petitioner therefore most humbly prays your Lordship would be pleased to order the major part of the commissioners named in the said commission, forth-with to appoint a time and place for your petitioner to appear and surrender himself before them, to make a full disclosure and discovery of his estate and effects, and finish his examination under the said commission, and that the said

com-

commissioners cause due notice of
such meeting to be given in the
London Gazette, that such of your
petitioner's creditors as shall think
proper, may be present at your petitioner's examination, and that the
said commissioner's may enter on
the proceedings had and taken under
the said commission, an account of
the cause which prevented your petitioner from surrendering himself,
and finishing his examination within
the time limited for that purpose,
or that your Lordship will be pleased
to make such other order for the relief of your petitioner, as to your
Lordship shall seem meet.

And your petitioner shall ever pray, &c.

Petition to sell an estate, and make a dividend.

In the matter of T S. a bankrupt.

To the Right Hon the Lord High Chancellor *of* Great Britain

The humble petition of J. B of   street, in the parish of   in the county of M gentleman, sole executor under the last will and testament of E. H. widow, one of the creditors of the said bankrupt, on behalf of himself and the rest of the creditors of the said bankrupt,

Sheweth,

THAT a commission of bankrupt under the
great seal of Great Britain, was duly awarded and issued
against the said T S. on the   of   17   whereupon he was duly found and declared a bankrupt, and
shortly afterwards at a meeting of the commissioners
named and authorized in and by the said commission,

I d 1

held at Guildhall, in the city of London, E S of London, falefman, and J G of   falefman, were duly chofen affignees of the faid bankrupt's eftate and effects, and it was agreed at a meeting of the commiffioners, named and authorized in the faid commiffion, by and between the creditors then prefent, and the faid affignees, that when they, or either of them, fhould have on account of the faid bankrupt's eftate, to the amount of 50 l or upwards, in their hands, it was to be paid into the bank, for the benefit of themfelves, and the reft of the faid bankrupt's creditors.

THAT your petitioner fometime afterwards received a dividend after the rate of 2 s. 8 d in the pound, upon the fum of   proved to be due to the faid E H from the faid bankrupt's eftate

THAT the faid J G one of the affignees of the faid bankrupt, on the   day of   17   (which was fubfequent to the making of the faid dividend) received from J F of   in the county of   the fum of   (being a legacy bequeathed to the faid T. S. the bankrupt, in and by the laft will and teftament of T H. deceafed,) for and on account of the faid bankrupt's eftate, which the faid J. G then faid would be appropriated to the paying another dividend of the faid bankrupt's effects, which was intended to be made in about a month afterwards, but the faid fum of   has ever fince remained in the hands of the faid J G. without being divided amongft the feveral creditors of the faid bankrupt, or placed in the bank to the credit of the faid eftate, and other fums of money have fince alfo come to the hands of the faid E. S and J G. on account of the faid bankrupt's eftate and effects, which they have employed in their refpective trades and bufinefs, or otherwife applied to their own ufe

THAT the faid E S. and J. G pretend they cannot make a further dividend of the faid bankrupt's eftate and effects, till the right and intereft of the faid bankrupt to   part of a meffuage and premifes fituate in   ftreet, Weftminfter, can be fold and difpofed of.

YOUR

YOUR petitioner therefore humbly prays your Lordship, that the said E. S. and J. G. may be directed to come to an account of all sum and sums of money received from time to time, by them, or either of them, as assignees of the estate and effects of the said T. S. the bankrupt, before the major part of the commissioners named in the said commission, and that they may pay all such sum and sums of money which have come to their and either of their hands, as aforesaid, with interest for the same, into the Bank of England; and that the said E. S. and J. G. may also be directed to sell and dispose of the said bankrupt's estate and interest in the said messuage and premises, either by public auction or private sale, with all convenient speed, and that the money to arise by such sale, may also be paid by the said E. S. and J. G. into the bank, and that the said commissioners, or the major part of them acting under the said commission, may be directed to make a dividend of all such monies when so paid into the bank, as aforesaid, to and amongst your petitioners, and all other the creditors of the said T. S. who have come in and sought relief under the said commission, or that your Lordship will be pleased to make such other order in the premises as to your Lordship, shall seem meet.

And your petitioner shall ever pray, &c.

Q

Form

Form of a petition for the sale of mortgaged premises, and for the petitioners to prove assets under the commission.

In the matter of **A H.** a bankrupt

To the Right Honourable the LORD HIGH CHANCELLOR *of* GREAT BRITAIN

The humble petition of S P. W. S ? R. and H. B executors of H H. deceased,

Sheweth,

THAT by indenture tripartite, bearing date the   day of   in the year of our Lord 17   made between K C as therein described, of the first part, A H the bankrupt, of the second part, and H H. is therein also described, since deceased, of the third part, *reciting* that by indenture of lease bearing date the   day of   17   and made between D B. therein mentioned, of the one part, and the said A. H. of the other part, the said D B did demise to the said A. H his executors, administrators, and assigns, all that messuage or tenement situate and being at   in the parish of   in the county of   called or known by the name of   together with the stables, outhouses, buildings, yard, gardens, orchards, and appurtenances, to hold the same to him the said A. H his executors, administrators, and assigns, from the feast day of the annunciation of the blessed Virgin-Mary, then next ensuing the date of the said indenture, for the full end and term of   years, thence next ensuing, under the rents and covenants therein mentioned, and also reciting that the said indenture of demise was then vested in the said K C for the remainder of the said term of   years, but subject to redemption by the said A H. upon payment to the said K C. of   pounds with legal interest, and that H H at the request of the said A H. had agreed to pay the said K C the said principal sum of   pounds; and also to lend and advance him so much more as would make up

in the whole the fum of   and that the faid A. H. had
given a bond and judgment for fecuring the fame, and
by way of better fecurity had propofed to affign the faid
indenture of leafe to the faid H H for the remainder of
the faid term   the faid K C in confideration of the faid
fum of   pounds, did by the direction of the faid A H
bargain, fell, affign, transfer, and fet over, and the faid
A H did bargain fell ratify and confirm unto the faid H.
H. his executors, adminiftrators, and affigns, as well the
faid recited indenture of leafe, as all mefne affignments
thereof, and the faid meffuage or tenement and premifes
therein comprized, and all right and title of them the faid
K C. and A. H. or either of them in or to the fame to
hold the fame to the faid H. H his executors, adminiftrators and affigns, from thence forth, for all the refidue and
remainder of the faid term of   years, fubject to redemption by the faid A H. upon payment to the faid H H.
of the fum of   pounds, and intereft for the fame, according to the condition of the faid recited bond

That the faid fum of   pounds, or any
part thereof, was not paid to the faid H. H at the time
fpecified in the faid indenture of mortgage, or at any time
during his life, except   pounds, or there-abouts

That the faid H H departed this life on
or about the   day of December, 17   having firft
duly made and executed his laft will and teftament in
writing, bearing date the   day of   in the year of
our Lord 17   and appointed your petitioners executors thereof, who have duly proved the fame in the proper ecclefiaftical court.

That a commiffion of bankrupt, bearing
date the   day of   laft, was awarded and iffued
againft the faid A H and he was thereupon duly found
and declared a bankrupt, and S N of   ftreet, in the
city of   vintner, and J O of   in the county of
     were chofen affignees of his eftate and effects

That at the time when the faid commiffion
of bankrupt was awarded and iffued againft the faid A H
there is due from him to your petitioners, as executors

Q   of

of the said H. H. on account of the said mortgage, the sum of   pounds   shillings and   pence.

THAT the said mortgaged premises are a very scanty and insufficient security for the said sum.

YOUR petitioners therefore humbly pray your Lordship, that the said mortgaged premises may be sold before the major part of the commissioners in the said commission named, and that what shall arise from the sale thereof, may be paid to your petitioners, in satisfaction of so much of the said sum of pounds   shillings   and pence, as the same will extend to satisfy, and that your petitioners may be at liberty to prove the remainder of the said sum of pounds   shillings and   pence, under the said commission.

And your petitioners shall ever pray, &c.

Petition for sale of mortgaged premises, before the master, and for other purposes.

In the matter of J. C a bankrupt

To the Right Honourable the LORD HIGH CHANCELLOR *of* GREAT BRITAIN.

The humble petition of T. M. W. R. and W. S. assignees of the said bankrupt,

Sheweth,

THAT A. F. widow, and sole executrix of C. F her late husband, deceased, preferred her petition to your Lordship, shewing, That in the year 17   the above named J. C. being seized of some freehold estates, at   in the county of   and having occasion to borrow a sum of money, had applied to a Mr. C. for the loan of pounds,

pounds, who had agreed to advance the fame, on having fome of the faid eftates conveyed to him, by way of moigage, and a friend's becoming jointly bound unto him, with the faid J, C. for the greater fecurity of repayment.

THAT on or about the   day of   17 the faid J C had received the fud fum of   pounds, and executed unto the faid Mr.C a mortgage, as agreed on, and the faid C F without any confideration or advantage, and merely through friendfhip, having been prevailed on to become fuch fecurity for the repayment thereof, with intereft, had joined with the faid J C. in executing a bond for that purpofe.

THAT on or about the   day of   17 a commiffion of bankiupt, under the great feal of Great Britain, had been awarded and iffued againft the faid J C and he had been thereupon declared a bankiupt, and his eftate and effects, both real and perfonal, had been accoidingly conveyed and affigned to your petitioners, being the affignees duly chofen under the fud commiffion.

THAT the faid bankrupt having neglected to pay off and difcharge the fud mortgage bond, the faid C F in his life time, and after the faid commiffion iffued was called on by the faid Mr. C and was obliged and actually did pay him the fum of   for the principal and intereft due thereon

THAT on the   day of   17   being the time the faid C. F paid the above fum the faid Mr. C had executed to him a conveyance of the fudmortgaged premifes, by leafe and releafe, and which fecurity was very infufficient to pay the faid A F as the executrix of the faid C. F. the faid monies, which he had actually advanced, or paid, to the faid Mr. C, and theieby praying that your Lordfhip would be pleafed to direct that the fud bankiupt's mortgaged eftates above mentioned, fhould be immediately fold, and that your petitioners fhould join with the faid A F. in executing a conveyance thereof, to the purchafer or purchafers, and that the whole puichafe

r u e,

money, should the same be insufficient to pay the said A. F. the said debt of   and interest, might be paid to the said A F. and she be ordered to be admitted as a creditor under the said commission, for so much as the money arising from the sale of the said estates, should turn out insufficient to answer the said debt   Upon hearing the said petition on the   day of   last past, your Lordship was pleased to order that it should be referred to the major part of the commissioners named in the commission of bankrupt, issued against the said J. C. to take an account of what was due to the said A F as executrix of her late husband, deceased, for principal and interest on the said mortgage, and that the premises comprized in the said mortgage, should be forthwith sold before the said commissioners, to the best purchaser or purchasers, that could be got for the same, and that the said commissioners should appoint a meeting for that purpose, of which due notice was to be given in the London Gazette, and your petitioners and all proper parties were to join with the said commissioners in the execution or a proper conveyance or conveyances to the purchaser or purchasers thereof, and all parties were to produce before the said commissioners all deeds and writings in their respective custody or power, relating to the title of the said premises, upon oath, as the said commissioners should direct, and that the money arising by such sale, should be applied in discharge of the principal and interest due to the said A. F. on the said mortgage, and the surplus thereof, if any, was to be paid to your petitioners, and in case the money to arise by such sale, should not be sufficient to pay and satisfy what should be found due, to the said A F for principal and interest, as aforesaid, your Lordship did order that the said A F should be at liberty to go before the said commissioners, and be admitted a creditor under the said commission, for such deficiency and that she should be paid a dividend or dividends in respect thereof, rateably and in equal proportion with the rest of the said bankrupt's creditors, seeking relief under the said commission

THAT

THAT the said C F. deceased, about the day of   17   prevailed on the tenants of the said mortgaged premises, to attorn to him, and pay him the rent then in arrear, and he and the said A F his widow, ever since have been and now are in the receipt of the rents and profits of the said mortgaged premises.

THAT the said A F is not by your Lord-ship's said order, ordered to account for the rents and profits of the said mortgaged premises, come to her hands, and to the hands of the said C, F. her late husband, deceased

THAT the said A. F. hath not proceeded under the said order nor taken any steps before the said commissioners, for the sale of the said mortgaged premises.

YOUR petitioners therefore humbly pray your Lordship, that it may be referred to one of the masters of this honourable court, to take an account of the rents and profits of the said mortgaged premises, come to the hands of, and received by the said C F deceased, in his life time, or to the hands of and received by the said A F his widow, since his decease, or to the hands of any other person on their account, and that the said order dated the   day of   17 may be altered and varied, as to such part thereof, whereby it is referred to the major part of the commissioners named in the said commission of bankrupt, to take an account of what is due to the said A F for the principal and interest, on the said mortgage, and that the premises comprized therein be forth-with fold befoie the faid commiſsioners, and that they ſhould appoint a meeting for that purpoſe, by notice in the London Gazette. And that it may be alſo referi ed to the faid maſter to take an account of what is due to the faid A F. as executrix of her late huſband, deceaſed, for principal and intereſt due on the faid mort-gage, and that the piemiſes com-piized in the faid mortgage may be forth-with fold before the faid maſtei, to the beſt puichaſer or purchaſeis, that can be got foi the ſame, to be allowed of by the faid maſter, and that the faid maſtei do appoint a time for that purpoſe, of which due notice is to be given in the London Gazette, and that proper paities may join in ſuch iale oi mortgage, and produce upon oath before the faid maſter, all deeds and writings in their cuſtody or powei, i elating thereto as he ſhall direct, an d that the money ariſing by ſuch ſale may in the fii ſt place be applied in diſ-charge of the piincipal and intei eſt due to the faid A. F. as executrix as aforeſaid, on the faid moitgag(i and that the iefidue thereof (if any) may be paid to your petition-ers.

And your petitioners ſhall evei piay, &c.

Petition to transfer money in the matter of the bankrupt to the credit of the cause

In the matter of M N. a bankrupt.

To the Right Hon the LORD HIGH CHANCELLOR *of* GREAT BRITAIN

The humble Petition of J M T H and T F. the surviving assignees of the said bankrupt,

Sheweth,

THAT by an order made in the matter on the day of 17 the sum of (being the amount of several dividends of the said bankrupt's estate upon a claim made by your petitioner] M. is the executor of W N deceased, of the sum of under the said commission) was paid by your petitioners H and F into the bank of England, with the privity of the accountant-general of this court, in trust in this matter, and by virtue of the same order hath been since laid out in the purchase of 3 per cent consolidated bank annuities, which with the dividends from time to time received thereon and since laid out, amount to the sum of of like annuities, which now stand in the name of the said accountant-general in trust in this matter, together with the sum of cash in the bank, which has arisen from dividends on the said annuities as yet uninvested, and which annuities and cash are by the said order declared to be in trust for the benefit of such person or persons as should appear to be intitled thereto, without prejudice to any of the parties interested therein

THAT a cause is now depending in this court, wherein G W. and A his wife, late A. H widow; and T. N. spinster, are plaintiffs, and your petitioner M the said M N (the bankrupt) your petitioners H and F and W B and M his wife are defendants, being all the parties interested in the said annuities, and cash, and dividends

THAT by an account taken in the said cause in which the master has made his report, a considerably

R   larger

larger fum than the faid fum of   has been found and reported due from the eftate of the faid M. N. to your petitioner M as fuch executor of W N.

THAT in order to accomplifh a fettlement between all the parties in the faid caufe, refpecting the faid annuities and dividends, your petitioners are advifed that it will be convenient that the fame fhould be tranfferred from the credit of the bankruptcy in this matter, to the credit of the faid caufe, in truft for the parties interefted therein, and fubject to fuch future order as fhall be made in the faid caufe.

YOUR petitioners therefore humbly pray your Lordfhip to order that the faid fum of 3 per cent. annuities, together with the faid fum of cafh now in the bank, and all dividends to be hereafter received on the faid annuities, may be transferred by the accountantgeneral of this court, from the credit of this matter to the credit of the faid caufe, in truft for all parties interefted therein, and fubject to the orders of this court in the faid caufe

And your petitioners fhall ever ever pray, &c.

Petition to fuperfede a commiffion, after paying 20s. in the pound.

In the matter of G K. a bankrupt

> *To the Right Honourable the* LORD HIGH CHANCELLOR *of* GREAT BRITAIN
>
> *The humble petition of the faid G K. the bankrupt,*

Sheweth.

THAT a commiffion of bankrupt under the great feal of Great Britain bearing date at Weftminfter the

the   day of   17   was awarded and issued forth against your petitioner upon the petition of A F of mercer, which commission was directed to C. N. C.--- F F---C. L esquires, A. I. and W. C. gentlemen, the major part of whom found and declared your petitioner a bankrupt

THAT T B. of London stationer, and A F. of London, printer, were duly chosen assignees under the said commission, and an assignment was thereupon made and executed to them by the major part of the commissioners in the said commission, named nd authorized, of all your petitioner's estate and effects,

THAT under and by virtue of such assignment, the said I B and A H possessed themselves of the whole of your petitioner's estate and effects, which produced monies sufficient to enable them to pay, and they actually did pay to the whole of your petitioner's creditors who proved their debts under the said commission, full twenty shillings in the pound upon their respective debts

YOUR petitioner therefore humbly prays your Lordship would be pleased to order that the said commission of bankrupt, awarded and issued against your petitioner as aforesaid, be immediately superseded, and that a writ of supersedeas do forthwith issue for that purpose at your petitioner's expence.

And your petitioner shall ever pray, &c

Petition to supersede a commission taken out by one partner against the other.

In the matter of J. S. the elder, a bankrupt.

To the Right Honourable the LORD HIGH CHANCELLOR *of* GREAT BRITAIN.

The humble petition of the said bankrupt,

Sheweth,

THAT your petitioner having for many years previous to the month of   in the year 17   been brought up to and conversant with the trade and business of a sugar-refiner, and having for   previous to the said month of   17   been established in the said business, and having fitted up a house in   in the   of   for the purpose of carrying on the said business, and of which house and premises your petitioner had obtained a lease for the term of   years from the   day of   17   it was in or about the said month of   proposed by M. W the elder of   brewer, to enter into partnership with your petitioner, for the purpose of carrying on the said trade and business of sugar refiners, as co-partners, in equal proportions, and which proposal being acceded to by your petitioner, it was therefore agreed between him and the said M. W. that each party should bring in an equal sum in goods, money, or good debts, to constitute a common stock or fund wherewith to carry on the said business, and that in consideration thereof, each party should receive and bear an equal proportion and share of the profits, benefit and advantage which should arise or be made from the said business, or the loss or damage which should or might be sustained therefrom in the course of the said partnership

THAT in consequence of the before stated proposal and agreement, an account was taken of the then stock in trade of your petitioner, the debts due and owing to him, and the value of the said lease, which

upon

upon a fair valuation thereof amounted to the sum of or thereabouts

THAT articles of agreement conformable to the said proposal and agreement were drawn up by the said M W between your petitioner and the said M. W. and figned by both parties, but only one part thereof being so drawn and figned, fuch part was kept by the faid M. W.

THAT the whole of the faid goods, ftock in trade, and debts were by your petitioner brought into and applied in the faid partnership, trade, and bufinefs, which was carried on for a confiderable time under the firm of S. and W but the faid M W enly brought into the faid co partnership-ftock the fum of and that, at several different periods, out of which faid fum, the faid M. W during the faid co partnership, drew out the fum of

THAT your petitioner being as before ftated, well experienced in the art and myftery of refining fugar, it was agreed between him and the faid M W that your petitioner fhould act as a boiler of the fugar, and in confideration thereof, and of his managing and attending the faid partnership concerns, fhould receive and be paid the fum of per annum over and befides his fhare of the profits of the faid co-partnership bufinefs

THAT your petitioner did in purfuance of the faid agreement, carry on the faid trade and bufinefs of a fugar-refiner, by buying of raw fugars and boiling and refining the fame, and felling and difpofing thereof for the beft price he could procure and get for the fame, and that with the privity and knowledge of the faid M W your petitioner from time to time entering or caufing to be entered in the partnership books, the real and true value of the prime cofts of the faid raw fugars and other materials, and of the monies received by fale thereof

THAT owing to the very high price of the raw materials and fundry loffes, the fame was a lofing trade, and the faid M W being diffatisfied thereat, urged your petitioner to diffolve the faid co-partnership

between

between them, to which your petitioner did consent and agree, and therefore on or about the   day of   17 their said co-partnership concerns were by mutual consent dissolved, and from which period your petitioner carried on the said trade and business of a sugar-refiner on his own separate account, until the time herein after particularly mentioned.

THAT on stating the partnership accounts between your petitioner and the said M. W. from the commencement thereof, until the said   day of   17 being one year and a quarter, it appeared a loss had been sustained of   and upwards, exclusive of the sum which your petitioner was to be allowed for his trouble and experience as a boiler of sugar and managing the said partnership concerns

THAT the said M. W. finding the said co-partnership, trade and business, had, contrary to his expectations, turned out a loosing instead of a profitable concern, he took the advantage of your petitioner not having any copy of the articles of partnership, which were as before stated, signed by them, and insisted that no partnership had ever subsisted between them, and that he would be paid by your petitioner the whole of the money which he had so as aforesaid advanced and brought into the said co-partnership, and having burnt or otherways destroyed the said articles, and taking advantage of the circumstances of your petitioner, being a foreigner without friends, and unacquainted with the laws of this kingdom, caused your petitioner to be arrested and held to bail for the sum of   and upwards, which he alledged was due to him as so much advanced to your petitioner.

THAT your petitioner being as before mentioned, a foreigner, unacquainted with the laws of this kingdom, without friends, and supposing that the said articles of co-partnership were destroyed, that therefore he could not insist upon the benefit thereof, and being urged by the said M. W. to come to an agreement with him, your petitioner was prevailed upon, through fear and

in

in order to obtain his releafe from the fpunging-houfe, to
give and execute to the faid M W a bond or obligation,
bearing date the   day of   17   for the payment of
      and intereft, on the   day of   17   and at the
fame time your petitioner was for the like reafons prevailed upon to fign a warrant of attorney, to confefs a
judgment on the faid bond, and alfo to affign over to the
faid M W. the leafe of your petitioner's faid fugar-houfe
as a collateral or further fecurity for payment of the faid
money.

THAT your petitioner had, previous to giving and figning the faid bond, warrant and affignment,
paid to the faid M W the fum of   which added to
the fum of   before drawn out by him from the faid
partnerfhip effects, rendered the money advanced by him,
on account of the faid partnerfhip, to the fum of   in f
as the loffes of the faid joint trade amounted to the fum
of   at the leaft, the whole of the faid money fo advanced and brought in by the faid M W was loft in f funk,
and more, as will appear upon the faid partnerfhips' accounts, being fairly taken, ftated and fettled

THAT your petitioner after the faid partnerfhip between him and the faid M W was to diffolved
as aforefaid, entered into partnerfhip with his fon J f
the younger, who advanced and brought into the faid
trade a confiderable fum of money, and articles of
co-partnerfhip were drawn up and executed between
them whereby it was amongft other things agreed between your petitioner and his faid fon, that in confideration of the monies fo brought into the faid trade by the
faid J S the younger, fhould be intituled to a moiety or
joint intereft with your petitioner of, in, and to the debts
then due and owing to your faid petitioner, and
of, in, and to a moiety of the ftock in trade,
utenfils, fixtures, and other things then being in and
upon your petitioner's faid fugar-houfe and premifes as
aforefaid

THAT your petitioner and his faid fon carried on the bufinefs of fugar-bakers in co-partnerfhip

from the   day of   17   until on or about the day of   laſt, in which time they contracted ſeveral large debts to divers perſons, and your petitioner having many times by himſelf and friends applied to the ſaid M W to come to a fair account and ſettlement reſpecting their ſaid partnerſhip concerns, but which he totally refuſed to do, and threatening to ſue out execution upon his ſaid bond, and the judgment ſigned upon the ſaid warrant of attorney, your petitioner in order to prevent his debts being taken in execution for a debt which he then thought and now thinks he did not or does not owe, and to prevent his real and bona fide creditors from being injured, did, in conjunction with his ſaid ſon, the ſaid J S the younger, cauſe a meeting to be held of their ſaid creditors, at which meeting it was propoſed and agreed that your petitioner and his ſaid ſon ſhould aſſign over the whole of their effects to R. H of   grocer, and R. D of   grocer, truſtees, nominated and appointed by the ſaid creditors, in truſt for the benefit of themſelves and the reſt of the ſaid creditors; and in purſuance of ſuch propoſal and agreement, your petitioner and his ſaid ſon did, by indenture, bearing date on or about the   day of   laſt, aſſign over the whole of their ſaid eſtate and effects to the ſaid R H and R D in truſt, and for the purpoſes aforeſaid, and in the ſaid indenture particularly mentioned

That the ſaid M W did in or about the   day of   laſt, ſue out a ſcire facias on the judgment ſigned by him on the ſaid warrant of attorney, and by virtue thereof ſeized and took poſſeſſion of the whole of the eſtate and effects of your petitioner and his ſaid ſon, but your petitioner's moiety of the ſame having been previouſly ſeized and taken poſſeſſion of by virtue of a writ of ſcire facias at the ſuit of the ſaid J S the younger, and the whole of ſuch effects having been aſſigned by your petitioner and his ſaid ſon, to the ſaid R H and R. D as aforeſaid, the ſaid M. W, thought proper to wave and give up his ſaid execution, and on or about the

the   day of   laſt, cauſed a commiſſion of bankrupt
under the great ſeal of Great Britain, to be awarded and
iſſued againſt your petitioner, and ſworn to and exhibi
ted his ſaid bond ſo unduly obtained from your petitioner,
as the foundation, and in proof of his ſaid debt, your petitioner was found and declared bankrupt by the major
part of the commiſſioners acting under the ſaid commiſſion.

THAT by virtue of the ſaid commiſſion, the
eſtate and effects of your petitioner then being in and
upon the ſaid premiſes in   aforeſaid, were ſeized and
taken by the meſſenger under the ſame commiſſion, but
the whole thereof, except a mill and ſome other fixtures
on the ſaid premiſes, were ſold by public auction by
the ſheriff of   under and by virtue of the ſaid writ of
fi ri facias, ſo iſſued at the ſuit of the ſaid J S. the younger, and the money ariſing by ſale thereof now remains
in the hands of the ſaid ſheriff for the ſaid R H and
R D. as truſtees as aforeſaid, by virtue of the aſſignment ſo to them made by your petitioner and the ſaid
J S the younger.

THAT your petitioner attended with his ſolicitor at the firſt meeting appointed to be held under the
ſaid commiſſion, and then ſtated to the commiſſioners
acting under the ſame, the nature of the tranſactions between your petitioner and the ſaid M. W and your petitioner's reaſons for aſſerting that there was not any debt
due and owing from him to the ſaid M. W. but the ſaid
commiſſioners being of opinion that they were not com-
petent to enter into the conſideration of the ſaid bond ſo
given by your petitioner to the ſaid M W as aforeſaid,
proceeded to act in the execution of the ſaid commiſſio ,
and the ſaid M. W s debt very greatly exceeding any
other debt proved under the ſaid commiſſion, he did
nominate and chuſe himſelf and J S. of the pariſh of

gentleman, his ſon-in-law but who is no creditor of
your petitioner, to be aſſignees of your petitioner's ſaid
eſtate and effects

S   THAT

THAT your petitioner having caufed the whole of the accounts between him and the faid M. W to be minutely examined and ftated, has the greateft reafon to believe it wi'l clearly appeal, that fo far from your petitioner being indebted to the faid M. W he will be found to be debtor to your petitioner or his eftate, and your petitioner has no doubt but he can prove that the faid bond, warrant of attorney and affignment, were obtained from him upon falfe fuggeftions, by threats and undue means, and that therefore the faid commiffion fo awarded and iffued againft him is unfounded and ought to be fuperfeded.

YOUR petitioner therefore moft humbly prays your Lordfhip, that it may be referred to one of the mafters of this honourable court, to take an account of the co-partnerfhip affairs and tranfactions between your petitioner and the faid M W and to ftate the ballance thereon, and if upon the taking of fuch account, after making all juft allowances, it fhall appear that your petitioner was not at the date and fuing forth of the faid commiffion, juftly and truly indebted to the faid M W. in the fum of
that the faid commiffion of bankrupt fo awarded and iffued againft your petitioner may be fuperfeded at the expence of the faid M. W and that the bond fo entered into by your petitioner to the faid M. W and alfo the faid affignment of the leafe of your faid petitioner's houfe and premifes, may be delivered up to your petitioner to be cancelled, and alfo that the bond entered into by the faid
M. W.

M. W on applying for and taking
out the said commission of bankrupt against your petitioner, may
be assigned to your petitioner, and
that the said M. W may pay to
your petitioner his costs of this
application, or that your Lordship would make such further and
other order in the premises as to
your Lordship shall seem meet
And your petitioner shall ever pray, &c,

In the matter of A Y V K and V W, bankrupts

To the Right Hon. the LORD HIGH CHANCELLOR
of GREAT BRITAIN

The humble Petition of D G *of   in*
Esq. a separate creditor of the said V K on
behalf of himself and all other the separate cre-
ditors of the said V K.

Sheweth,

THAT on or about the   day of   last
a joint commission of bankrupt under the great seal of
Great Britain, was awarded and issued against the said
A Y, V K and V W of   silk weavers and co-partners, and they have thereupon been duly found and declared bankrupts, and their estate and effects, as well joint
as separate are intended to be assigned to assignees, to be
duly chosen under the said commission, without distinguishing or dividing the joint estates and effects from the
separate estate and effects of the said bankrupts

THAT before the date and suing forth of the
said commission, the said V K was and still is indebted
to your petitioner on his separate account, in the sum of
upon a judgment recovered against the said V K by
your petitioner in Easter term last, in his majesty's court
of King's bench, at Westminster, and also in a very

S 2   considera-

confiderable further fum on the ballance of an account betwixt your petitioner and the faid V. K

THAT there are other feparate creditors of the faid V K. who with your petitioner cannot be admitted to prove their feparate debts under the faid joint commiffion, without your Lordfhip's order for that purpofe.

YOUR petitioner therefore moft humbly prays, that your Lordfhip would be pleafed to order that your petitioner and the other feparate creditors of the faid V K may be at liberty to come in and prove their debts under the faid joint commiffion, iffued againft the above named bankrupts, and that it may be referred to the major part of the commiffioners named and authorized in and by the faid commiffion, to take joint and feparate accounts of the joint and feparate eftates of the faid bankrupts, and of the faid V K and that what fhall be found on fuch accounts to belong to the feparate eftate of the faid V K may be applied towards fatisfaction of the debt due to your petitioner and the feveral other feparate creditors of the faid V K. and that in cafe fuch feparate eftate fhall not be fufficient to pay and fatisfy the demands of your petitioner and the other feparate creditors of the faid V K and in cafe there fhall be any furplus of the joint eftate remaining after payment of all the debts due to the joint creditors of the faid bankrupts, that one third part of fuch furplus

furplus fhall be carried to the account of the feparate eftate of the faid V. K. and be applied towards fatisfaction of the debts of the feparate creditors of the faid V. K. and that the cofts of taking fuch accounts of this application may be paid out of fuch feparate eftate of the faid V. K. or out of fuch furplus of the joint eftate, or that your lordfhip will be pleafed to make fuch further or other order in the matter for the relief of your petitioners and the other feparate creditors of the faid V. K. as to your Lordfhip fhall feem meet

And your petitioner fhall ever pray, &c.

In the matter of A. L. a bankrupt.

To the Right Honourable the LORD HIGH CHANCELLOR *of* GREAT BRITAIN

The humble Petition of A K. the elder, and J K. the younger, creditors of the faid bankrupt,

Sheweth,

THAT in or about the month of the faid A. L. being indebted in the way of his trade of an ironmonger and brazier to feveral perfons to a large amount, and particularly to your petitioners in the fum or were about to fue out a commiffion againft him, but to fave the expence of fuing out fuch commiffion, it was propofed to call a previous meeting of his creditors, and after feveral meetings, his creditors at the laft of fuch meetings propofed and agreed to accept of the faid A L's promiffory notes for in the pound, for the amount of their refpective debts which notes are to be

drawn by the said A L payable at   months and your
petitioners were to indorse the same, upon whose indorsement the said A L's then creditors agreed to give him a
release and discharge, to which proposal (and in order to
extricate the said A L out of his then difficulties, your
petitioners as his friends, and at his request, agreed to such
proposals, and accordingly indorsed the said A L's promissory notes to secure to his then creditors   shillings in the pound, to the amount of the said A. L's.
debts, and which such creditors accepted in full thereof,
and gave the said A L a discharge.

That in order to reimburse your petitioners the money they should advance to the other creditors of the said A. L (and for securing whereof they had
given then indorsed notes payable as aforesaid) he the
said A L. prepared to assign to your petitioners the
lease of his then dwelling-house and shop by way of
mortgage and also to execute to them a bond and warrant
of attorney, to confess judgment thereon by way of collateral security, and on your petitioners indorsing such
notes the said A L executed such securities to your petitioners accordingly, and the said A L. thereupon continued in his shop and business as usual.

That when the first of such promissory
notes became due, the said A. L. (with the assistance of
your petitioners) provided for payment thereof, and your
petitioners in the interim had (to keep up his credit) let
him have goods upon fresh credit

That on or about the   day of   last,
the said A. L called on your petitioners and informed
them that it would be impossible for him to provide cash
to take up and pay their last indorsed notes (which became due on the   day of   then next) which greatly
alarmed your petitioners, whereupon they immediately
went to the said A L's house and shop, and examined
his stock in trade, and notwithstanding your petitioners
had sent him in goods upon fresh credit, found a very
great deficiency in his stock in trade, and that a large

quantity

quantity of goods were then ready packed up to be ſhipp'd for Holland

THAT on the   day of   laſt your pe-
titioners in order to ſecure themſelves part of their debt,
cauſed judgment to be entered up, upon the ſaid A L's.
bond and warrant of attorney, and ſued out a fieri facias thereon.

THAT in order to get rid of your petitioners' execution, the ſaid A L on the   day of
laſt, cauſed a commiſſion of bankrupt to be taken
out againſt him by one H P of   in   victualler,
the brother-in-law to the ſaid A L and who till the ſuing
of the ſaid commiſſion never appeared as one of the
ſaid A. L's creditors, and whoſe debt was then alledged
to be for money lent to the ſaid bankrupt ſo long ago as
the   of   17

THAT on the   day of   17   (when
the laſt of the ſaid payments became due) your petitioners took up and paid their indorſed notes.

THAT on the   day of   (being the
firſt meeting of the commiſſioners under the ſaid commiſſion) the ſaid H P. proved a debt under the ſaid
A. L's commiſſion of   for money lent and advanced
by the ſaid H. P. to the ſaid A L and inter alia thereon, in
whoſe depoſition is in exception of a promiſſory note,
dated the   day of   17   drawn by the ſaid bankrupt, whereby on demand he promiſed to pay the ſaid
deponent by the name of H P   for value received

THAT on the   day of   17   your petitioner J K the elder, on behalf of himſelf and the
other petitioner J K the younger, his partner, proved
a debt of   under the ſaid commiſſion for goods ſold
and delivered, and for money paid, laid out, and expended by your petitioners to and for the uſe of the ſaid
bankrupt, in whoſe depoſition is an exception of the
ſaid aſſignment of leaſe by way of mortgage, and the ſaid
bond and judgment, and which the ſecurities your petitioner
J K the elder, on proving of his and partner's debt,
agreed to relinquiſh and give up, and immediately with-
                                        drew

drew their execution and gave up their securities, and your petitioner J. K the elder was thereupon chosen sole assignee of the said bankrupt's estate and effects

THAT there is now due and owing to your petitioners from the estate of the said A L the bankrupt (exclusive of the said sum of   by them already proved under the said commission, the sum of   for money by your petitioners advanced and paid in taking up their said indorsed notes, which they had given to the said bankrupt's creditors on his first failure, and which notes did not (from the time they had to run) become due and payable 'till   17

THAT the remainder of the said bankrupt's debts proved under the said commission do not amount to more than the sum of

YOUR petitioners therefore most humbly pray your Lordship, that they may be permitted to prove, under the said commission, the said sum of   so by them paid to the several other creditors of the said A L in discharge of the remainder of his debts upon his former failure, and for his use and on his account, and that your petitioners may (as having paid such creditors) be considered as standing in their place and stead under the said commission, and may be permitted to receive a dividend of the said bankrupt's estate or the produce thereof, rateably and in proportion to their said debt with the other creditors of the said bankrupt, or that your Lordship will be pleased to make such other order therein as to your Lordship shall seem meet

And your petitioners shall ever pray, &c.

Petition

In the matter of S. P. the younger, and S P. of
in the county of   merchants, dealers, chapmen, and partners, bankrupts,

To the Right Hon. the Lord High Chancellor
of Great Britain.

The humble Petition of H P.

Sheweth,

THAT your petitioner on or about the
day of   17   entered into a copartnership with the
said S. P. and S. P. the bankrupts, in the business of
merchants and factors, for and during the term of 21
years, from that time, in case the said bankrupts and
your petitioner should so long live, and a memorandum
of such agreement was signed on that occasion, but was
afterwards destroyed on the execution of the deed of
dissolution after-mentioned.

THAT by a certain indenture bearing date
day of   17   and made between the petitioner
of the one part, and the said bankrupts of the other
part, your petitioner and the said bankrupts respectively
covenanted, declared, and agreed, that the partnership
then subsisting between them should, from the day of
the date thereof, be bona fide dissolved, and determined,
and that the parties thereto should be precluded from
continuing and carrying on the trade or business of
merchants and factors, and your petitioner in consideration of   secured in manner therein mentioned (being
the money advanced by your petitioner into the said
copartnership trade), and of the further sum of   for
interest of the said sum of   during the time the same
remained in the said co-partnership trade, and of an
indemnity therein contained, thereby bargained, sold,
and assigned unto the said S P and S P. their executors, administrators, and assigns, his undivided third
part or share of the capital joint stock and trade, whether
consisting of ready money, bills, notes, or securities for
money, debts, or any other matter or thing, and the

T   profits,

profits, gains, and increase, and advantage arising or to arise from the said joint trade, and of all contracts made and entered into upon account of the said joint trade, and all benefit and advantage whatsoever arising therefrom—to hold the same unto the said S P and S. P their executors, administrators and assigns, from thenceforth absolutely to their own use, and as their property, and the said S P and S. P. thereby covenanted with your petitioner in consequence of the said assignment, that they would, with their own proper monies, as the same should become due and payable, pay off and discharge all such debts and sums of money as were then due and owing upon the said joint trade, and would perform and keep all contracts, agreements and engagements made and entered into on account of the said joint trade, and indemnify your petitioner from the same and all costs of suit relating thereto.

THAT on or about the   day of   17 a commission of bankrupt under the great seal of Great Britain, founded on a debt contracted partly before the said co-partnership, with your petitioner, and partly after the determination of the said co-partnership, was awarded and issued against the said S. P. and S. P as partners, whereupon they were found and duly declared bankrupts, and their estate and effects were duly assigned by the commissioners or the major part of them acting under the said commission to A. M T. A and L. W all of   aforesaid, who were duly chosen assignees thereof

THAT the said bankrupts did not in pursuance and performance of their said covenant entered into with your petitioner, pay off, satisfy and discharge the debts contracted and due and owing from your petitioner, and the said bankrupts, at the time of their dissolving partnership, so that at the time of issuing the said commission there remained due and owing to the creditors of the said partnership between your petitioner and the said bankrupts, debts to a very considerable amount. And your petitioner having in consequence of the said bankruptcy been called upon to pay off and satisfy such

debts,

debts, your petitioner hath already paid several of such debts to the amount of   or thereabouts And your petitioner apprehends there are other debts of the said partnership to a considerable amount still unsatisfied, which your petitioner will be obliged to pay

THAT several parts of the effects and credits belonging to the late co-partnership between your petitioner and the said bankrupts, were remaining in specie and outstanding at the time of the issuing of the said commission, and the said assignees have possessed and received several of such credits and effects, and your petitioner submits he is entitled to have all such credits and effects, applied towards the payment of the unsatisfied debts owing from the late partnership between your petitioner and the said bankrupts, and towards reimbursing your petitioner what he has paid in discharge of debts as aforesaid; and your petitioner also submits that he is entitled to stand in the place of such of the creditors of the said late co-partnership whose debts have been or shall be paid by him, as shall not be satisfied by means of the said effects and credits remaining in specie.

THAT at the respective times of your petitioner's paying off and discharging the several debts to the creditors of your petitioner and the said bankrupts as aforesaid, it was understood and agreed, as well by your petitioner, as by the said creditors themselves and also by the commissioners acting under the said commission, and the assignees of the said bankrupts, that your petitioner should stand in the place of the several creditors whose debts he should discharge out of his private estate, and have the full benefit which the creditors themselves would be entitled to under the said commission

Your petitioner therefore humbly prays
that your Lordship will be pleased
to direct an account to be taken
of the several effects and credits
belonging to the said co-partner-

ship

ship between your petitioner and the said bankrupts, which were remaining in specie at the time of the issuing of the said commission, and have been possessed by or received by the said A M T A and L W. and also of the debts owing from the said late partnership at the time of the issuing of the said commission, and of the monies paid by your petitioner towards the discharge thereof, and that the said effects and credits remaining in specie may be applied in payment of the unsatisfied debts of the said late partnership, and in reimbursing your petitioner which he has paid or shall pay in discharging of any of such debts, and that your petitioner may stand in the place of such of the creditors of the said late partnership paid or to be paid by him, and for so much of their debts as he shall not be reimbursed out of the late partnership's effects, and be admitted a creditor for the same under the said commission of bankrupt, and may receive a dividend or dividends of the said bankrupts' estate and effects in respect thereof, rateably with the said bankrupts' other creditors And that such further or other order may be made in the premises as your Lordship shall seem meet.

And your petitioner shall ever pray, &c

In the matter of A. L. and K. L. bankrupts.

To the Right Hon. the LORD HIGH CHANCELLOR
of GREAT BRITAIN

The humble Petition of V. W. of   in the   Weaver,
J. W. of   Mercer, and J. C. W. of   Merchant,

Sheweth,

THAT your petitioners did on the   day
of   last prefer their petition to your lordship, stating
that your petitioner V. W. in the way of his trade as a
weaver, became acquainted and had several dealings and
transactions with A. L. and K. L. of   street, London, merchants and co-partners (who were lately become
bankrupts) and on or about the   day of   17
your petitioner V. W. then standing indebted unto the said
A. L. and K. L. in the sum of   for goods fold and delivered by them in the way of their trade, and in the further sum of   for money lent and advanced to your said
petitioner V. W. they, the said A. L. and K. L. applied
to him and requested him to accommodate them with paper to the amount of   payable some short time after
the demand that they then had upon him should become due, and to ante-date the same that it might appear
to be a note given for goods in the regular course of business, whereby they could get the same more regularly
discounted, and accordingly in order to serve the said
A. L. and K. L. he drew his promissory note, bearing
date the   day of   17   payable   months after date
to the said Messrs. A. L. and K. L. or order for   which
he fully expected would have been entered to the credit
of his account with them, in diminution of their said demand upon him.

AND also stating, That your petitioner V. W.
being in habits of intimacy with the said A. L. and K. L.
and being desirous of serving them as much as in his
power, was again applied to by them to accommodate
them with more paper to the amount of   which he
from motives of friendship   was   induced to do, and
accordingly

accordingly on the   day of   in like manner, and
for the like reafon, drew another promiffory note, bearing
date the   day of   17   for the faid fum of   payable to the faid Meffis A L. and K L. or order   months
after date, and delivered the fame to them or one of them,
and they in order to indemnify him from being prejudi-
ced thereby, indorted over to him a promiffory note,
bearing date the   day of   17   drawn by D F
and Y C of   weavers and partners (who are fince
alfo become bankrupts) and payable   months after date
to the faid Meffrs A L and K L. or order for   which
faid laft mentioned note fo drawn by the faid D. E and
Y. C as aforefaid, was to become due   days before
the faid note for   fo drawn by your petitioner V W.
in favor of the faid A. L and K L fo as to make a
provifion for the payment thereof when the fame fhould
become due.

AND alfo ftating, That a commiffion of bankrupt under the great feal of Great Britain bearing date
the   day of   laft had been awarded and iffued
againft the faid A L and K L. and they had been thereupon found and declared bankrupts, and an affignment of
their eftate and effects had been executed by the major
part of the commiffioners, acting under the faid commiffion, to J. T. of   merchant, and R. K of   in
merchant, the affignees chofen under the faid commiffion.

AND alfo ftating, That the notes for   and
fo given by your petitioner V W to the faid A L.
and K L as aforefaid, had been negotiated by the faid
A L and K. L and were become due fince the iffuing
of the faid commiffion againft the faid A L and K. L
and that they had been taken up and duly paid by your
faid petitioner V W.

AND alfo ftating, That your petitioner V W
having as aforefaid duly paid the faid two promiffory
notes for   and   fo given by him as aforefaid to the
faid A. L and K L became a creditor of the faid A L
and K. L. on balance, to the amount of the fum of   and
thereupon,

thereupon, and as the said note of the said D. E and Y C. so indorsed to your said petitioner V. W. as aforesaid was not paid, he applied to prove the same under the said commission awarded and issued against them the said A L and K L. which he insisted he was intitled to do at least to the extent of the said   but the major part of the commissioners acting under the said commission had rejected such proof.

AND further stating, That your petitioner V W from the loss and misfortune aforesaid, had been under the necessity of convening a meeting of his creditors, and had by indenture, bearing date the   day of   last, actually assigned over his estate and effects of what nature and kind soever to the said J W. and J C W. two of his principal creditors, in trust for themselves and the rest of the creditors seeking relief under the said trust-deed, and that they had accordingly begun to carry the intention of the said trust into execution.

AND also stating, That your said petitioners J W and J C. W. the said trustees, had caused application to be made to the assignees chosen under the said commission awarded and issued against the said A L and K L. in order to adjust the account between the said A L and K L and your said petitioner V W. but that the assignees chosen under the said commission had refused to state such account, and insisted that they had a right to consider themselves as creditors under the estate of your petitioner S W. for the whole sum of   appearing to be unsatisfied upon the books of the said A L and K L. and that your petitioners might be left to pursue such remedy for relief as they thought proper

AND further stating, That your petitioners contended that they were intitled to a fair statement of accounts from the assignees acting under the said commission issued against the said A. L and K L and that they had a right to set off the said two promissory notes so given by your petitioner V W. to the said A L and K L. against the said demand of   so claimed by the said assignees upon the estate of your said petitioner V W.

and

and that your petitioner V W. having duly taken up the said two several notes when the same respectively became due as aforesaid, and the estate of the said A L and K. L. having been benefited to the amount of the said two notes, your petitioners conceived they ought to be admitted creditors under the said commission so awarded and issued against the said A. L. and K. L as aforesaid, to the full amount of the balance which should appear to be due to your petitioners as trustees as aforesaid upon the statement of such account.

AND therefore your petitioners did pray that your Lordship would order that the said assignees chosen under the said commission awarded and issued against the said A. L and K. L might state the said accounts between them and your petitioner V. W and that in stating the same, the said two promissory notes for   and making together the sum of   so given and duly taken up as aforesaid by your petitioner V W might be considered as so much money paid by him to the use of the said A. L. and K. L. and that as to   part thereof, that your petitioners might be allowed to set off the same against the said sum of   being the demand of the said assignees against your petitioner V W. and that as to the surplus being   that it might be considered as a balance due from the said estate of the said bankrupts to your petitioners J. W and J C W as trustees as aforesaid, that they might be admitted creditors for such balance and be at liberty to prove the same under the said commission awarded against the said A. L. and K L. and that your Lordship would make such further or other order in the premises as to your Lordship should seem meet. Whereupon your Lordship ordered all parties concerned to attend your Lordship on the matter of your petitioners' said petition upon the next day of petitions, and counsel for your petitioners and for the assignees of the estate and effects of A. L. and K L. the bankrupts on Saturday the   day of   17   attending accordingly, your Lordship, upon hearing your petitioners' said petition, an affidavit of your petitioner V W. and an affidavit

affidavit of your petitioner J. C W. read, and what was
alledged by the counsel on both sides, did order that it
should be referred to Mr. M. one of the masters of this
court, to take an account of all dealings and transactions
between your petitioner V W and the said bankrupts,
and the said master was to ascertain the dates and facts as
to the delivering and negotiating the securities in your
petitioner's said petition mentioned, and whether any,
and what use was made of the indorsements of such securities, or any and which of them.

THAT the said master having by his report,
dated the   day of   been attended by the solicitor
for your petitioners, and also by the solicitors for the
assignees of the said bankrupts, found that an account
had been made up and settled between the trustees of
your petitioner V. W. and the assignees of the said bankrupts relating to the said securities, and that there remained due from the estate of the said bankrupts to the
estate of your petitioner V. W. in respect thereof, the sum
of   as it had been admitted before him the said master,
which he humbly certified to your Lordship.

YOUR petitioners therefore most humbly
pray your Lordship to grant an
order to confirm the said report,
and that they may be admitted
creditors for the said sum of
and be at liberty to prove the
same under the said commission
awarded against the said A L and
K L and that your petitioners may
have the benefit of any dividend
already declared or made, or which
shall hereafter be declared or made
to the creditors under the said
commission, in an equal proportion with the rest of the creditors
of the said A L and K L. seeking relief under the said commission, and that the costs of this and
U   the

the former applications of your
petitioners may be paid to your
petitioners out of the estate and
effects of the said bankrupts, or
that your Lordship will make such
further or other order in the pre
mises as to your Lordship shall
feem meet

And your petitioners shall ever pray, &c.

In the matter of A P and W. I bankrupts.

To the Right Honourable the LORD HIGH
CHANCELLOR *of* GREAT BRITAIN.

The humble Petition of E. I *of*   *in the county of*
gentleman.

Sheweth,

THAT a commission of bankrupt hath been
awarded and issued forth against A P. and A. L. of
carriers and co-partners, bearing date on or about the
day of in the year of our Lord 17

THAT they were thereupon found and declared bankrupts, and W C of in the county of
and L P of London, gentleman, were duly
chosen assignees of the said bankrupts' estate and effects,
and the usual assignment thereof hath been made to them
accordingly.

THAT that the said A P. was justly and
truly indebted to your petitioner before and at the time
of the issuing of the said commission in the sum of
principal money, on bond, bearing date the day of
17 part thereof (to wit) the sum of pounds
shillings, for so much money really and bona fide
lent and advanced, and the remaining part thereof, being the sum of for money then really and bona fide
due

due on the balance of account from the said A P and A L. to your petitioner

THAT the said sum of advanced to the said A P. by your petitioner as aforesaid, was, as your petitioner apprehends and believes, thrown and put into the joint trade, and carried to the joint account of them the said A P and A L and that they had jointly the benefit and advantage of the said sum of in their said trade

THAT the said A P. and A L were justly and truly indebted to your petitioner before and at the time of the suing forth the said commission in the sum of (after allowing all money claimed by the said A P and A L as due to them from your petitioner), part whereof for money received by the said bankrupts, to and for the use of your petitioner, and the other part for the hire and use of a diligence for fifty-two weeks, borrowed by the said A L of your petitioner, for carrying on the said bankrupt's trade or business

THAT your petitioner hath by his agent applied to the commissioners named in the said commission at a meeting held at the Guildhall, London, in pursuance of an advertisement for that purpose and did there cause to be exhibited to the said commissioners your petitioner's affidavits of his said debts and his said bond, and desired to be admitted to prove said several debts under the said commission, but was not permitted to prove the same or either of them.

YOUR petitioner therefore humbly prays your Lordship that he may be at liberty to prove his said bond debt of and interest, under the said joint commission up to the date thereof, and also his said debt of under the said joint commission, and to be paid a rateable share of the dividends to be made out of the joint estate of the said A P and A L in equal proportion

U 2

tion with the reft of the joint creditors, and that the affignees may
produce the proceedings under
the faid commiffion, and alfo the
bankrupts' book or books of account in which the faid bond debt
was carried to the joint account
of the faid bankrupts, and that
the coft of this application may be
paid out of the faid bankrupts'
eftate and effects, but if your
Lordfhip fhall be of opinion that
your petitioner's faid debts are not
joint debts of the faid bankrupts,
but that any part thereof is the
feparate debt of either of the faid
bankrupts, then that feparate accounts may be directed to be taken
as part of the joint and feparate
eftates of the faid bankrupts, and
that fo much of your petitioner's
faid debt as fhall appear to be (if
any) a feparate debt of the faid
bankrupts, may be paid to your
petitioner in proportion with their
other feparate creditors, and that
the ufual directions may be given
for that purpofe

And your petitioner fhall ever pray, &c.

In

In the matter of W. T. late of   in the county of
          a bankrupt.

To the Right Hon. the Lord High Chancellor
  of Great Britain.

*The humble Petition of A. P. of   in the county of
  widow and executrix of D P late of   aforesaid,
  deceased, who was one of the creditors of the said W. T*

Sheweth,

THAT your petitioner preferred her petition in this honourable court on the   day of   in the year 17   therein stating, amongst other things, that the said W T before he became bankrupt, was indebted to the said D P by bond, in the sum of   with an arrear of interest due thereon; and the said W T. being a creditor for   on the estate of one T R a bankrupt, the said W. T. before he committed any act of bankruptcy, for better securing to the said D P the payment of the said debt of   and interest, executed to the said D P a letter of attorney, empowering him to receive the dividends which should become due to him in respect of his said debt from the estate of the said T. R. and by an indorsement on the said letter of attorney, the said W. T. assigned all his interest in the said dividends to the said D P and the said D. P thereby agreed, that on receiving his principal interest and costs out of said dividends, he would cancel or deliver up his security for the said

And your petitioner further shewed unto your Lordship, That the said W T. after the execution of the said letter of attorney and assignment, became bankrupt, and a commission of bankrupt having issued against him, he was thereupon found and declared a bankrupt, and an assignment of his estate and effects was made to W. G then of   in the county of   T. B of   in the said county of

And your petitioner further shewed unto your Lordship, that a dividend had then lately been d

clared and made of the effects of the faid I R. and that
the fum of   being a dividend upon the faid debt for
     affigned as aforefaid to the faid D P. had been re-
ceived by the faid W G and T. B or was retained by
S R the folicitor employed in taking out the faid commiffion of bankruptcy iffued againft the faid W. T.
which your petitioner had a right to receive as executrix
of the faid D P deceafed.

AND therefore prayed your Lordfhip to
order that the faid fum of   fho ld be paid to your
petitioner, in payment of the fum of   and all the arrears of interest due thereon, as far as the fame would
extend, and that your petitioner might be a creditor to
prove what fhould remain due as a debt under the commiffion of the faid W T your petitioner being ready,
and thereby offering, on payment thereof, to cancel or
deliver up the faid bond, and all other fecurities in her
poffeffion, which were given by the faid W I to the
faid D. P. for fecuring the faid   and interest.

AND your petitioner further fheweth unto
your Lordfhip, That the faid S R of   in the county
of   folicitor to the faid commiffion of bankrupt, being
made a party to the faid petition, did make an affidavit
againft W. T. admitting (amongft other things) that he
had, on the   then laft, received of the affignees of
the faid T. R, the fum of   as and for a dividend made
on the faid debt of   for the purpofe of paying the fame
over to the faid affignees of the faid W. I

AND your petitioner further fheweth, That
by an order, bearing date the   day of   17   made
on the hearing of the faid petition and affidavit, your
Lordfhip was pleafed to order that after deducting the
fum of   for money paid to one R R the refidue of
the faid fum of   amounting to   fhould be paid to
your petitioner towards fatisfaction of the faid debt of
     and interest due thereon, and that your petitioner
fhould be admitted a creditor under the commiffion of
bankrupt iffued againft the faid W. T for what fhould
then remain due to her for her faid debt, and be paid

out of the estate of the said bankrupt a dividend or dividends in respect thereof, rateably and in equal proportion with the rest of his creditors, as by the said petition and affidavit duly filed of record, relation being thereunto had, will more fully appear.

AND your petitioner further sheweth unto your Lordship, That your petitioner hath applied to the said S. R. to pay the said sum of   to your petitioner, in pursuance of such order, who hath refused or declined to pay the same to your petitioner, and still retains the same in his hands, notwithstanding he hath had a copy of such order delivered to him, and the said sum of   remains unpaid to your petitioner.

YOUR petitioner therefore humbly prays your Lordship, to order the said S. R. the solicitor to the commission of bankrupt issued against the said W. T. to pay to your petitioner the said sum of   now remaining in his hands, and unpaid, to your petitioner; and also that the said S. R. may pay to your petitioner the costs of this her application.

And your petitioner shall ever pray, &c.

In the matter of H. K. a bankrupt.

To the Right Hon. the LORD HIGH CHANCELLOR *of* GREAT BRITAIN.

The humble Petition of T. C. and K. H. trustees of the joint estate and effects of A. M. and J. H.

Sheweth,

THAT in   17   the said A. M. and J. H. became jointly concerned in the purchase of a

ship

ſhip called the Thames, and in the loading her with a cargo of proviſions and ſtores, which they agreed to ſend as an adventure upon their joint and equal account in profit and loſs, to the Weſt-Indies, and back again to London, and that the ſaid J. H. ſhould go as maſter of the ſaid ſhip on the ſaid voyage.

THAT the ſaid A. M. and J H. accordingly purchaſed goods, proviſions, and ſtores for the cargo and outfit of the ſaid ſhip, and the ſaid J H ſailed therein to St. Lucia in the Weſt-Indies

THAT the ſaid J. H. ſold part of the ſaid cargo at St. Lucia, but not finding a ſale for the remainder, he, in   17   left the ſame in the hands of J B a broker there, and agent to Meſſrs D and D with directions to ſell the ſame, and remit the produce to him the ſaid J. H in London.

THAT that the ſaid J. H. while he was in the Weſt-Indies, and after his coming from thence, the ſaid J B received part of the produce of the ſaid cargo, and made remittances on account thereof to the ſaid J. H.

THAT the ſaid ſhip Thames being loaded with a cargo for her voyage back to London, was, in her return home, taken by an American privateer, and carried into Boſton, and there condemned

THAT from the loſs of the ſaid ſhip, and other misfortunes, the ſaid J H became inſolvent, and in   17   aſſigned all his ſeparate eſtate and effects to truſtees for his ſeparate creditors

THAT the ſaid A. M. and J H being unable to pay the debts due to their joint creditors, by indenture, dated   17   aſſigned over all their joint eſtate and effects to your petitioners, in truſt for themſelves and all other their joint, who, in conſideration thereof by that deed releaſed them from the payment of their ſaid joint debts.

THAT the the ſaid A M. being indebted in his ſeparate capacity to the ſaid Meſſrs. D and D. in the ſum of   they, upon hearing of A M's failure, poſ
ſeſſed

sessed themselves of effects belonging to A. M of the value of   and have ever since kept the whole of the sum in discharge of the debt of   due from A M. to them as aforesaid, and they refuse even to account for the surplus, though frequent applications have been made to them for that purpose

THAT in   17   the said A. M being considerably indebted on his separate account, a commission of bankruptcy was awarded and issued against him, an assignment of his separate estate was made to W. C J B. and T. B who had been chosen to be assignees thereof.

THAT at the time of issuing the said commission there was a ballance of   due from the separate estate of the said A. to the joint estate of the said A. and M.

THAT your petitioners are advised that they, as trustees of the joint estate of the said A M. ought to receive a like dividend out of the separate estate of the said A. for the said sum of   as the said D D would have been entitled to in case they had not proved their debt under the commission against the said A. and also a dividend on the said sum of   out of the said A's separate estate in proportion with his other separate creditors

THAT no dividend has yet been declared under the said commission against the said A

YOUR petitioners therefore humbly pray your Lordship that they may be at liberty to go before the commissioners named in the said commission against the said A and prove the said sums of   and   as debts due to them from the said A's separate estate, and receive a dividend on both the said sums for the benefit of the joint creditors of the said A and M.

X

M. or that your Lordſhip will be pleaſed to make ſuch other order in the premiſes as to your Lordſhip ſhall ſeem meet.

And your petitioners ſhall ever pray, &c.

In the matter of L W and L K. againſt whom a commiſſion of bankrupt hath been awarded and now in proſecution.

To the Right Hon. the LORD HIGH CHANCELLOR *of* GREAT BRITAIN

The humble Petition of the ſaid L W.

Sheweth,

THAT a commiſſion of bankrupt under the great ſeal of Great Britain, bearing date at Weſtminſter the   day of   laſt, upon the petition of W P. of   in the county of   and M his wife, and J C. of   in the county of   and S. his wife, adminiſtrator and adminiſtratrixs of J S late of   London   was awarded and iſſued againſt your petitioner jointly with the ſaid L. K. by the names and deſcriptions of L W. and L. K. of   London   and co-partners, which commiſſion was directed to J E. F H. W. R A. eſquires, S O. and W T gentlemen, as commiſſioners to execute the ſame.

THAT your petitioner hath been declared a bankrupt jointly with the ſaid L. K his co-partner, by the major part of the ſaid commiſſioners acting under the ſaid commiſſion, and by ſummons under their hand and alſo by notice in the London Gazette of   the   day of   17   was required to ſurrender himſelf to the ſaid commiſſioners or the major part of them at Guildhall, London, to be examined by them on the firſt and fourteenth days of   then next reſpectively, at ten of the clock in the forenoon on each of the ſaid

days,

days, touching the disclosure and discovery of his estate and effects, and on the   day of   next ensuing, your petitioner is by such summons and notice required to finish his examination under the said commission.

THAT your petitioner hath not at any time committed any act of bankruptcy within the true intent and meaning of the statute made in the fifth year of the reign of his late majesty king George the second, or any other statute now in force concerning bankrupts, so as to make him liable to the said commission so awarded and now in prosecution against him jointly with the said L. K. as aforesaid.

YOUR petitioner therefore most humbly prays that in consideration of the premises, your Lordship will be pleased to order the said commission, which is so improvidently issued as aforesaid, to be superseded at the expence of the said W. P. and M. his wife, J. C. and S. his wife, the petitioning creditors, and that the bond which has been entered into by the said W. P. and M. his wife J. C and S. his wife, may be assigned to your petitioner; or that your Lordship will be pleased to order and direct one or more issue or issues to try the validity of the said commission, or that your Lordship will be pleased to make such other order in the premises for the relief of your petitioner as to your Lordship shall seem meet

And your petitioner as in duty bound shall ever pray, &c.

Of prefenting Petitions,
Filing Affidavits,
Obtaining Orders, &c.

ALL petitions in bankruptcy are to be engroffed on treble fixpenny ftamped paper, and carried to the fecretary of bankrupt's office for the Lord Chancellor's fiat for the parties' attendance, which is generally in the following form,

     th of 17

Let the parties concerned,
or their agents, attend me,
on the matter of this petition,
upon the next day of petitions:
Hereof give notice forthwith.
  THURLOW, C.

When the petition is figned, which is ufually in a day or two after leaving it, you apply for it, and pay 13s 6d having a copy of fuch petition upon unftamped paper, which muft be left on taking away the original Petitions are required to be ferved on all proper parties at leaft two clear days before the appointed day of hearing the petition (but in the country a much longer notice is neceffary) by delivering copies on unftamped paper to the perfon
        concerned,

concern d, or leaving such copy with a wife, servant, &c at the dwelling-house or last place of abode. An affidavit of which service, the affidavit of facts in support of the petition, together with all other affidavits in the matter, must be filed at the secretary's office, copies of which are there made on three halfpenny stamped paper, and marked with the office seal. This must always be done before the affidavits can be read in court, for which is paid according to the length, for the first sheet 2s. and for every subsequent sheet 8d. (ninety words to the sheet.)

Form of an Affidavit of the Service of a Petition.

In Chancery.

In the matter of E. R. a bankrupt.

J L of   in the county of   gentleman, maketh oath, that he this deponent did on the   day of   instant, served T A one of the assignees of the said bankrupt L K and W. I. assignees of the estate and effects of the said T. A and J. S with a petition preferred by J B. of   aforesaid, builder, the other assignee of the estate and effects of the said E. R. the bankrupt in this matter, to the right honourable the Lord High Chancellor of Great Britain, with his Lordship's order thereon, bearing date the   day of the said month of   whereby it was ordered that the parties concerned, or their agents, attend his Lordship on the matter of the said petition upon the next day of petitions, whereof notice was forthwith to be given in manner following, that is to say, by personally delivering to the said T A L K W. I and J S respectively, a true copy of the said petition and order thereon, and at the same time shewing them respectively the said original petition and order thereon, and this defendant further saith that the said L. K, and
W I

W. T. are the affignees of the eftate and effects of the faid T, A as this deponent hath been informed and believes.

J.— L.—

Sworn at   in the county of   this
day of   in the year of our Lord, one
thoufand feven hundred and   before
me,

T. H

A Mafter Extraordinary in Chancery.

In the affidavit of the fervice of a petition, it frequently happens that inftead of the above form, the words (petition hereunto annexed) are inferted, which fhould always be avoided, as it fubjects the petition to be filed with the affidavit, which is an unneceffary expence It is proper that affidavits fhould be filed as long a time before the day of petitions as poffible, that each party may have time to take copies, and file further affidavits. Where it becomes neceffary to file affidavits clofe upon the hearing of a petition, it will be proper (or at any period of the bufinefs) for the follicitor or his clerk to carry copies with the original to the office, and the clerk there will mark the copy with the office feal, which will then be ready to be read in court, and fave the time it would neceffarily take for the office to copy them. After the petition is heard, the order muft be befpoke at the fecretary's office, for which you pay 17s 6d. befides the duty, thefe orders are all entered in the books at the office and figned by the Lord Chancellor, copies of which may be had, or the minutes of any fuch order

When an order is made by the Lord Chancellor for the payment of money, or any other matter therein directed, and which fhall have been duly ferved, and the party bound by fuch order do not obey the directions therein; to inforce the fame, a petition muft be carried to the office, with an affidavit of the facts, praying that within fourteen days (the ufual time given) after being ferved with the order then to be obtained, which you will have

of

of courfe (without a hearing) if the party do not perform the directions of the former order, that he, A. B. the party, may ftand committed to his Majefty's prifon of the Fleet for his contempt This order being obtained, muft be ferved on the party, and on non-compliance you muft prepare another petition and affidavit, ftating fuch neglect and refufal, and pray that a warrant may iffue for his or their commitment to the Fleet for fuch contempt You will then obtain an order for the warrant and the partys' commitment, which you carry as directed to the Warden of the Fleet or his deputy, and they will take them into cuftody, and there remain without bail or mainprize, until they have complied with the directions of the firft order, together with payment of all the cofts of fuch feveral applications.

Form of the Warrant of Commitment.

In the matter of W. V. a bankrupt.

WHEREAS by my order made in this matter, dated the   day of   upon the petition of the petitioners, it was ordered that J. S. in the faid order named, fhould ftand committed to his Majefty's prifon of the Fleet for his contempt in the faid order mentioned, and that a warrant for his commitment fhould iffue accordingly Thefe are therefore in purfuance of the faid order, to will and require you forthwith upon receipt hereof, to make diligent fearch after the body of the faid J S. and wherefoever you fhall find him, to arreft and apprehend him, and to carry him to his Majefty's prifon of the Fleet, there to remain until further order, willing and requiring all mayors, fheriffs, juftices of the peace, conftables, headboroughs, and all other his Majefty's officers and loving fubjects, to be aiding and affifting to you in the due execution of the premifes, as thefe tender his Majefty's fervice, and will anfwer the contrary hereof at their peril· And this fhall be to you, or any of you, who fhall do the fame, a fufficient warrant, dated this   day of   in the

the   year of our Sovereign Lord King George the
third, and in the year of our Lord Christ 17

To

    J. E esq Warden of the Fleet prison, or his
    deputy attending the High Court of Chan-
    cery, and also to all his Majesty's justices
    of the peace, mayors, sheriffs, bailiffs,
    constables, headboroughs, and all other
    officers whom it may concern.

Order for Striking Docquets.

LORD CHANCELLOR.

The 12th day of February, 1774.

Ordo Curiæ.

There having been of late many commissions of bankruptcy fraudulently taken out with intent to deceive
honest creditors, whereby the good intent of the bankrupt laws has been in some measure defeated, in order
to prevent as far as may be the like frauds and misdoings
for the future, I do hereby order and direct the secretary
for the commissions of bankruptcy forthwith to signify
to the gentlemen named in the several standing lists of
commissioners, that it is my desire and recommendation
to them to be careful in examining into the reality of the
debts of the petitioning creditors coming to prove their
debts under the commission   And in case it be a single
commission, to enquire whether the bankrupt was concerned in any and what partnership at the time of his bankruptcy? And in case the same be a joint-commission,
then to enquire of how long standing the partnership has
been? And whether any separate commission has before
issued and be then depending against either, and which

of

of the faid partners? And that they do likewife in all
cafes enquire whether the bankrupt ever, and how long
before, had obtained a certificate under any former
commiffion, or been difcharged under any act for the
relief of infolvent debtors? And in cafe, upon fuch
enquiries, they have reafon to apprehend, that the
bankrupt in a fingle commiffion has been concerned in
any partnerfhip, or that a feparate commiffion has before iffued againft either of the bankrupts in a joint-
commiffion; or that the bankrupt has before obtained
his certificate under a former commiffion, or been difcharged by any act for the relief of infolvent debtors,
that the commiffioners do proceed upon fuch enquiry,
and to hear the evidence thereon in the prefence of the
bankrupt, who is to be informed of the fubject of the
enquiry, and to be at liberty to lay evidence before
them relating thereto, and in cafe any of the matters
aforefaid do appear to them, that they do, at the time
of making their certificate, alfo feparately certify to me,
fuch of the aforefaid matters as they find to be true.
And that they tranfmit fuch feparate certificate to the
fecretary of bankrupts, to be laid before me at the fame
time with the other certificate. I do alfo order, That
when any commiffion is applied for, the fecretary do
examine whether any previous application has been
made, and by whom, for a commiffion againft the fame
perfon, and that he do give notice thereof by letter to the
commiffioners to whom the commiffion is directed, that
they may enquire into the fame. I do further order,
that when any certificate is brought to the fecretary, in
order for him to get my allowance thereof, he do fearch
for and certify to me, whether he can find any previous
certificate having been before allowed to the fame
bankrupt. I do alfo order, that where any commiffion has iffued, and the commiffioners have not
found the perfon againft whom iffued to be a bankrupt,
in cafe another commiffion be granted (whether on the
petition of the fame or any other creditor) the fecretary
do take care that fuch fecond commiffion be directed

Y

to the fame commiffioners to whom the firft commiffion was directed. I do alfo order, that the fecretary do never deliver out any affidavit made, or bond given, by any petitioning creditor, without my particular order for his fo doing. And laftly, I do order and declare, That a docquet being ftruck, and no commiffion iffued thereon, fhall in no cafe prevent the iffuing of a commiffion on the petition of any other creditor, fo as fuch fecond application be not made in lefs than four days after fuch docquet ftruck, exclufive of the day of ftriking the fame, any former practice to the contrary notwithftanding.

APSLEY, C.

Of Striking the Docquet.

THE firft ftep to be taken towards fuing out a commiffion of bankruptcy, is for the creditor to apply to his attorney or folicitor, and he will draw up an affidavit on a treble fixpenny ftamp as follows:

Petitioning Creditor's Affidavit.

JOHN SMITH, of Leadenhall-ftreet, in the city of London, warehoufeman, maketh oath and faith, That John Brown, of the Strand, in the county of Middlefex, haberdafher, dealer, and chapman, is juftly and truly indebted to this deponent in the fum, of one hundred pounds and upwards, and that the faid John Brown is become bankrupt within the true intent and meaning of fome or one of the ftatutes made and now in force concerning bankrupts, as this deponent hath been informed and verily believes.

JOHN SMITH,   Sworn at the Public Office,
the   day of   17
before   P. H.

THIS affidavit is fworn before a Mafter in Chancery, at the Public Office in Symond's Inn, Chancery-Lane, or at a Mafter's dwelling-houfe. It is then taken to the

fecretary

fecretary of bankrupts' office, in Bell-yard, where the creditor enters into a bond to the Great Seal as follows:

KNOW ALL MEN by thefe prefents, that I John Smith, of Leadenhall-ftreet, in the city of London, warehoufe-man, am held and firmly bound to the Right Honour-able Lord Thurlow, Lord High Chancellor of Great Britain, in the fum of two hundred pounds of good and lawful money of Great Britain, to be paid to the faid Lord Chancellor, or to his certain attorney, executors, adminiftrators, or affigns; to which payment well and truly to be made, I bind myfelf, my heirs, executors, and adminiftrators, firmly by thefe prefents, fealed with my feal, dated the   day of   in the   year of the reign of our fovereign Lord King George the Third, and the year of our Lord one thoufand feven hundred and

THE CONDITION of this obligation is fuch, that if the above bound John Smith fhall prove as well before the major part of the commiffioners to be appointed in a commiffion of bankruptcy againft John Brown, of the Strand, in the county of Middlefex, haberdafher, dealer, and chapman, as upon a trial at law, in cafe the due iffuing forth of the faid commiffion fhall be contefted and tried, that the faid John Brown is juftly and truly indebted to the faid John Smith in the fum of one hundred pounds, or upwards, and is become bankrupt within the true intent and meaning of the ftatutes made and now in force concerning bankrupts, fome or one of them; and if the faid John Smith fhall caufe the faid commiffion to be executed according to the directions of an act parliament made in the fifth year of the reign of his late Majefty King George the Second, intitled, " An act to prevent the committing of frauds by bank-" rupts;" then this obligation to be void.

Sealed and delivered
(being firft duly ftamp-   JOHN SMITH, (L.S.)
ed) in the prefence of
    A. B.
    C. D.

THIS

THIS bond is provided at the office, and when exe-cuted by the creditor, is witneffed by the clerk, likewife by the attorney or his clerk attending the creditor, who pay two guineas. Thefe papers are left and remain at the office, and are entered in the books, which is called *ftriking the docquet.* The commiffion muft be ordered to be fealed within four days after ftriking the docquet, or any other creditor may apply and fue out a commif-fion. It is the cuftom when a commiffion is ordered at the office to be fealed, to pay the fees. The petition is always provided by the office, and is conftantly an-nexed to the commiffion when it is paffed the great feal. The commiffion is delivered at the office in a tin box, with the following bill of fees:

Commiffion, *John Brown.*

	£.	s.	d.			£.	s.	d.
Bond and duty	0	9	6	If at a private feal,				
Petition and duty	0	7	0					
Secretary's fee and filing af-fidavit	1	2	0			1	3	0
Commifsion and hanaper fee	4	18	2			4	18	8
Deputy fecretary	0	5	0	private feal		2	2	0
Box	0	1	6					
	7	3	2					

IF the creditor do not proceed to fue out a commif-fion, upon applying to the clerk, he will return half a guinea, which is called the drawback.

HAVING got the commiffion fealed, or whilft the commiffion is preparing and fealing, fpeak to your meffenger to be ready to fummon the commiffioners. The commiffion is directed to five commiffioners (as they come in courfe in the lift of commiffioners, if to be executed in London) two or more of whom are bar-rifters,

rifters, and the meffenger being informed of their names
at the office, will fummon any three of them to meet
as can attend   the firft meeting is ufually at a tavern or
a coffee-houfe.

THE form of the proceedings on a commiffion of
bankrupt where the clerk to the commiffion has not
time to write or draw them out, may be had at any of
the law ftationers ready printed, which render the bufinefs eafy, having nothing more than the blanks to fill
up, which fometimes, efpecially on the opening of a
commiffion where it is of great moment to gain poffeffion of the bankrupt's effects, it is neceffary and faves a
great deal of time.

AT this private meeting the clerk to the commiffion
attends with the petitioning creditor who is to prove his
debt, and the neceffary witneffes to prove the trading
and act of bankruptcy, thefe points being eftablifhed to
the fatisfaction of the comm.ffioners, they will fign their
warrant to the meffenger, by virtue whereof he enters the
bankrupt's houfe, &c and holds poffeffion of all his books
and effects wherever he can find them, until the choice of
affignees.   The commiffioners then proceed to appoint
the three feveral meetings under the commiffion, and
fign the fummons for the bankrupt to furrender, which
the meffenger takes with him and delivers to the bankrupt, that he may be protected, to conftitute the petitioning creditor's debts, the bankrupt muft be indebted to
one perfon in 100l. or upwards, to two perfons in 150l.
or upwards, and being indebted to three or more in
200l. their feveral names and the amount of the debts
due to them, their partners' names (if any) muft be inferted in the affidavit and bond.

ALL commiffions of bankrupt where the trader lives
within forty miles of London, are executed at Guildhall, London   but if a commiffion is intended to be
executed in the country, it muft be fo expreffed in the
affidavit and bond, as follows

(Or

(On a treble fix-penny ftamped fheet of paper.)

A, B. of the city of Briftol, merchant, and C. D. of the fame place, banker, feverally make oath and fay; And firft this deponent A B for himfelf faith, that John Smith, of High-ftreet in the city of Briftol, linen draper, dealer and chapman, is juftly and truly indebted unto him, this deponent, and o W. F. of the faid city of Briftol, this deponent's partner in trade, in the fum of eighty pounds, for goods fold and delivered by this deponent, and his faid par ner, to the faid John Smith, And this deponent C. D. for himfelf faith, that the faid John Smith is juftly and truly indebted unto him, this deponent, and to W. C. and F. Y of the faid city of Briftol, this deponent's partners in trade, in the fum of feventy pounds ten fhillings, for money lent and advanced by this deponent and his faid partners to the faid John Smith, for which faid fum of feventy pounds ten fhillings, he, this deponent nor his faid partners have not received any fecurity or fatisfaction, fave and except a promiffory note under the hand of the faid John Smith, for the faid fum of feventy pounds ten fhillings, long fince due and unpaid. And both thefe deponents fay, that they verily believe the faid John Smith is become a bankrupt within the true intent and meaning of fome or one of the ftatutes made and now in force concerning bankrupts, and thefe deponents further fay, that the commiffion, when obtained, is intended to be executed in the faid city of Briftol, or within ten miles of the fame, and not within forty miles of the city of London.

A. B.　　　　Sworn at the city of Briftol by
C. D.　　　　both deponents this　　day
　　　　　　of　　17　　before me,
　　　　　　Jacob Kirby, a Mafter Ex-
　　　　　　traordinary in Chancery.

(On

(On a fix shilling stamped sheet of paper.)

KNOW ALL MEN by these presents, That we A. B. and W. F. of the city of Bristol, merchants and partners; C D. W. C. and F. Y. of the said city, bankers and partners, are jointly and severally held and firmly to the right honourable Edward Lord Thurlow, Lord High Chancellor of Great Britain, in the sum of 300l. of good and lawful money of Great Britain, to be paid to the said Lord Chancellor, or to his certain attorney, executors, administrators, or assigns, for which payment well and truly to be made, we bind ourselves and each of us, our, and each of our heirs, executors, and administrators, firmly by these presents, sealed with our seals, dated the   day of   in the twenty-eighth year of the reign of our sovereign Lord, king George the third, and in the year of our Lord one thousand seven hundred and eighty

THE CONDITION of this obligation is such that if the above bounden A. B. W. F. C. D. W. C. and F. Y. shall prove as well before the major part of the commissioners to be appointed in a commission of bankruptcy against John Smith, of High Street, in the city of Bristol, linen draper, dealer and chapman, as upon a trial at law, in case the due issuing forth of the said commission shall be contested and tried, that the said John Smith is justly and truly indebted to the said A. B. and W F. C D. W. C and F. Y in   or upwards, and is become bankrupt within the true intent and meaning of the statutes made and now in force concerning bankrupts, some or one of them, and if the said A B. W F C D W. C and F. Y. shall cause the said commission to be executed according to the directions of an act of parliament made in the fifth year of the reign of his late majesty, king George the second, intituled "an act to prevent the committing of frauds by bankrupts," at the city of Bristol,

Briftol, aforefaid, or within ten miles of the fame, and not with forty miles of London, then this obligation to be void.

Sealed and delivered (being firft ⎫ A. B. ()
duly ftamped) in the prefence of ⎬
  JACOB KIRBY. ⎬ C. D. ()
  JAMES SCOTT. ⎭ ()
                           ()
                           ()

WHERE there are three or more creditors whofe debts amount to two hundred pounds, the fame form muft be obferved, fpecifying the fums due to each, and defcribing partners, if any, one partner may always fwear the affidavit for the reft, and execute the bond As foon as the affidavit and bond to ground a commiffion are executed, the attorney in the country fends them to his agent in London, by poft or exprefs, according to the urgency of the bufinefs, who immediately carries them to the office to fecure the right to the commiffion. It fometimes happens that two or three applications are made for a commiffion againft the fame perfon; the firft in priority of courfe takes out the commiffion.

IN all commiffions to be executed in the country, the clerk to the commiffion muft fend up the commiffioners' names with the affidavit and bond, two of whom muft be barrifters at law, and the other three acting attornies, whofe refidence fhould be as near the place of executing the commiffion as poffible A copy of the affidavit is moftly neceffary to be fent with the commiffion.

A docquet being ftruck, does not operate as a caveat even for the four days, if any other creditor applies to the office, and gives notice, that he is ready to take out a commiffion, the firft applicant muft give up the benefit of his docquet, or immediately have the docquet fealed.

A creditor taking out a commiffion, and holding it in his hands, and not caufing the fame to be opened and proceeded on, fuch commiffion may be fuperfeded by any other creditor after the publication of the eighth

Gazette

Gazette from the date thereof (Vide form for that purpose, page 179.)

In case a creditor strikes a docquet against any person,
and the business is made up, and no commission intended
to be taken out thereon (as it frequently happens) it would
be to the interest of the party, against whom the docquet
was entered, to have the same withdrawn by the attorney
who lodged such docquet for although the papers cannot
be taken out of the office, if any other creditor of the
party should search at the office for that purpose, it will
appear in favour of such parties' circumstances, which
is done by the attorney or his clerk, writing on the back
of the bond in the office, after this manner, " I do consent to withdraw this docquet against the within named
A B dated this   day of   17   "

                                        C D attorney for E F.

Any Person by searching the books at the office may
know if any docquet is struck against any one, or commission taken out, certificate granted, &c &c and for
every such search pay one shilling

So likewise if a commission be sealed and the parties
settle the business, so that it is agreed on and not intended
that such commission be proceeded in, it will be to the
interest of the party against whom such commission was
sued out, to supersede the same, which may be done of
course, and at a little expence [Form for which, with
bill of fees for the same, as under] No notice of which
is to be given in the Gazette

In the matter of A B against whom a commission of
bankrupt hath been lately awarded and issued.

To the Right Hon the LORD HIGH CHANCELLOR
  of GREAT BRITAIN,

The humble petition of the above named A. B

Sheweth,

THAT a commission of bankrupt under the great seal
of Great Britain, was awarded and issued against your

                    L   petitioner

petitioner on the petition of C D of   bearing
date at Weftminfter the   day of   directed to (infert
the commifsioners' names) as commifsioners to execute
the fame

THAT no proceedings whatever hath been had under
the faid commifsion, as by the affidavit of J. S. hereunto
annexed, doth appear.

THAT fince the ifsuing the faid commifsion, your petitioner has fettled and agreed with the faid C D all demands he had on your petitioner, and he is willing that
the faid commifsion fhould be fuperfeded, for which purpofe he has figned his confent at the foot hereof

> YOUR petitioner therefore moft humbly
> prays your Lordfhip, that the faid
> commifsion of bankrupt fo awar-
> ded and ifsued againft your peti-
> tioner, be forthwith fuperfeded,
> and that a writ of fuperfedeas do
> ifsue for that purpofe at your pe-
> titioner's expence

And your petitioner fhall ever pray.   A. B.

Day of   17
I do hereby confent to the prayer of the above petition, if your Lordfhip pleafe to order the fame.

C. D.

———————

Affidavit to be annexed to the Petition.

In the matter of A. B. againft whom a commifsion of
bankrupt hath been awarded

JOHN SMITH of Clement's Inn, in the county of Middlefex, gentleman, maketh oath and faith · That a commifsion of bankrupt on the petition of C. D of   was
awarded and ifsued againft the above named A. B. bearing

ing date the   day of   17   and that no proceeding whatever hath been had under the said commission;
and further saith that he this deponent did see C. D sign
his name to a consent in writing to the prayer of a petition of the said A, B. to the Right Honourable the Lord,
High Chancellor of Great Britain, humbly praying that
his Lordship would please to order the said commission to
be superseded; and that the name, of the said C. D.
signed and subscribed to the said consent in writing, is of
the proper hand writing of the said C. D.

    JOHN SMITH.

      Sworn at the public office
        this   day of   17
        before me   P. H.

Answering petition	12s. 6d.	
Filing Affidavit	2s. 8d.	
Order for supersedeas and duty	19s.	*if at a private seal*
Supersedeas	2l. 2d.	2l. 8d.
Deputy secretary	5s	private seal 2l. 2s.
Box	1s.	

                    4l. 4d.

In the matter of A, B against whom a commission of
bankrupt hath been awarded and issued.

    To the Right Hon, the LORD HIGH CHANCELLOR
    of GREAT BRITAIN,

    *The humble petition of C D a creditor of the above
    named A. B,*

Sheweth,

    THAT on the second day of June instant, a commis-
sion of bankrupt under the Great Seal of Great Britain,
was awarded and issued against the said A. B. on the peti-

             Z 2   tion

tion of E. F. of   in the city of London, directed to
certain commissioners therein named to execute the
same

THAT your petitioner hath caused the London
Gazette to be searched from the said second day of June,
to the twenty-sixth day of June, both days instant inclusive, making together eight Gazettes, as by the affidavit
of John Smith hereunto annexed doth appear, and doth
not find that the said A B hath been declared a bankrupt in any of such Gazettes

THAT your petitioner hath made an affidavit that the
said A. B. is justly and truly indebted unto him in the
sum of one hundred pounds or upwards, and is ready to
enter into the usual bond to your Lordship, to ground a
commission of bankrupt against the said A B which your
petitioner hereby undertakes to prosecute with effect, for
the benefit of himself and the rest of the creditors of the
said A. B.

> YOUR petitioner therefore most humbly
> prays your Lordship will be pleased
> to order the commission of bank-
> rupt so awarded and issued against
> the said A B to be forthwith su-
> perseded, and that a writ of su-
> persedeas do issue for that pur-
> pose, and that a new commission
> may issue against the said A. B.
> upon the petition of your peti-
> tioner.

And your petitioner shall ever pray, &c.

JOHN SMITH of Clements Inn, in the county of
Middlesex, gentleman, maketh oath and faith, That he
hath carefully searched the London Gazette, published
from the second day of June instant, to this day, both
days inclusive, making together eight Gazettes, to see if
a commission of bankrupt issued against A. B. by the
name and description of A. B. of   street, in the city
of

of London, merchant, was inserted in such Gazettes, but does not find that the said commission hath been published in any of such Gazettes,

> JOHN SMITH.
>
> Sworn at the public office
> this   day of June 17 ,
> before me   P. H.

IN case A takes out a commission against B. and cannot proceed to open the same, because B. had not committed an act of bankruptcy before the date of such commission, he cannot have it resealed as used to be the practice, till my Lord Thurlow came to the Great Seal, who ordered that such commission must be superseded by petition of the said A. praying a new commission to be granted him, neither should the same creditor have a second commission, unless he stated in such petition, that before the date and suing forth thereof, he was not able to prove the said B a bankrupt, but that he was now possessed of an act of bankruptcy, having been committed by B. which act of bankruptcy is to be set forth in his petition, and in the affidavit accompanying the petition. A commission may be resealed if there should be a mistake in the name of a commissioner therein named, &c. but the original date of such commission will remain, the fees for which come to 1l 6s 10d

---

Some remarks on ACTS *of* BANKRUPTCY; *and who* are *and who are* not BANKRUPTS.

DEPARTING the realm.
Withdrawing out of the king's dominions, to any foreign parts, to the intent thereby to remain, in defraud of creditors, and not returning within three months after proclamation

Beginning to keep house.

Absenting

Abfenting.

Taking fanctuary.

Willingly or fraudulently procuring himfelf to be arrefted.

Suffering himfelf to be outlawed.

Yielding himfelf to a prifon.

Departing from his dwelling-houfe.

Willingly or fraudulently procuring his goods, money, or chattles to be attached or fequeftered.

Making any fraudulent grant or conveyance of his lands or chattels.

Obtaining any protection (otherwife than being lawfully protected by parliament)

Preferring unto his majefty, or unto any of the king's courts, any petition or bill againft his creditors, or any of them, thereby defiring or endeavouring to compel them to accept lefs than their juft and principal debts, or to procure time or longer [more] days of payment, than was given at the time of their original contracts.

Being arrefted for debt, after his arreft, lying in prifon two months upon *that*, or any other arreft or detention for debt.

Being arrefted for one hundred pounds or more, of juft debt, after fuch arreft, efcaping out of prifon.

Paying to the petitioning creditor, or delivering to him goods or fecurity for his debt, whereby he fhall privately have more in the pound, than the other creditors.

Neglecting to make fatisfaction for any juft debt to the amount of one hundred pounds, within two months after fervice of legal procefs, for fuch debt, upon any trader having privilege of parliament---

Are deemed acts of bankruptcy.

An *infant*, tho' a trader, cannot be a bankrupt; for an infant can owe only for neceffaries: and the ftatutes of bankruptcy create no new debts, but give a fpeedier and more effectual remedy for recovering fuch as were before due. And no perfon can be made a bankrupt for

debts,

debts, which he is not liable at law to pay. 2 *Blackst. c.* 31

The daughter of a freeman of London being a *married* woman, if she trades separately from her husband, may be a bankrupt. 1 *Atk.* 206

Using the trade of merchandize, as by exercising the calling of a merchant, a grocer, mercer, or in one general word a *chapman*, who is one that buys and sells any thing. 2 *Blackst. c.* 31.

A *brickmaker* may be a bankrupt, because the earth is manufactured, and turned into quite another thing before it is sold. By Lord Chancellor *Camden.* Wilson's Rep C. B. 162.

Persons using the trade or profession of a scrivener, receiving other mens' monies or estates into their trust or custody, shall be adjudged bankrupts. 21 *Jac. c.* 19. *s.* 2

Though dealing merely in smuggling and running of goods is an offence, and contrary to act of parliament, yet still it is a trading within the meaning of the bankrupt acts, and such trader is liable to a commission. *Atk Rep.* 198, 199.

But one single act of buying and selling will not make a man a trader; there must be a repeated practice, and profit by it. *Id*

Persons who adventure any money in the East-India company, and receive their dividend in merchandize, and who sell or exchange the same, shall not be judged thereby a merchant or trader within any statute for bankrupts 13 & 14 *C* 2. *c.* 24 *s* 3, 4

Buying and selling stock in the public funds, or government securities, will not make a man a bankrupt; the same being not goods, wares, or merchandise, within the intent of the statute, by which a profit may be fairly made. 2 *Blackst c* 31

So also the members of the corporation of the English Linen company (for making cambricks and lawns), shall

not

not upon that account only be liable to bankruptcy.
4 G. 3 c 37.

He that buys only, or sells only, is not within this description; but it must be both buying and selling, and also getting a livelihood by it.   2 *Blackst.* c. 31

By 5 G. 2. c 30. No *farmer*, *grazier*, or *drover* of cattle, shall be deemed a bankrupt *s.* 40———But if such farmer or other shall deal in wool, hops, or the like, he shall be deemed a bankrupt; otherwise any person by taking a farm, might avoid the statutes. And in the case of *Mayo* and *Archer*, *E* 8 G. a farmer who planted potatoes, but also bought divers large quantities of potatoes, and sold the same again, was adjudged a bankrupt. *Str* 513

No *handicraft occupation*, where nothing is bought and sold, will make a man a bankrupt, as that of a husbandman, a gardener, and the like, who are paid for their work and labour   2 *Blackst* c. 31.

Also, an *innkeeper* cannot, as an innkeeper, be a bankrupt; for his gain or livelihood does not arise from buying and selling in the way of merchandize, but greatly from the use of his house, furniture, attendance, and the like · and tho' he may buy corn and victuals, to sell again at a profit, yet that no more makes him a trader, than a schoolmaster or other person is, that keeps a boarding house, and makes considerable gains by buying and selling what he uses in the house, and such an one is clearly not within the statutes.   *Id*

But where persons buy goods, and make them up into saleable commodities, as *shoemakers*, *smiths*, *bakers*, and the like; here, tho' part of the gain is by bodily labour, and not by buying and selling; yet they are within the statutes of bankrupts. for the labour is only in melioration of the commodity, and rendering it more fit for sale.   *Id.*

But where a person bought a *coal mine*, and worked the mine, and sold the coals, he was adjudged not to be within the statutes for bankrupts But it would have
been

been otherwife if he had bought the coals and fold the fame again. 2 *Wilfon* 169.

Bankers, brokers, and factors are within this defcription 5 *G* 2. *c.* 30. *f.* 39.

So alfo *pawnbrokers*, being comprehended under the general word *brokers*, which includes the feveral fpecies of brokerage. 1 *Atk.* 206.

But no receiver-general of any taxes granted by act of parliament, fhall be deemed a bankrupt. 5 *G* 2. *c* 30. *f.* 40.

If a man keeps his houfe for a long time, this doth not immediately make him a bankrupt; but if he conceals himfelf within his houfe for a day or hour, to delay or defraud his creditors, he is a bankrupt. *Bac Abr.* 250

It muft be proved, that the perfon, to whom the party was denied, was a creditor *Jackman* v. *Nightingale, Eaft* 13 *Geo.* 2 *B. R*

If a man abfents himfelf for felony, it is an act of bankruptcy, if his creditors are thereby delayed of their juft debts, otherwife not

If a bankrupt might convey all to a favourite and friendly creditor, juft before committing an act of bankruptcy, the whole power of felling his effects, calling in his debts, and fettling his accompts, muft be in fuch fingle and particular creditor, he muft have a right even to the cuftody of the books and papers, whereby the worft and moft dangerous priority would prevail, depending merely upon the unjuft or corrupt partiality of the bankrupt *Bur Rep* 447

No man can be an evidence to prove an act of bankruptcy committed by himfelf, but he may be admitted to give evidence as to the time of the act of bankruptcy, his confeffion to a third perfon, that he had gone out of the way, to avoid being arrefted, is evidence. *Evans* and *Gould.* 8 *Geo* 2

The law does not look upon perfons, whofe debts amount to lefs than 100l to a fingle creditor, or two or more partners, 150l. to two creditors, or 200l or more

A 4   to

three petitioning creditors, to be traders confiderable enough either to enjoy the benefit of the ftatute
themfelves, or to intitle the creditors, for the benefit of
publick commerce, to demand the diftribution of their effects. 2 Black. Rep. 475.

Enlarging Commiffions.

IT frequently becomes neceffary to enlarge the time
for the bankrupt's finifhing his laft examination, for feveral reafons, viz. The bankrupt's accounts being large
and intricate, being confined by illnefs, being at too
great a diftance, &c. therefore the allegations muft be
varied accordingly.

THE petition muft be left at the fecretary of bankrupt's office, fix clear days before the day appointed in
the Gazette for the finifhing his laft examination. The
petition for that purpofe may be in the name of the bankrupt himfelf, or in the names of his affignees. At the time
of leaving the petition at the office, you pay 12s and 6d.
The enlargement muft be advertifed in the Gazette, and
granted by the Commiffioners at the third fitting, at Guildhall in London, in the country, at the place the commiffioners meet to take the bankrupt's laft examination.

The Assignees' Petition.

In the matter of John Smith a bankrupt.

> To the *Right Honourable* EDWARD LORD THUR
> LOW, LORD HIGH CHANCELLOR *of* GREAT
> BRITAIN.

> *The humble Petition of* J B *and* C. F. *assignees of
> the estate and effects of the said bankrupt.*

Sheweth,

THAT a commission of bankrupt, under the great
seal of Great Britain, bearing date at Westminster the
          day of   last, was awarded and issued against
the said John Smith, by the name and description of John
Smith of Cheapside, in the city of London, linen-draper,
dealer, and chapman, directed to R C. W. B. C. E.
A. O. esquires, and R. H. gentleman, as commissioners to
execute the same

THAT the said commissioners duly found and declared
the said John Smith bankrupt, and by summons under
their hands, and by notice in the London Gazette of
Saturday the   day of   last, was required to
surrender himself to the said commissioners or the major
part of them, at Guildhall, London, to be examined
on the   and   days of the said month of
respectively on each of the said days, touching the disclosure and discovery of his estate and effects, and on the
          day of   was required to finish his examina-
tion under the said commission

THAT your petitioners have been duly chosen assignees of the said bankrupt's estate and effects, and find that
on account of the intricacy and perplexity of the said
bankrupt's accounts, he will not be able to complete the
same so as to finish his last examination by the time limited
by such summons and notice for that purpose,

YOUR

Your petitioners therefore moſt humbly pray your Lordſhip will be pleaſed to order that the time the ſaid bankrupt's ſurrend ring himſelf to the commiſſioners in the ſaid commiſſion named or the major part of them, and finiſhing his laſt examination under the ſaid commiſſion. may be enlarged for the ſpace of forty-nine days, to be computed from the ſaid day of

And your petitioners ſhall ever pray.

Bankrupt's Petition.

In the matter of John Smith a bankrupt.

To the *Right Honourable* EDWARD LORD THURLOW, LORD HIGH CHANCELLOR *of* GREAT BRITAIN

The humble petition of the ſaid bankrupt;

SHEWETH,

That a commiſſion of bankrupt, under the great ſeal of Great Britain, bearing date the   day of   laſt, upon the petition of I. B. of Gracechurch-ſtreet, in the city of London linen-draper, was awarded and iſſuing againſt your petitioner by the name and deſcription of John Smith, of Cheapſide, in the city of London, linen-draper, dealer and chapman, which commiſſion is directed to R C W B C B. A O. eſquires, and R H gentleman, as commiſſioners to execute the ſame.

That your petitioner hath been duly declared bankrupt by the major part of the ſaid commiſſioners, and by commiſſion under their hands, and alſo by notice in the London

London Gazette of Tuesday the   of   last, was
required to surrender himself to the said commissioners,
or the major part of them, at Guildhall London, to be
examined by them on the   and   day of
last respectively, at eleven of the clock in the forenoon,
on each of the said days, touching the disclosure and discovery of his estate and effects, and on the   day of
      instant your petitioner was by such summons and
notice required to finish his examination under the said
commission

THAT your petitioner did surrender himself to the said
commissioners on the said   day of   last, and on
the   day of   , and submitted to be examined
touching the disclosure and discovery of his estate and
effects, and to conform himself to the several statutes made
and now in force concerning bankrupts.

THAT your petitioner is preparing and settling his accounts, in order to make a full and true disclosure and
discovery of all his estate and effects, but finds his accounts to very long, intricate, and perplexed, that he
cannot possibly finish the same by the time limited by the
said commissioners' summons and notice for that purpose.

> YOUR petitioner therefore humbly
> prays that your Lordship would be
> pleased to order that the time for
> your petitioner's surrendering him-
> self to the commissioners in the said
> commission named or the major part
> of them, and disclosing and discover-
> ing his estate and effects, and finish-
> ing his last examination under the
> said commission, may be enlarged
> for the space of forty-nine days, to
> be computed from the   day of
>   instant

And your petitioner shall ever pray

Copy of the Order on these Petitions.

Day of   17

LET the time for the bankrupt's surrendering himself and disclosing and discovering his estate and effects
to the commissioners in the said commission named, or
the major part of them, and finishing his last examination under the said commission, be enlarged for the space
of *forty-nine days, to be computed from the said
day of   , but such surrender is to be made between
the hours of eleven and one of the clock of the forty-
ninth day. Hereof give notice to the commissioners
forthwith.

THURLOW, C

―――――――――――

Of Renewed Commissions.

ON the death of the major part of the commissioners, or the whole of them, it becomes necessary to have a renewed commission, before any
further proceedings can be had. A petition for a renewed commission, with an affidavit of the death of the commissioners annexed, is to be engrossed, and carried to
                                                    the

―――――――――――

* Or the time prayed for

the secretary's office, upon which a renewed commission is obtained, which, together with the former commission, and proceedings, are laid before the new commissioners. The fees paid for it at the office are

Answering petition	12s	6d.
Filing Affidavit	2s	8d.
Renewed commission	3l. 1s.	7d.
Deputy secretary	5s	
Box	1s.	6d.

4l. 3s. 3d.

Petition for a renewed commission

In the matter of A B a bankrupt

To the Right Honourable the LORD HIGH CHAN-
CELLOR OF GREAT BRITAIN.

*The humble petition of J. B. of   Street in the city of Lon-
don, merchant, a creditor of the said bankrupt,*

Sheweth,

THAT upon the petition of your petitioner, a commission of bankrupt, under the great seal of Great Britain, bearing date the   day of   17   was awarded and issued against the said A B directed to [name the commissioners] whereupon the said A. B. was duly found and declared bankrupt.

THAT several proceedings hath been had under the said commission.

THAT since the date and suing forth of the said commission [names of the commissioners] the major part of the said commissioners have departed this life, and further proceedings are wanting to be had under the said commission

Your

YOUR petitioner therefore humbly prays your Lordſhip that the ſaid commiſſion may be renewed and be directed to [names of the ſurviving commiſſioners] and to ſuch other commiſſioners as to your Lordſhip ſhall ſeem meet.

And your petitioner ſhall ever pray, &c.

THE meſſenger employed to the commiſſion is the moſt proper perſon to make an affidavit of the death of the commiſſioners, as follows:

In the matter of A. B. a bankrupt.

THOMAS VAUGHAN, of Chancery-lane, London, Gentleman, maketh oath and ſaith, That [names of the deceaſed commiſſioners], three of the commiſſioners named in the commiſſion of bankrupt, iſſued againſt the ſaid A B bearing date the   day of   178 , are all ſince deceaſed, as this deponent hath been informed and verily believes.

THOMAS VAUGHAN.
Sworn at the Public office
this   day of   178
beforeme   P. H.

A renewed commiſſion is directed to the two ſurviving commiſſioners, together with three others, on the Lord Chancellor's tam quam liſt appointed for that purpoſe, but in the country, the clerk to the renewed commiſſion muſt put the names of the new commiſſioners in the prayer of the petition.

THE

Petition for a renewed commission of bankruptcy in the country.

In the matter of I G. a bankrupt

To the Right Honourable the LORD HIGH CHAN-
CELLOR OF GREAT BRITAIN.

*The humble petition of A B. and C D affignees of the faid
bankrupt's estate and effects,*

Sheweth,

THAT a commiffion of bankruptcy, under the great
feal of Great Britain, was, on or about the   day
of   17   , awarded and iffued againft the
faid I G by the name and defcription of I G of Liverpool, in the county of Lancafter, merchant, directed to
R T. R M R P efquires, G E. and B. J. gentlemen,
as commiffioners to execute the fame

THAT your petitioners were duly chofen affignees of
the faid bankrupt's eftate and effects, and feveral proceedings have been had under the faid commiffion

THAT the faid R T R M and R P efquires the
major part of the faid commiffioners, are fince deceafed,
as by the affidavit of John Smith hereunto annexed, doth
appear

THAT your petitioners have collected and got in all
the outftanding debts, and effects of the faid bankrupt,
and are ready to make a final dividend unto and amongft
the faid bankrupt's creditors, who have come in and
proved their debts under the faid commiffion, but on account of the death of the faid commiffioners, your
petitioners are advifed they cannot proceed to the making fuch final dividend, without the faid commiffion be
renewed.

B b   YOUR

YOUR petitioners therefore moſt humbly pray your Lordſhip would be pleaſed to order that the ſaid be renewed, and directed to the ſaid G. E and B. J the ſaid two ſurviving commiſſioners, and to A B C. D. and E F. eſquires

And your petitioner ſhall ever pray, &c.

May 12th 178

Filing the affidavit of John Smith.—Let the ſaid commiſſion be renewed and directed to A. B. C. D E F. eſquires G. E. and B. J. gentlemen.

THURLOW C.

Affidavit to be annexed to the petition.

JOHN SMITH of Liverpool, in the county of Lancaſter, gentleman, maketh oath and ſaith, That R. F. R. M. and R. P. eſquires, three of the commiſſioners, named in a commiſſion of bankrupt awarded and iſſued againſt I. G. of Liverpool, aforeſaid, merchant, bearing date at Mancheſter the   day of   17 are all ſince deceaſed, as this deponent hath been informed and really believes.

JOHN SMITH.

Sworn at Liverpool aforeſaid this   day of May 178 before

W L.
A maſter in chancery extraordinary.

Of Superseding Commissions of Bankruptcy.

Superseding a commission by consent of creditors.

In the matter of G P a bankrupt

To the Right Hon the LORD HIGH CHANCELLOR
of GREAT BRITAIN

The humble petition of the said G P. the bankrupt.

Sheweth,

THAT a commission of bankrupt under the great seal of Great Britain, bearing date at Westminster the day of 17 , was awarded and issued against your petitioner, by the name and description of G P of in the county of Kent, butcher, dealer, and chapman, upon the petition of I. S of in the county of , farmer, and J. G of aforesaid, victualler, which commission was directed to certain commissioners therein specially named and authorized, the major part of whom found and declared your petitioner a bankrupt.

THAT the several persons whose names are hereunto subscribed, are all the creditors of your petitioner who have proved or claimed any debts under the said commission, as by the certificate of the said commissioners hereunto annexed appears, and all the said creditors of your petitioner are consenting the said commission should be superseded, and for that purpose have signified their said respective consents in writing to the prayer of this petition, at the foot hereof, as by affidavit also annexed appears.

Your

YOUR petitioner therefore most humbly prays your Lordship will be pleased to order the said commission of bankrupt, awarded and against your petitioner aforesaid, be superseded, and that a writ of supersedeas forthwith issue for that purpose.

And your petitioner shall ever pray, &c   G. P

WE whose names are hereunder subscribed, do hereby most humbly certify and declare our consent to the prayer of the above petition, in case your Lordship shall be pleased to grant the same.

Witness our hands the   day of May 17

· T. S.
J G.
T S.
H. L,

Affidavit.

In the matter of G. P. a bankrupt.

T L of   in the county of   gentleman, maketh oath, That he this deponent, did on the 12th day of this instant May, see T S J G T S and this 14th day of May, H L severally sign their names to a consent in writing, subscribed to the prayer of a petition of the said G P directed and intended to be preferred to the Lord High Chancellor of Great Britain, most humbly praying that his Lordship would be pleased to order that the said commission of bankrupt therein mentioned to have been awarded and issued, be immediately superseded, and that a writ of supersedeas might forthwith issue for that purpose or to that effect, and this deponent fur-

ther

their faith, That the names I S J G T S. and
H L figned and fubfcribed to the faid content in writing
of the refpective proper hand writings of the faid
T.S. J G T.S and H.L

I. L.

Sworn this   day of May 17   at
the public office in Symonds Inn
before me   r W.

In the matter of G P a bankrupt.

To the Right Hon the LORD HIGH CHANCELLOR
of GREAT BRITAIN.

We whofe names are hereunto fubfcribed, being the
major part of the commiffioners named in and authorized
in and by a commiffion of bankrupt, bearing date at
Weftminfter the   day of   17 , banker and ift
findagainft G P late of   in the county of   , butcher dealer, and chapman, directed to T T N and
W C efquires together with S D efquire, and J P.
gentleman, do humbly certify to your Lordfhip, that
we the major part of the faid commiffioners on the
day of the faid month of   , have begun to put the
faid commiffion into execution againft the faid G P did
find that the faid G. P and before the date and fuing forth
of the faid commiffion, become bankrupt, within the
intent and meaning of the feveral ftatutes made and now
in force concerning bankrupts, fome or one of them,
and did therefore declare the faid G P bankrupt accordingly, and we the faid commiffioners humbly certify to
your Lordfhip, that I S J G T S and H L are
the only creditors of the faid G. P. who have proved
debts under the faid commiffion

And we the faid commiffioners do further certify to
your Lordfhip, that we did meet purfuant to notice on
the faid   day of   17   for the proof of debts,
                                                    and

and on the day of then next following, for the choice of affignees of the faid bankrupt's eftate and e⁻fects, when no other creditors proved or claimed any debts under the faid commiffion, at any of the faid fittings, and that on the day of the faid bankrupt finifhed his examination under the faid commiffion.

Witnefs our hands this day of

E P
J N
W C.

Of the Certificate.

Form of the Commiffioner's Certificate of Bankrupt's conformity *.*

To the Right Honourable EDWARD LORD THUR-LOW, LORD HIGH CHANCELLOR OF GREAT BRITAIN.

WE whofe names and feals are hereunto fubfcribed and fet, being the major part of the commiffioners named and authorized in and by a commiffion of bankrupt, awarded and iffued againft John Smith, of Cheapfide, in the city of London, linen-draper, dealer and chapman, bearing date at Weftminfter the day of in the year of his prefent Majefty's reign, directed to R. C W B. C B. A O efquires, and R H. gentleman, do humbly certify to your Lordfhip, that the major part of the commiffioners, by the faid commiffion

* To be engroffed on a treble fixpenny ftamped fkin of parchment.

miffion authorized, having begun to put the faid commiffion into execution, did find that the faid John Smith
became bankrupt fince the   day of   , and before
the date and fuing forth of the faid commiffion, within
the true intent and meaning of the ftatutes made, and
in force concerning bankrupts, or fome of them, and did
thereupon declare him bankrupt accordingly, and we
further humbly certify to your Lordfhip, that the faid
John Smith being fo declared bankrupt, the major part
of the commiffioners by the faid commiffion authorized,
purfuant to the Act of Parliament made in the 5th year
of the reign of his late Majefty, King George the Second, entitled " an act to prevent the committing of
" frauds by bankrupts" did caufe due notice to be
given and publifhed in the London Gazette of fuch commiffion being iffued, and of the times and place of three
feveral meetings, of the faid commiffioners, within forty-
two days next after fuch notice, the laft of which meetings was appointed to be on the forty-fecond day †, at
which the faid John Smith was required to furrender
himfelf to the faid commiffioners named in the faid commiffion, or the major part of them, and to make a full difclofure and difcovery of his eftate and effects, and the
creditors of the faid John Smith were defired to come
prepared to prove their debts, and to affent or to diffent
from the making this certificate And we further humbly certify to your Lordfhip, that fuch three feveral
meetings of the major part of the faid commiffioners,
by the faid commiffion authorized, were had purfuant to
fuch notice fo given and publifhed, and that at one of
thofe meetings, the faid John Smith did furrender himfelf to the major part of the faid commiffioners, by the
faid commiffion authorized, and did fign or fubfcribe
fuch furrender, and did fubmit to be examined from
time to time upon oath, by and before the major part of
the

---

† If the bankrupt obtains an order for the enlargement of the time •
furrender, fuch order muft be inferted in the certificate, and the time given
by the faid order, mentioned.

the commissioners by the said commission authorized, and in all things did conform to the several statutes made and now in force concerning bankrupts, and particularly to the said act made in the fifth year of his said late Majesty's reign. And we further humbly certify to your Lordship, that at the last of the said three meetings, the said John Smith finished his last examination before the major part of the said commissioners by the said commission authorized, according to the direction of the said last mentioned act, and upon such his examination, made a full discovery of his estate and effects, and in all things conformed himself to the several statutes made and now in force concerning bankrupts, and particularly according to the directions of the said act made in the fifth year of his said late Majesty's reign, and there doth not appear to us any reason to doubt of the truth of such discovery, or that the same is not a discovery of all the estate and effects of the said John Smith, and we further humbly certify, that the creditors whose names or marks are subscribed to this certificate, are full four parts in five in number and value of the creditors of the above named John Smith, who are creditors for not less than twenty pounds respectively, and who have duly proved their debts under the said commission, and that it doth appear to us by due proof, by affidavit in writing that such several subscribing creditors, or some person by them respectively duly authorized thereunto, did, before our signing thereof, sign this certificate, and testify their consent to our signing the same, and to the said John Smith his having such allowance and benefit as by the said last mentioned act are allowed to bankrupts, and to the said John Smith his discharge in pursuance of the said last mentioned act. In witness whereof we have hereunto set our hands and seals this   day of   in the   year of the reign of   and the year of our Lord one thousand seven hundred and

W2

WE the creditors of the above named John Smith, whose names or marks are hereunto subscribed, do hereby testify and declare our consent that the major part of the commissioners by the above named commission authorized, may sign and seal the certificate above written, and that the said John Smith may have such allowance and benefit as are given to bankrupts by the act of parliament last above mentioned, and the said * John Smith his discharge in pursuance of the same act.

Charles Bragge ()
Arthur Onflow ()
Robert Haffell ()

John Brown }
Charles Scott } *Affignees*
Thomas Smith
William Grant
Peter Murray, for felf and partner
John Emery, for Samuel Newton by letter of attorney
Thomas Riley
Edward Warner

Affidavit of feeing creditors fign their consent to the certificate

In the matter of John Smith a bankrupt.

A. B. of   maketh oath and faith, That he did fee John Brown of   Charles Scott of   affignees of the faid bankrupt's eftate and effects, Thomas Smith of William Grant of   Peter Murray of   for himfelf and Charles Murray his partner, John Emery of   by virtue of a power of attorney from Samuel Newton of   Thomas Riley of   and Edward Warner of   feverally fubfcribe their refpective names to a confent at

* In cafes of partnerfhip, where all the partners are to be difcharged by a joint certificate, the names and defcriptions of the parties are to be carried through the form of the certificate, but as it often happens that the creditors will give a feparate certificate only to one of the partners, the name of fuch partner muft be here inferted.

C c

the

the foot of a certain instrument in writing, intended to be a certificate under the hands and seals of the major part of the commissioners named and authorized in and by a commission of bankrupt awarded and issued against J S of Cheapside in the City of London, linen-draper, dealer and chapman, that the said John Smith hath in all things conformed himself to the several statutes made and now in force concerning bankrupts, whereby they do severally testify and declare their consent to the said commissioners signing and sealing the said certificate, and that the said John Smith may have such allowance and benefit as are given to bankrupts by an act of parliament made in the fifth year of the reign of his late Majesty King George the Second, entitled, " an act to prevent the committing of frauds by bankrupts," and be discharged from his debts in pursuance of the said act.

A. B.   Sworn at the public office,
                                      the   day of   173
                                      before me,

Affidavits of two persons seeing creditors sign.

A. B. of   and C D. of   severally maketh oath as follows   and first this deponent A. B. for himself saith, That he was present and did see John Brown of William Grant of   Peter Murray of   for himself and Charles Murray his partner, severally subscribe their respective names to a consent at the foot of a certain instrument in writing intended to be a certificate under the hands and seals of the major part of the commissioners named and authorized in and by a commission of bankrupt awarded and issued against John Smith of Cheapside in the city of London, linen-draper, dealer, and chapman, that the said John Smith hath in all things conformed himself to the several statutes made and now in force concerning bankrupts   hereby they do severally testify and declare their consent to the said commissioners signing and sealing the said certificate, and that the said John Smith may have such allowance and bene-

ne

fit as are given to bankrupts by an act of parliament made in the fifth year of the reign of his late Majesty King George the Second, intitled "an act to prevent "the committing of frauds by bankrupts," and be discharged from his debts in pursuance of the said act. And this deponent C D for himself saith, That h was present and did see John Emery of by virtue of a letter of attorney from Samuel Newton, Thomas Riley of and Edward Warner of severally subscribe their names to the said consent.

A B.
C. D.   Sworn at the Public office by both
         deponents, this   day of   17
         before me

Form of a general power of attorney.

Know all men by these presents, that I Samuel Newton of a creditor of John Smith of Cheapside, in the city of London, linen-draper, dealer, and chapman, the person against whom a commission of bankrupt is awarded and issued, and now in prosecution, and have duly proved my debt under the said commission, have made, ordained, authorized, constituted, appointed, and by these presents, do make, ordain, authorize, constitute, appoint, and in my place and stead, put John Emery of to be my true and lawful attorney, for and in my name, to vote in the choice of any new assignee or assignees of the said bankrupt's estate and effects, in case of any alteration or change of the present assignees, and also for me, and in my name, place and stead, to consent with whom the monies to be received from time to time out of the said bankrupt's estate and effects, shall remain until the same be divided, and also for me and in my name place and stead, to consent to the commissioners, in and by the said commission named and authorized,

or

or the major part of them, figning a certificate for the
faid bankrup's having the allowance and benefit given
to bankrup's by an act of parliament made in the fifth
year of the reign of his late Majesty King George the
Second, intitled " an act to prevent the committing of
frauds by bankrup s " and that the faid bankrupt may
be difcharged from his debts in purfuance of the faid
act. And alfo for me, and in my name, to confent not
only to the commencing of any fuit or fuits in equity,
by the affignee or affignees under the faid commiffion,
touching the faid bankrupt's effate, but alfo to the fub-
mitting of any difpute or difference between fuch affignee
or affignees or any other perfon or perfons whatfoever,
for or on account, or by reafon, or means of any matter caufe or thing whatfoever, relating to the faid bankrupt's effate or effects, and likewife to fuch affignee or
affignees, making any compofition with any perfon or
perfons, debtors or accomptants, to the faid bankrupt;
where the fame fhall appear neceffary and reafonable
Alfo for me and in my name, place and ftead, and for
my own proper ufe and benefit, to afk, demand, fue
for, and receive of, and from the affignee or affignees of
the effate and effects of the faid bankrupt, or whom elfe
thefe prefents do, fhall, or may concern, all and every
fum and fums of money, as now is, or are, or fhall
hereafter become due or payable to me, for my dividend
or fhare of the effate and effects of the faid bankrupt,
on my debt duly proved under the faid commiffion as
aforefaid, and on receipt thereof for me, and in my
name, to fign, feal, execute, and deliver, all and every
fuch good and fufficient receipts, acquittances, releafes,
and difcharges, to the faid affignees, as fhall and may be
lawful, fit and convenient to be done ; and generally to
do all and every fuch further and lawful act and deed,
matters and things in the law, for the better executing
and difcharging the power and authority hereby
given, as fully and amply, to all intents and purpofe,
as I myfelf might or could do, if perfonally prefent

fent and did the fame hereby ratifying, allowing, and confirming all and whatfoever my faid attorney fhall or may lawfully do, or caufe to be done, in and about the faid premifes, for the better executing the purpofes aforefaid, by virtue of thefe prefents. In witnefs whereof I have to thefe prefents fet my hand and feal this   day of   17

SAMUEL NEWTON. (l.s.)

Signed, fealed and delivered (being
 firft duly ftamped) in the prefence
 of   A B.
                                 C. D.

An affidavit of the due execution of the letter of attorney
 muft be made and annexed thereunto.

F O R M.

A B. of   maketh oath, That he was prefent, and did fee Samuel Newton of   duly fign, feal, and as his act and deed, deliver, the letter of attorney hereunto annexed and that the name, Samuel Newton, fubfcribed againft the feal of the faid letter of attorney, is of the proper hand-writing of the faid Samuel Newton, and that the name of this deponent, and C D. fubfcribed to the faid letter of attorney, as witneffes to the execution thereof, are of this deponent's and of the faid C D's own proper refpective hand-writings.

Sworn, &c.   A B

Another form of a general letter of attorney

Know all men by these presents, that we, A B C D. E F G H. I. K. L M. of   and N O P Q of   creditors of R S of   the person against whom a commission of bankrupt is awarded and issued, and now in prosecution, and who have duly proved our respective debts under the said commission, have made, ordained, authorized, constituted, and appointed, and by these presents do make, ordain, authorize, constitute, appoint, and in our places and steads respectively put T U of   to be our true and lawful attorney, for and in our names respectively, to vote in the choice of any new assignee or assignees, of the said bankrupt's estate and effects, in case of any alteration or change of the present assignee; And also for us and in our names, places and steads respectively, to consent with whom the monies to be received from time to time out of the said bankrupt's estate and effects shall remain until the same be divided. And also for us, and in our names, places and steads respectively, to consent to the commissioners, in and by the said commission named and authorized or the major part of them, signing a certificate for the said bankrupt having the allowance and benefit given to bankrupts, by an act of parliament in the fifth year of the reign of King George the Second, intitled, " An act to prevent " the committing of frauds by bankrupts," and that the said bankrupt may be discharged from his debts, in pursuance of the said act. And also for us and in our names respectively to consent not only to the commencing of any suit, or suits in equity, by the assignee or assignees, under the said commission, touching the said bankrupt's estate, but also to the submitting of any dispute or difference between such assignee and assignees or any person or persons whatsoever, for or on account, or by reason or means of any matter, cause, or thing whatsoever relating to the said bankrupt's estate or effects, and likewise to such assignee or assignees, making any composition

position with any person or persons, debtors, or accomptants to the said bankrupt, where the same shall appear necessary and reasonable. And also for us and in our names, places and steads respectively, and for our own proper uses and benefits respectively to ask, demand, sue for, and receive of and from the assignee or assignees of the estate and effects of the said bankrupt, or whom else these presents do, shall, or may concern, all and every sum and sums of money, as now is or are, or shall hereafter become due or payable to us the said A B &c. respectively, for our respective debts, dividends or shares of the estate and effects of the said bankrupt, on our said respective debts duly proved under the said commission as aforesaid, and on receipt thereof for us, and in our respective names to sign, seal, execute and deliver, and and every such good and sufficient receipts, acquittances, releases, and discharges to the said assignees, as shall and may be lawful, fit, and convenient to be done, and generally to do all and every such further and lawful act and deed, matters and things in the law, for the better executing and discharging the power and authority hereby given, as fully and amply to all intents and purposes as we or either of us might or could do if personally present and did the same, hereby ratifying, allowing, and confirming, all and whatsoever our said attorney, shall or may lawfully do, or cause to be done, in and about the said premises, for the better executing the purposes aforesaid, by virtue of these presents. In witness whereof we the said A B. C D. E F G. H I K. L M. and N O P Q have to these presents set our hands and seals this   day of   in the year of our Lord 17

Form of a letter of attorney for the purpose only of signing the certificate.

Know all men by these presents that I Samuel New—
e...... a creditor of John Smith of   the person against
whom

whom a commission of bankrupt is awarded and iſſued and now in proſecution, and have duly proved my debt under the ſaid commiſſion, have made, ordained, authoriſed, conſtituted, and appointed, and by theſe preſents do make, ordain, authorize, conſtitute, appoint, and in my place and ſtead, put John Emery of   to be my true and lawful attorney, for me and in my name, place and ſtead, to ſubſcribe his conſent to the commiſſioners in and by the ſaid commiſſion named and authorized, or the major part of them, ſigning a certificate for the ſaid bankrupt having the allowance and benefit given to bankrupts, by an act of parliament made in the ninth year of the reign of his late Majeſty King George the Second, intitled, " An act to prevent the committing of frauds by bankrupts," and that the ſaid bankrupt may be diſcharged from his debts, purſuant to the directions of the ſaid act.

Signed, &c.

Samuel Newton.　()

A general power of attorney being wanted for many purpoſes, it is often neceſſary to have one executed for the above purpoſe only, to be filed with the certificate. When the commiſſioners ſign the certificate, the affidavit of ſeeing the creditors ſign letters of attorney, with affidavits of the due execution annexed to them, &c are exhibited to the commiſſioners, who authenticate ſuch papers, by underwriting each in the following manner

　　" Exhibited to us, under a commiſſion of bank-
　　" rupt againſt A B the　　day of　　17

Charles Bragge.
Arthur Onſlow
Robert Hayeld.

When

When the certificate and the papers are so completed, you take them or send them by the messenger to the secretary's office, and the clerk gives a warrant, for which you pay 2s. and 6d. which is a notice to the Gazette, that the certificate is left at the office, take this to the Gazette-office, and the printer will insert the advertisement in the usual manner, that the certificate will be allowed and confirmed, unless cause be shewn to the contrary within twenty-one days from the date of the said advertisement.

In the mean time the bankrupt must make an affidavit in the following form

In the matter of John Smith, a bankrupt.

In Chancery

JOHN SMITH, of   the person against whom a commission of bankrupt was awarded and issued on the   day of   maketh oath and saith that the certificate bearing date the   day of   17   under the hands and seals of Charles Bragge, Arthur Onslow, esquires, and Robert Hassell, gentleman, the major part of the commissioners in the said commission named and authorised, whereby they have certified to the Right Honourable Edward Lord Thurlow, Lord High Chancellor of Great Britain, that he, this deponent, hath in all things conformed himself according to the directions of an act of parliament made and passed in the fifth year of the reign of his late Majesty King George the second, intituled, " An act to prevent the committing of frauds by bankrupts," and the consent of all this deponent's creditors who have signed their names at the foot of the said certificate, that the commissioners may sign and seal the same, and that this deponent may have such allowance and benefit as are given to bankrupts by the said act, and be

Dd   discharged

difcharged from his debts in purfuance thereof, was obtained fairly and without fraud.

JOHN SMITH.

        Sworn at the Public Office, the
           day of   17   before

After the expiration of the twenty-one days, take this affidavit to the office, and if there is no petition lodged againft the certificate, befpeak the allowance thereof, and in a day or two after it will be allowed, by the Lord Chancellor's figning the allocator, in the following manner:

day of   17

WHEREAS the ufual notice hath been given in the London Gazette of   the   day of   laft, and none of the creditors of the above named John Smith having fhewn any caufe to the contrary, I do allow and confirm this certificate.

                 THURLOW, C

The affidavits, &c. are left and filed in the office, and you pay for the allowance of the certificate, with two affidavits, 1l. 14s. and 2s. more for every other affidavit or letter of attorney belonging thereto.

INROLMENT.

INROLMENT.

Of Inrolling Proceedings under Commissions of Bankruptcy.

IN order to secure the title to purchasers of estates sold under commissions of bankruptcy, it is necessary to have part of the proceedings entered of record, an attested copy of which will at all times be admitted in evidence. The method of doing which is as follows. Draw up a petition in the subsequent form, in the names of the assignees, together with such parts of the proceedings as are mentioned in the prayer of the petition, take these to the secretary of bankrupts' office where the books of record are generally kept, and the deputy to the clerk of the inrolments will obtain the Lord Chancellor's fiat to the petition, enter the same, and make an attested copy thereof.

PETITION.

In the matter of S. M. a bankrupt.

To the Right Honorable the LORD HIGH CHAN-CELLOR OF GREAT BRITAIN.

The humble petition of T S and R B. assignees of the estate and effects of the said bankrupt,

Sheweth,

THAT on the   day of   a commission of bankrupt was awarded and issued against the said S M. and your petitioners were duly chosen assignees of his estate and effects, and the major part of the commissioners in the said commission named and authorised, have executed an assignment of the personal estate, and also a bargain

D d 2   and

and sole of the real estate of the said bankrupt, to your petitioners accordingly

THAT the said bankrupt was seized of, or entitled unto him, and his heirs, of and in the equity of redemption, of a freehold estate in ____ which has been sold, and in order to complete the sale thereof, your petitioners are advised that several parts of the proceedings under the said commission should be entered of record

> YOUR petitioner therefore most humbly prays your Lordship to order, that the stile and title of the proceedings of the commissioners under the said commission, the memorandum of the said commissioners taking the usual oath to qualify themselves to act under the said commission, the deposition of the petitioning creditor's debt, the depositions of the trading and act of bankruptcy of the said S M together with the commissioners' adjudication and declaration of the said S M having become bankrupt, the memorandum of the choice of your petitioners to be assignees of the estate and effects of the said S M and your petitioners' acceptance of the trust thereof may be entered of record, pursuant to the directions of the act of parliament in that case made and provided.

And your petitioners shall ever pray.

AFTER

AFTER the petition and proceedings are inrolled, each deposition or memorandum is indorsed, and signed by the deputy thus

THE memorandum within written hath been entered of record, by virtue of an order of the Rt. Hon. Edward Lord Thurlow, Lord High Chancellor of Great Britain, made upon the petition of I S and R B assignees of the estate and effects of S M the within named bankrupt, bearing date the   day of   17   according to the directions of an act of parliament made and passed in the fifth year of the reign of his late Majesty King George the second, intitled, " An act to prevent the committing of frauds by bankrupts."

A B
Deputy to Henry Hemoool, esquire,
clerk of the inrolments in bankruptcy.

THE fees to be paid for the above are, 12s 6d for inrolling the petition, for each hundred words contracts to the roll, and ninety words to the sheet; and for each memorandum as inrolled, and for the copy on treble fix-penny, according to the length, 6d per sheet.

OF INROLLING THE CERTIFICATE.

THE E are several reasons for inrolling bankrupts certificates such as being afraid to trust to accident or loss where a joint certificate is granted to partners, each bankrupt should have a duplicate copy, or where prisoners, and where the bankrupts are obliged to go into parts beyond the seas, &c.

Petition of a bankrupt to have the certificate inrolled.

To the *Right Hon.* the LORD HIGH CHANCELLOR of GREAT BRITAIN

The humble petition of S. M. a bankrupt,

Sheweth,

THAT on the   day of   17   a commission of bankrupt was awarded and issued against your petitioner, whereupon your petitioner was duly found and declared bankrupt.

THAT your petitioner has obtained a certificate under the hands and seals of the major part of the commissioners named in and acting under the said commission, whereby they have certified, that your petitioner hath in all things conformed himself to the acts of Parliament made and now in force concerning bankrupts, and four-fifths in number and value of the creditors of your petitioner who have proved their debts under the said commission, have signed their names at the foot of the said certificate, testifying their consent that your petitioner may have such allowance and benefit as are given to bankrupts by the said acts.

THAT the said certificate hath been allowed and confirmed by your Lordship.

THAT your petitioner is desirous that the said certificate so allowed and confirmed by your Lordship, as aforesaid may be entered of record.

YOUR petitioner therefore most humbly prays your Lordship, that the said certificate, together with your petitioner's affidavit of having obtained the same fairly and without fraud, may be entered of record, pursuant to the act of parliament in that case made and provided.

And your petitioner shall ever pray, &c

Proceedings

Proceedings under a Commiſſion of Bankruptcy.

Examinations, depoſitions, and proceedings had and taken under a commiſſion of bankruptcy, awarded and iſſued againſt S. M. of ſtreet, London, oilman, dealer, and chapman, bearing date at Weſtminſter the day of 17 directed to Thomas Mulſo, Randle Ford, Auguſtus Pechell, John Calthorpe Gough, and Henry Jodrell, eſquires, on the petition of I. S. of Alderſgate-ſtreet, London, oilman.

At the Baptiſt-head coffee-houſe, Chancery-lane, the day of 17

MEMORANDUM.

THAT we Thomas Mulſo, Auguſtus Pechell, and Henry Jodrell, eſquires, being three of the commiſſioners named and authorized in a commiſſion of bankrupt awarded and iſſued againſt S. M. of ſtreet, London, oilman, dealer and chapman, adminiſtered to and ſeverally took before each other the oath of a commiſſioner of bankrupt, preſcribed and ſpecified in and by an act of parliament made in the fifth year of the reign of his late Majeſty King George the ſecond, intitled, " An act to prevent the committing of frauds by bankrupts," before we proceeded to act in the execution of the ſaid commiſſion according to the directions of the ſaid act

Witneſs,
George Miller.

Thomas Mulſo,
Auguſtus Pechell.
Henry Jodrell.

At

At the Baptiſt Head coffee-houſe, Chancery lane, th
  day of   17

Thos. Mulſo.

Aug. Pechell.

Henry Jodrell.

T. S. of Aldergate-ſtreet, London, oilman, being ſworn, and examined, the day, and year, and at the place aforeſaid, upon his oath ſaith, That S. M. of Aldergate-ſtreet, London, oilman, dealer and chapman, the perſon againſt whom this commiſſion of bankruptcy is awarded and iſſued, was at and before the date and iſſuing forth of the ſaid commiſſion, and ſtill is juſtly and truly indebted unto this deponent in the ſum of one hundred pounds and upwards for goods ſold and delivered by this deponent to the ſaid bankrupt.

I S.

At the Baptiſt Head coffee-houſe Chancery-lane, the
  day of   17

Thos Mulſo.

Aug Pechell.

Henry Jodrell.

EDWARD HILL, clerk to T S. of Aldergate-ſtreet, London, oilman, being ſworn and examined the day, and year and at the place aboveſaid, upon his oath ſaith, That he hath known S M of   ſtreet, London, oilman, dealer and chapman the perſon againſt whom this commiſſion of bankrupt is awarded and iſſued, for the ſpace of   years laſt paſt, and upwards, during all which time the ſaid S. M. did follow the trade or buſineſs of an oilman, in buying and ſelling of oils, pickles, ſalt, ſoap, vinegar, and various other things, and thereby ſought and endeavoured to get his living as others, of the ſame trade uſually do.

EDWARD HILL

At the Baptist Head coffee-house, Chancery-lane, the   day of

J C. thopman to S M of   ftreet,

Thos Mulfo   Lord n, oilman, dealer and chapman, being fworn and examined the day, and year, and at the place abovefaid, upon his oath faith, That he hath been employed by the faid S M the perfon againft whom this commiffion of bankrupt is awarded for the fpace of   laft paft, and upwards and this deponent faith, that th faid S. M. during all that time did foll w the trade of an oilman, by buying and felling of oils, pickles, falt, foap, vinegar, and various other things, and thereby fought and endeavoured to get his living, as others of the fame trade ufually do And this deponent faith, That the faid S M did on Monday the day of   inform this deponent, that he expected Mr.

to whom he owed money, would call at his houfe, and enquire for him, and he did then defire this deponent to deny him to the faid Mr   or

Mag. Pechell.   any other perfon that fhould call at his houfe and enquire for him, although he might at the fame be at home And this deponent faith, That the faid Mr.   did foon after, as, on the fame day, come to the faid S M's houfe and did then enquire of this deponent for the faid S M when this deponent informed the faid Mr.   that the faid S. M. was not at home, although the faid S M was at th fame time up ftairs in the dining-room of his faid houfe, and the faid Mr   told this deponent that he came to fettle with the faid S. M or to that effect, and this deponent foon afterwards acquainted the faid S M that he had fo denied him to the faid Mr   in he feemed well fatisfied therewith, and faid this deponent had done right And this deponent further faith, That the faid S M does fecrete himfelf, and h s abfconded for fear of being arrefted by fome or one of his

H nry Pechell   creditors as this deponent verily believes.

J C

*At the Baptift Head coffee houfe, Chancery lane, the
day of   17*

MEMORANDUM —We whofe names are hereunto
fubfcribed, being the major part of the commiffioners
named and authorifed in a commiffion of bankrupt,
awarded againft S M of   ftreet, London, oilman,
dealer and chapman, bearing date at Weftminfter, the
      day of   in the   year of his prefent Maj fty's reign,
having begun to put the faid commiffion into execution,
upon examination of witneffes upon oath, taken before
us, do find that the faid S. M. did, before the date and
fuing forth of the faid commiffion, become bankrupt
within the true intent and meaning of the feveral ftatutes
made and now in force concerning bankrupts, fome or
one of them, and we do accordingly adjudge and declare
the faid S. M. bankrupt, to all intents and purpofes

Thos Milfo,
Aug Pechell,
Henry Jodrell

THIS bufinefs conftitutes the firft meeting of the commiffioners, at which time, as it has been before obferved,
they execute the war ant of feizure, and the fummons
for the bankrupt to furrender, and the ufual notice of
the bankruptcy in the London Gazette.

———————

Proceedings at the firft public meeting at Guildhall.

At Guildhall, London, the   day of   17

MEMORANDUM.—THAT Randle
Thos. Muifo.   Ford, efquire, one of the commiffioners
named and authorifed in and by the
commiffion of bankrupt awarded againft S M did, be
fore he proceeded to act in the faid commiffion, take the

oath

oath of a commissioner prescribed and specified in and
by an act of parliament passed in the fifth year of the
reign of his late Majesty King George the second, intitled. 'An act to prevent the committing
of frauds by bankrupts," according to
the directions of the said act.

A g Pechell.

RANDLE FORD.

Witness,
Geo Miller.

Proof of Debts.

W C of Holborn-bridge, London, colourman, being
sworn and examined the day and year and at the place
aforesaid, upon his oath saith, That S. M. the person
against whom this commission of bankruptcy is awarded
and issued forth, was at and before the
Thos. Mulso.   date and issuing forth of the said commission, and still is justly and truly in-
debted unto this deponent, and to J. C this deponent's
partner, in the sum of   pounds   shillings and pence,
for goods sold and delivered, for which said sum of
pounds   shillings and pence, or any part thereof, he
this deponent hath not, nor hath this deponent's said
partner, to the knowledge and belief of this deponent,
received any security or satisfaction whatsoever.

W. C.

I. A of White-chapel, Brush maker, being sworn
and examined the day and year, and at the place aforesaid upon his oath faith, That S. M. against whom this
commission of bankruptcy is awarded and issued forth,
was at and before the date and issuing forth of the said
commission, and still is justly and truly
Randle Ford.   indebted unto this deponent in the sum
of   pounds   shillings and pence

E e 2

for

for goods sold and delivered, for which said sum of pounds shillings and pence or any part thereof, this deponent hath not received any security or satisfaction whatsoever.

Aug. Pechell.

I A.

Petitioning Creditor's d[?]t.

T S of Aldersgate-street, London, oilman, being sworn and examined the day, and year and at the place aforesaid, upon his oath faith, That S M the person against whom this commission of bankruptcy is awarded and issued forth, was at and before the date and suing forth of the said commission, and still is justly and truly indebted to this deponent and I P, this deponent's late partner, in the sum of pounds shillings and pence, for which said sum of pounds shillings and pence or any part thereof, he this deponent hath not nor hath this deponent's said late partner to the knowledge or belief of this deponent received any security or satisfaction whatsoever, except one promissory note under the hand of the said bankrupt dated whereby he promised to pay to this deponent' said late partner and this deponent, or order, the sum of pounds on demand, one other promissory note under the said bankrupt's hand, dated whereby he two months after date, promised to pay to this deponent's said late partner and to this deponent or order pounds shillings and pence, value received, and a bill of exchange dated drawn by the said bankrupt on and accepted by B. E payable six weeks after date to the said bankrupt's order and indorsed by him for pounds shillings and pence, and this deponent upon his oath further faith, that the said bankrupt is justly and truly indebted unto this deponent in

Thos. Mulso.

Randle Ford.

the

the sum of   pounds   shillings and pence, for goods
sold and delivered, for which said sum of   pounds
shillings and pence or any part thereof this deponent
hath not received any security or satisfaction whatsoever,
except one bill of exchange dated   drawn by J. L. P
                on and accepted by Messrs. C   n   F
Aug Pechell.   payable six months after date to the
                drawer's order, and indorsed by him
and the said bankrupt for   pounds   shillings

                                        J. S.

        Bankrupt's surrender.

                At Guildhall   day of   17

Thos Mulso.   MEMORANDUM—THAT S. M.
                the person against whom the commis-
sion of bankrupt hath been awarded this,   day of
                17 voluntarily surrendered him-
Randle Ford   self to us, the major part of the com-
                missioners named and authorized in and
by the said commission of bankrupt awarded against
him, pursuant to notice in the London Gazette for that
purpose, and submitted to be examined, and in all
things to conform himself to the directions of the several statutes made concerning bankrupts, and particularly to the late statute made in the fifth year of the
                reign of his late Majesty King George
Aug Pechell   the second, intitled, " An act to pre-
                vent the committing of frauds, by bank-
rupts," in order to have the benefit of the said
act.

                                        S M,

                                        Second

Second meeting of the Commissioners for taking further proofs of Debts, the choice of Assignees, &c

At Guildhall, London   day of   17

R W Bermondsey-street, Southwark, in the county of Surry, gluemaker, being sworn *Thos. Mulfo.* and examined the day, and year, and at the place aforesaid, upon his oath saith That S M the person against whom this commission of bankruptcy is awarded and issued forth, was at and before the date and suing forth of the said commission, and still is justly and truly indebted to this deponent in the sum of   pounds   shillings and pence, for goods sold and delivered, for which said sum of   or any part thereof, this deponent hath not received any security, or satisfaction whatsoever, save and except one promissory note under the said bankrupt's hand, dated   whereby he two months after date, promised to pay this deponent, or order,   pounds shillings, value received.

R W

G C of   being sworn, &c that S M the person, &c was at and before the date and suing forth of the said commission, and still is justly and truly indebted to this deponent in the sum of   for money lent by this deponent to the said S M to which said sum of   or any part thereof this deponent hath not received any security or satisfaction whatsoever, save and except a bill of exchange drawn by this deponent on and accepted by the said bankrupt, dated   at six weeks after date, for the sum of

G C

Debts of creditors at a distance from London must be proved by affidavits, sworn before a master extraordinary

traordinary in chancery, and produced and exhibited to the commissioners at Guildhall, on the security (if any) must be annexed to the affidavit of debt, and the persons impowered by letter of attorney to prove debts and vote in the choice of assignees, must attend therewith at the second meeting of the commissioners.

At Guildhall London, the   day of   17

MEMORANDUM—This being the day appointed in the London Gazette for the choice of assignees of the estate and effects of S. M. the person against whom the commission of bankrupt is awarded, we whose names are here underwritten, being the major part in value of the creditors of the said S. M. present at this meeting, and who have proved our debts to be ten pounds or upwards, have chosen, and do hereby nominate and chuse T S of   and K B of   to be assignees of the estate and effects of the said S M and we do hereby desire the commissioners to make an assignment thereof to them accordingly.

Thos Ma's.

A z. Ped's'l.

Henry Jochell.

We do accept of the said
trust and promise to
execute a counterpart
of the said assignment.
　　　I S
　　　R B.

T S.
R P.
W C for self and partner.
P W
G C
A. B by letter of attorney
　　from C D

MEMORANDUM.—Unanimoufly agreed by the creditors prefent, that as often as the money received by the faid affignees arifing from the bankrupt's effect, fhall amount to one hundred pounds, the fame fhall be placed in the hands Meffieurs of B. K. A. and company, bankers, in ——— ftreet, London, in the joint names of the faid affignees.

A. P.

Solicitor's bill of Fees and Difbursments, under commiffion of bankruptcy againft S. M.

		£	s	d
ATTENDING petitioning creditor feveral times, advifing and confulting as to taking out commiffion againft S. M. examining witneffes as to proving act of bankruptcy, taking inftructions for commiffion, and attending ftriking docket		0	13	4
Affidavit of debt, duty, and oath		0	7	6
Bond to Lord Chancellor, and duty		0	13	6
Secretary's fee and filing affidavit		1	3	0
Petition for commiffion and duty		1	1	0
Commiffion and hamper fee, box, deputy fecretary private feal, and expedition at patent office		7	14	2
Fee fuing out commiffion		1	1	0
A meeting being appointed to open commiffion at Baptift Head coffee houfe, at two o'clock attending accordingly, when only two commiffioners attended		0	6	8
Expences there		0	1	0
Commiffioners and clerk fitting when bankruptcy proved		4	0	0
The like firft fitting at Guildhall		4	0	0
The like fecond fitting		4	0	0
Drawing affignment of bankrupt's effects and engroffing two parts		2	2	0
Parchment and duty		0	17	0
Commiffioners and clerk fitting on executing affignment		4	0	0
Letters		0	2	0
		32	2	2
	Deduct	0	5	0
	£	31	17	2

We

We have perufed and allowed the above bill at the fum of £ 31 17 2 and direct the affignees to pay the fame

T. M.
A P.
H. J.

ASSIGNMENT.

Affignment from Commiffioners to Affignees

THIS INDENTURE, made the   in the   year of the reign of our fovereign Lord George the third, by the grace of God of Great Britain, France and Ireland, King, Defender of the Faith, &c. and in the year of our Lord one thoufand feven hundred and   BETWEEN Thomas Mulfo, Auguftus Pechell, and Henry Jodrell, efquires, of the one part, T S of ftreet, London, oilman, and R B. of   in the county of   diftiller, of the other part.—WHEREAS his Majefty's commiffion under the great feal of Great Britain, grounded upon the feveral ftatutes made and now in force concerning bankrupts, bearing date at Weftminfter the   day of   laft, hath been awarded and iffued againft S M. of   ftreet, London, oilman, dealer and chapman, directed unto the faid Thomas Mulfo, Auguftus Pechell, and Henry Jodrell, and alfo to Randle Ford, and John Calthorpe Gough, efquires, thereby giving full power and authority unto them, the faid commiffioners, four or three of them, to execute the fame, as in and by the faid commiffion, rela-

F f

tion

tion being thereunto had, may appear AND WHEREAS the said S M did for some time last past before the date and suing forth of the said commission, use, exercise and carry on the trade and business of an oilman, dealer and chapman, and thereby sought and endeavoured to get his living as others of the same trade and business are used to do, and that during such time of his the said S M.'s trading and dealing as aforesaid he the said S M became justly and truly indebted to the said I S in the sum of one hundred pounds and upwards, and being so indebted, he the said S M. did also, before the date and suing forth of the said commission, in the judgment of the said Thomas Mulso, Augustus Pechell, and Henry Jodrell, the major part of the said commissioners, become a bankrupt to all intents and purposes within the true intent and meaning of the several statutes in the said commission mentioned, or within some or one them   AND WHEREAS it appeared to the major part of the said commissioners, that the said S M at the time he became a bankrupt, was possessed of, interested in, or entitled unto, divers houshold goods, and other goods, wares and merchandizes, then remaining and being in or about his dwelling house, and premises situate in   street aforesaid, which have been seized by virtue of a warrant under the hands and seals of the major part of the said commissioners, and also of, in, and to divers book-debts, and other debts and sums of money, due, owing and payable to the said S M and his estate by and from divers and sundry persons, and likewise of, in, and to other personal estate and effects AND WHEREAS on this   day of   being the day appointed in the London Gazette for the creditors of the said S M to come before the major part of the said commissioners at Guildhall, London, to prove their debts and chuse assignees of the said S. M.'s estate and effects, the major part in value of the creditors of the said S M who are creditors for not less than the sum of 10l. and upwards respectively, and who have duly proved

their

their debts under the said commission, did nominate,
elect, and chute the said T S and R B to be assignees
of the said S M.'s estate and effects, and requested the
said Thomas Mallo, Augustus Pechell, and Henry Jodrell, to assign the same to them accordingly Now
this Indenture witnesseth, that they the said commissioners, parties to these presents, in pursuance of the
above recited commission, and of the statutes therein
mentioned, and also for and in consideration of 5s. a piece
to them the said commissioners parties hereto in hand
respectively, well and truly paid before the sealing and
delivering of these presents by the said T. S. and R. B.
the receipt whereof is hereby acknowledged, and also
for and in consideration of the covenants herein after
referved and contained on the part and behalf of the said
T S. and R. B. their executors, administrators, and
assigns, to be kept done and performed, HAVE ordained, bargained, sold, assigned, transferred, and sett
over, and by these presents do (as much as in them the
said commissioners and they lawfully may) order, bargain,
fell, assign, transfer, and sett over unto the said T S and
R B their executors, administrators, assigns, all and
singular the goods, merchandizes, debts, sum and sums
of money, and all other the personal estate and effects of
him, the said S M. whatsoever and wheresoever, To
HAVE and To HOLD, receive and enjoy, the said goods,
wares, and merchandizes, debts, sum and sums of
money, and all other the personal estate and effects
herein before ordered, bargained, sold, assigned, transferred, and sett over unto the said T S. and R B. their
executors, administrators, and assigns, for ever, IN
TRUST, nevertheless to and for the use, benefit, and
advantage of themselves, and all and every other the
creditors of the said S M who already have, or hereafter shall, or may, in due time come in, and seek relief
under the said commission, according to the limitations
and directions of the said several statutes made concerning bankrupts as aforesaid   And the said T S and

R. B.

R. B. for themselves, their executors and administrators, do covenant, promise, grant, and agree to, and with the said commissioners, parties hereto, their executors and administrators, and to and with every of them, by these presents in manner and form following (that is to say) That they the said I S and R B their executors, administrators, and assigns, shall and will use his and their utmost endeavours, and means, by suit at law or otherwise, to get in, collect, and receive, all the debts, personal estate and effects of S. M. with what care and speed they can. And also that the said I S, and R B their executors and administrators, shall and will, from time to time, and at all times hereafter, upon reasonable request and notice to them for that purpose, given under the hands and seals of the said commissioners, in the said commission named and authorized, give and render unto them, the said commissioners, or the major part of them, a just and true account of all and every such sum and sums of money, or other satisfaction as they the said I S and R b their executors, and administrators, shall or may have raised, obtained, or received, by force, virtue, or means of this present deed of assignment, or otherwise, out of the estate and effects of the said S M and all such money and other satisfaction, as upon such account shall appear to have been raised, obtained, and received, as aforesaid, shall and will, well and truly pay and deliver up, or cause to be paid and delivered up, unto the said commissioners, in the said commission named and authorized, or the major part of them, or to such other person or persons as they the said commissioners or the major part of them, shall, by writing under their hands, direct and appoint, to the end the same, or such other satisfaction may be by them, the said commissioners or the major part of them, ordered and disposed, distributed and divided, to and amongst all and singular the creditors of the said S. M who already have, or shall, or may hereafter come in and seek relief under the said commission, pro-

portionally

portionally to their several debts. And that they the
said T. S. and R. B. their heirs, executors, administrators and assigns, to all and every, from time to time, and
at all times hereafter, save, defend, and keep harmless
and indemnified as well the said commissioners, parties to
these presents named, by the said recited commission named and
authorized, their agents, servants and attornies, and
their heirs, executors and administrators, and every of
them, as their and every of their goods, chattels,
lands, and tenements, of from and against all and all
manner of actions, suits, costs, charges, and damages whatsoever, that shall or may at any time or times hereafter
arise, happen or come to them the said commissioners, or any or either of them, or any or
either of their executors or administrators, for, or
by reason or means of this present deed or assignment,
or any act, matter, or thing by them any or either of
them, lawfully acted or done, by virtue of the said recited commission, only their or any of their lawful intermeddling in and of the estate and effects of the said ———. In
witness, &c.

At Guildhall, London, the   day of   17

MEMORANDUM.—That the major part of the
commissioners named and authorized in and by the
commission of bankrupt, awarded against S———, met at
the time and place above-mentioned, and settled and
executed an assignment of the said bankrupt's estate and
effects to T. S. and R. B. being the persons chosen for
that purpose, and likewise settled the charges of suing
out and prosecuting the said commission to this time, by
settling the clerk's attendance to it, viz. clerk's suit,
——; the messenger's suit, ——; amounting
together 44l. 13s.

Thomas Tulp,
Abigail Peart,
Henry Jones

Third meeting of the Commissioners for taking further Proofs of Debts, the Bankrupt's last Examination, &c.

At Guildhall, London, the   day of   17

R Y. of   being sworn and examined the day, and year, and at the place aforesaid, upon his oath saith, That S M. the person, &c. and still is justly

Thos Maulso.   and truly indebted unto this deponent, and to R G this deponent's partner, in the sum of   for, &c. for which said sum of   or any part thereof, this deponent hath not, nor hath this deponent's partner, to the knowledge or belief of this deponent, received any security or satis-

Aug. Pechell.   faction whatsoever, save and except one bond or obligation dated   under the hand and seal of R H whereby he became bound to the said S M in   conditioned for payment of   with interest on   and except one promissory note, under the hand of the said S. M. dated   whereby he six months after due, promised to pay this deponent and partner, by

    names of Mess. Y. and Co. or order,

Henry Jodrell.   pounds, value received by him.

                       R. Y.

Bankrupt's last Examination.

At Guildhall, London, the   day of   17

    MEMORANDUM ---- That S M.

Thos Maulso.   the person against whom the commission of bankrupt is awarded, appearing again before us, the major part of the commissioners in the said

said commission named and authorized, in order to finish his examination pursuant to notice in the London Gazette, for that purpose given, and being now sworn and examined upon his oath, saith, That the paper writing hereunto annexed, marked with the letter A and signed by this examinant, and the books, goods, and effects, seized and taken by and under the said commission, and delivered to, or to the order of the assignees chosen thereunder, together with the books, papers, and writings, delivered by this examinant to the said assignees, together with one gold watch and seal, a mourning ring, a stone shirt-buckle, one pair of silver buckles, one pair of plated buckles, and three guineas and four shillings now delivered up to the said commissioners, do contain a full and true disclosure and discovery of all his estate and effects, real and personal, and how and in what manner, and to whom, and upon what considerations, and at what time or times he had disposed of, assigned or transferred any of his goods, wares, merchandizes, money or other estate, and of all books, papers and writings, relating thereto, of which he was pos-

Aug. Pechell. sessed, or in, or to which he was any ways interested for his estate, or which any person or persons had or hath in trust for him or for his use, at any time before or after the suing out of the said commission, or whereby he or any stands seized with or have, or may have or expect any profit, possibility of profit, benefit or advantage whatsoever, except that part only of his estate and effects sold, given really and bona fide sold or disposed of in the way of his trade and business, and except such sums and sums of money as have been laid out in the ordinary and necessary expence of himself and family. And this examinant further saith, That at the time of his former examination, or since, and at this the time of his latter examination, he hath delivered up to the said commissioners or some or one of them, or to the said assignees, all such part of this examinant's goods, wares, merchandizes, money, estate and effects,

and

and all books, papers and writings relating thereto, that at the time of such his examination, now are, or then were in his possession, custody or power (the necessary wearing apparel of this examinant, his wife and children, only excepted) and the said examinant further saith, that he hath not removed, concealed or embezzled, any part of his estate and effects, either real or personal, or any books of account, papers or writings relating thereto, with intent to defraud his creditors or *Henry Jodrell* whereby, he expects or can receive any benefit to himself or family.

S M.

MEMORANDUM The watch, seal, ring, shirt buckle, buckles and cash, above mentioned, were returned to the bankrupt, by consent of the creditors present.

Order of Dividend.

At Guildhall, London, the   day of   17

MEMORANDUM —This being the day appointed in the London Gazette for making a dividend of the estate and effects of S M. the person against whom a commission of bankrupt hath been issued, it appeared to us, the major part of the commissioners, named and authorized in and by the said commission, that the debts proved under the said commission, do amount in the whole to the sum of   and it appeared to us by the accounts of F. S. and R. B the assignees under the said commission, this day exhibited to us, upon oath, that the sum total of the bankrupt's estate now remaining in their hands, doth amount to the sum of   Now we do order and direct, that out of the monies remaining in the hands of the assignees as aforesaid a dividend of   shillings in the pound be paid to such of the bankrupt's bankrupt's creditors, as have already proved their debts under the said commission, in proportion to their several debts; which said dividend of   shillings in the pound, amounts to the sum of   as we compute the same, and after payment thereof, there will remain in the hands of the said assignees, the sum of   subject to our further order.

Thos. Mulfo.
Randle Ford
Aug Pechell.

Order for final Dividend.

At Guildhall, London, the   day of   17

BE IT REMEMBERED, that we whose names are hereunto subscribed, being the major part of the commissioners named and authorized in and by a commission of bankrupt, awarded and issued, and now in prosecution against S. M. of   street, London, oilman, dealer and chapman having met together the day, and year, and at the place above-mentioned, in order to make a final dividend of the estate and effects of the said bankrupt, pursuant to notice in the London Gazette for that purpose given, and it appearing to us that by an order of dividend made the   day of 17   the assignees under the said commission admitted that they then had sufficient money in their hands, to pay all the creditors of the said bankrupt, who had proved or claimed debts under the said commission, the sum of   shillings in the pound, for every pound so proved or claimed, the said commissioners did therefore, pursuant to the said admission, and at the desire of the creditors, order and direct that the assignees should pay and divide unto, and amongst all and every the creditors of the said bankrupt who have proved their debts, and unto the claimants when they should have

G g   proved

proved their claims under the said commission, the sum of   shillings in the pound, in proportion to their several and respective debts   and it also appearing to us by the account of T. S. and R. B. assignees of the said bankrupt this day exhibited to us, upon oath, that the sum total of the said bankrupt's estate remaining in their hands, doth amount to the sum of   and after payment of the solicitor's and messenger's bills to the sum of   and being deducted from the sum of   reduced the same to the sum of   which said sum now remains in the hands of the said assignees to be divided   Now we order and direct that the said dividend of   shillings in the pound, shall be paid to such of the said bankrupt's creditors who have this day proved their debts, which will amount to the sum of   and after payment thereof there will remain in the hands of the said assignees the sum of   to be divided among the creditors of the said bankrupt, and we do order and direct that out of the monies so remaining in the hands of the said assignees, a further dividend of   shillings in the pound, to be paid all the bankrupt's creditors who have already proved their debts, and sought relief under the said commission in proportion to their several debts, which said dividend of   shillings in the pound amounts to the sum of   as we compute the same, and after the payment thereof there will remain in the hands of the said assignees the sum of   and no more subject to our further order.

Thos Mulso.
Aug. Pechell.
Henry Jodrell.

Alphabetical Abstract

OF THE

WHOLE STATUTE LAW

RELATING TO

BANKRUPTS.

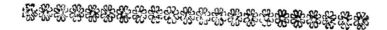

A C T S

RELATING TO BANKRUPTS.

34 and 35 Hen VIII. chap. 4.
13 Eliz chap. 7.
1 Jac I chap 15.
21 Jac. I chap 19.
7 Anne, chap. 12
10 Anne, chap. 15.
7 Geo. I chap 31
5 Geo. II. chap 30.
19 Geo. II chap 32.
24 Geo II chap. 57
4 Geo. III chap 33
12 Geo III chap 47.
13 Geo III chap. 77.

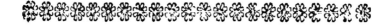

Alphabetical Abſtract, &c.

ALLOWANCE.

ALL bankrupts who ſhall ſurrender and conform, as by this act is directed, ſhall be allowed 5l per cent. out of the neat produce of the eſtate that ſhall be received, in caſe the neat produce of the eſtate, after ſuch allowance made, ſhall be ſufficient to pay 10s in the pound, and ſo as the ſaid 5l. per cent. ſhall not amount to above 20l., and in caſe the neat produce of the eſtate ſhall be ſufficient to pay 12s 6d in the pound, then all perſons ſo conforming ſhall be allowed 7l. 10s. per cent. ſo as ſuch allowance ſhall not amount to above 250l., and in caſe the neat produce ſhall, over and above the allowance, be ſufficient to pay 15s. in the pound, then perſons ſo conforming ſhall be allowed 10l per cent ſo as ſuch 10l per cent ſhall not amount to above 300l., and every ſuch bankrupt ſhall be diſcharged from all debts owing at the time that he did become bankrupt. 5 Geo 2. cap. 30 ſec. 7

If the neat produce of ſuch bankrupt's eſtate ſhall not amount to 10s. in the pound, ſuch bankrupt ſhall not be allowed 5l per cent but ſhall be allowed ſo much as the aſſignees and commiſſioners ſhall think fit, not exceeding 3l. per cent. 5 Geo. 2. cap. 30. ſec 8.

ARREST.

ARREST.

Bankrupt fhall be free from all arrefts, reftraint or imprifonment, of any of his creditors, in coming to furrender, and from his actual furrender to the commiffioners for the forty-two days, or fuch further time as fhall be allowed him, for finifhing his examination, provided he was not in cuftody at the time of his furrender, and fubmiffion to be examined.

If fuch bankrupt fhall be arrefted for debt, or on an efcape warrant, coming to furrender himfelf to the commiffioners, or after his furrender fhall be fo arrefted within the time before-mentioned, that then, on producing the fummons, under the hands of the commiffioners, or affignees, to the officer who fhall arreft him, and making it appear to him, that fuch notice or fummons was figned by the commiffioners, or affignees, and giving him a copy thereof, he fhall be immediately difcharged.

If any officer fhall detain fuch bankrupt (after he fhall have fhewn fuch notice or fummons to him, and made it appear it was figned as aforefaid) in his cuftody, he fhall forfeit and pay to fuch bankrupt for his own ufe, 5l for every day he fhall detain him, to be recovered by action of debt in any court of record at Weftminfter, in the name of fuch bankrupt, with full cofts of fuit. *5 Geo.* 2. *cap* 30. *fec.* 5.

In cafe any bankrupt (after certificate fairly obtained) fhall be arrefted, profecuted, or impleaded, for any debt due before fuch time as he became bankrupt, he fhall be difcharged upon common bail, and may plead in general, that the caufe of action did accrue before he became a bankrupt, and may give this act, and the fpecial matter in evidence. *Sec.* 7.

ASSIGNEES

ASSIGNEES OF BANKRUPT's ESTATES

Are impowered to appoint perfons to attend bankrupts in prifon under execution with books, papers, and writings, in order to prepare bankrupt's laft examination. 5 *Geo.* 2 *cap* 30 *fe.* 6.

May adjuft accounts that remain unbalanced between bankrupts and their creditors, and take the balance in full difcharge thereof. *Sec.* 28.

When a commiffion is iffued, the commiffioners fhall forthwith after they have declared the perfon a bankrupt, caufe a notice to be given in the *London Gazette*, and appoint a time and place for the creditors to meet (which meeting for London and the bills of mortality fhall be at Guildhall) to choofe affignees of the bankrupt's eftate; at which meeting the commiffioners fhall admit the proof of any perfon's debt by affidavit, and permit any perfon, duly authorized by letters of attorney from any creditor (oath or affirmation being made of the due execution thereof) to vote in the choice of affignees; and the affignees fhall keep books of account, in which they fhall enter all fums of money and other effects, which they fhall receive out of the bankrupt's eftate, which books, creditors who have proved their debts may infpect as often as they pleafe. *Sec* 26

No creditor, or other perfon for him, fhall vote in the choice of affignees whofe debt amounts not to 10l. or upwards. *Sec* 27

The commiffioners may immediately appoint affignees, who may be removed at the meeting of the creditors, if the major part of them think fit, and the affignees fo removed fhall deliver up and affign all the effects of the bankrupt, which fhall have come to their hands, to the affignees fo chofen by the creditors, and all fuch effects fhall be vefted in fuch new affignees. and if any

H h of

of the firft afsignees fhall by the fpace of ten days after notice of the choice of fuch new afsignees, and of their confent to accept fuch afsignment, refufe or neglect to make fuch afsignment and deliver, every fuch afsigne fhall forfeit 200l to be divided among the creditors, and recovered by action of debt, &c. by fuch perfons as the commifsioners fhall appoint, with full cofts, &c *Sec* 30.

The afsignees are to reimburfe the petitioning creditors, all cofts and charges they have been at in fuing out the commifsion, out of the firft monies or effects of the bankrupt, that fhall come into their hands *Sec*. 25.

If after any afsignment made purfuant to the choice of the creditors, it be found necefsary to vacate fuch afsignment, the Lord Chancellor, upon the petition of any creditors, may make fuch order therein, as he fhould think reafonable And if a new afsignment be ordered to be made by the creditors, the debts, effects and eftate of the bankrupt fhall be vefted in fuch new afsignees, who fue for the fame in their own names, difcharge any action, &c. *Sec*. 30.

The commifsioners fhall give notice in the two London Gazettes, immediately following the removal of fuch afsignees, and the appointment of new ones, that fuch afsignees are removed, and fuch others appointed in their ftead. *Sec*. 31.

Before the choice of afsignees, the major part in value of the creditors fhall, if they think fit, direct where and with whom the monies arifing from the bankrupts eftate fhall be depofited, till a dividend is made thereof, and every afsignee, as often as 100l come into his hands, fhall conform to fuch order and direction. *Sec*. 32.

The

The affignees fhall fome time after the expiration of
four months, and within twelve months from the time of
iffuing a commiffion, caufe 21 days public notice to
be given in the Gazette, of the time and place the commiffioners intend to meet and make a dividend of the
bankrupt's eftate (which meeting for the city of London
and the bills of mortality fhall be at Guildhall) when and
where creditors who have not proved their debts, may
prove the fame and the affignes fhall deliver to the
commiffioners and creditors, a fair account of the bankrupt's eftate, and may be examined upon oath, or
being Quakers, upon folemn affirmation, touching the
faid accounts They fhall be reimbursed their expences,
and have a reafonable allowance for their trouble, and
the commiffioners fhall order fo much of the neat produce of the bankrupt's eftate, as appears to be in the
hands of the affignees, to be divided amongft fuch of
the creditors as have proved their debts, which order
fhall be in writing under the hands of the commiffioners, to be filed amongft the proceedings of the commiffion, and a duplicate thereof delivered to each of
the affignees containing an account of the time, and
place of making fuch diftribution, the fum total of all
the debts proved under the commiffion, the fum
total of the money remaining in the hands of the affignees, and how much in the pound is then ordered to be
paid to every creditor, and the affignees, purfuant to
fuch order, are forthwith to make a dividend accordingly, and take receipts in a book to be kept for that
purpofe, from each creditor, which faid order and receipt fhall be an effectual difcharge to every affignee
for fo much as he pays purfuant thereunto. Sec. 33

The affignees may (with confent of the major part in
value of the bankrupt's creditors) fubmit matters in difpute to arbitration. Sec. 34.

May make compofition with the bankrupt's debtors, and take fuch reafonable part as can be gotten, in full difcharge of their debts *Sec.* 35.

The third claufe in the act of 5 Geo 2. relating to afsignees enacted in the act of 4 and 5 *Anne*, *cap* 17.

The like claufe in the act of 3 Geo. 1 *cap* 12.

The 4th, 5th, and 6th claufes, in the act of 5 *Anne* *cap* 13.

The 4th, 5th, 6th, 8th, 9th, and 13th claufes in the act of 5 *Geo.* 1. *cap.* 24

To make the final dividend within eighteen months after commifsion iffued; unlefs any fuit at law or equity be depending, or any part of the eftate not difpofed of, or fome future eftate to come to the afsignees, in which cafe they are to convert it into money as foon as pofsible, and within two months, by order of the commifsioners, divide the fame amongft the creditors. 5 *Geo.* 2. *cap.* 30. *fec* 37.

ASSURANCE.

No governor, director, or other officer of either of the corporations to be erected by this act, fhall in refpect of his fhare therein only be ajudged liable to be a bankrupt 6 *Geo* 1. *cap.* 18.

Affured, admitted to make claim before lofs happens, 19 *Geo.* 2. *cap.* 32.

BANKERS

BANKERS BROKERS.

Bankers, brokers and factors entrusted with money, goods and effects belonging to other persons, shall be liable to this and other statutes made concerning bankrupts 5 Geo. 2 cap 30 sec 39.

The like clause in the act of 5 Geo 1. cap 24.

BANK of ENGLAND.

No member of the land bank shall, in respect of his stock therein only, be adjudged liable to be a bankrupt. 7 and 8 W. 3 cap 31

Like clause for the Bank of England, in the act of 8 and 9 W 3 cap 19

Like clause in the act of 5 Ann, cap 13
Like clause in the act of 7 Ann, cap 7.
Like clause in the act of 3 Geo 1 cap 8.

BANKRUPTS

Described by 13 Eliz cap 7.
By 1 Jac cap. 15
Further described by 21 Jac 1 cap 19

Bankrupt to be deemed out of the King's protection, if he does not surrender himself within three months after the proclamation 34 and 35 Hen 8 cap 4

Like clause in the act of 13 Eliz cap 7

To be apprehended upon non-compliance with the proclamation and imprisoned upon refusing to be examined by the commissioners 1 Jac 1 cap 15

Bankrupts

Bankrupt convicted of perjury, to stand in the pillory, and have one of his ears cut off. 1 *Jac.* 1 *cap.* 15.

His wife to be examined by the commissioners, and liable to the same penalties as other persons for refusing to obey their orders. 21 *Jac* 1. *cap.* 19

A bankrupt convicted of endeavouring to defraud his creditors, by concealing or embezzling his effects, and refusing to surrender them to the commissioners, or not rendering some probable reason why he became a bankrupt, to stand in the pillory, &c 21 *Jac* 1 *cap.* 15

Not surrendering within forty two days after notice given in the London Gazette, and submitting to be examined, to be declared guilty of felony, and suffer as such without benefit of clergy. 5 *G o* 2 *cap* 30 *Jac* 1

To deliver up to the assignees all their books of accounts, writings, &c. not before delivered to the commissioners *Sec.* 4.

Not in prison, or custody, to attend assignees, to assist them in making out the accounts of their estate and effects *Sec.* 4

Have liberty to inspect their books and accounts, in presence of one or more of the assignees, and make extract from thence, in order to their making a full and true discovery of their effects, and to be free from all arrests of restraint during the time of their examination, if not in custody at the time of their surrender *Sec.* 5.

If in custody at the time of issuing the commission, and can be brought before the commissioners to be examined, the expence shall be paid by the assignees, but if under execution the commissioners are to attend them in prison *Sec.* 6.

Like

Like clause in the act of 4 *and* 5 *Anne, cap* 27.
Like clause in the act of 5 *Geo* 1 *cap* 24.

Discharged by this act, to be freed from arrests or prosecutions for any debts due at the time of his becoming a bankrupt. And if arrested or impleaded, may plead in general that the cause of such action did accrue before he became a bankrupt, and may give this act and the special matter in evidence, and shall recover his costs, &c. Nevertheless his future effects still liable. 5 *Geo* 2 *cap* 30. *sec.* 9.

No bankrupt whatsoever shall receive any benefit by this act, who, within a year before his becoming a bankrupt, has lost the sum of 100l. by contracts for the sale or purchase of any stock of any company or corporation, or any shares of government or public funds, if the contract was not to be performed within one week after the making such contract, or where the stock so bought or sold was not actually transferred in pursuance of such contract. *Sec* 12

If a bankrupt apprehended within the time limited, submits to be examined, and conforms in all respects to the directions of this act, he shall receive the same benefit thereby, as though he had voluntarily surrendered. *Sec* 13

The bankrupt is required, of and allowance of his certificate, to attend the assignees, in order to settle accounts; and if he refuses to attend or just to abscond, (without good and sufficient account given for such neglect or refusal) he is to be committed to gaol without bail, &c *Sec* 36

Like clause in the act of 5 *Geo* 1 *cap* 24.

Allow 2 s. 6 d. *per diem* for such attendance. 5 *Geo* 2. *cap* 30. *sec.* 16.

BILLS, BONDS, PROMISSORY NOTES &c.

Perfons who have fold goods upon credit, and taken bills, bonds, promissory notes, or other perfonal fecurities for their money, payable on future days of payment, if commiffions of bankruptcy be awarded againft the buyers of fuch goods, before the money due on fuch bills, &c is become payable, the perfons fo giving credit upon a good and valuable confideration for money or other thing whatfoever, which fhall not be due before the time of the buyer's becoming a bankrupt, fhall be admitted to prove their bills, &c in like manner as if they had been made payable prefently, and fhall be intitled to a proportionable fhare and dividend of fuch bankrupt's eftate, in proportion to the other creditors, deducting only a rebate of intereft, and difcounting fuch fecurities after the rate of 5l *per cent per annum*, for what he fhall fo receive, to be computed from the payment thereof, to the time fuch debt would have become payable by fuch fecurities 7 Geo. 1 *cap* 31

Every bankrupt fhall be difcharged from fuch bond, note, or other fecurity, and have the benefit of the feveral ftatutes againft bankrupts in like manner as if fuch money had been due before the time of his becoming bankrupt *Same ect.*

So much of the act of 7 Geo 1. *cap* 31. as difables any perfon poffeffed of fuch bonds, bills, promiffory notes, &c from petitioning for, or joining in any petition for a commiffion of bankruptcy, is by this act repealed, and it fhall and may be lawful for any fuch perfon to petition for, or join in petitioning for any fuch commiffion, any thing in the faid act contained to the contrary notwithftanding 5 Geo. 2 *cap.* 30. *fc* 22.

The creditors petitioning for a commiffion, fhall give bond to the Lord Chancellor in the penalty of 200l. conditioned for proving their debts, &c *Sec* 23

CERTI-

CERTIFICATE.

No bankrupt fhall be intitled to the benefit of this act, unlefs the commiffioners fhall certify to the Lord Chancellor, that he hath made a full difcovery of his effects, and in all things conformed himfelf to the directions of this act, and that there does not appear to them any reafon to doubt of the truth of fuch difcovery, or that it is not a full difcovery of all the bankrupt's eftate and effects, and unlefs four parts in five, in number and value of the creditors, fhall fign the certificate, and teftify their content to fuch allowance and certificate, and to the bankrupt's difcharge, to be alfo certified by the commiffioners, who are not to certify till they have proof by affidavit, or affirmation in writing, of the creditors figning fuch certificate, and the power by which any perfon fhall be authorized to fign for them, which fhall be laid before the Lord Chancellor, &c. with the certificate, in order to the allowing and confirming the fame, and unlefs the bankrupt make oath, or affirmation, that fuch certificate and confent were obtained fairly, and without fraud, and unlefs fuch certificate, after fuch oath or affirmation, be allowed by the Lord Chancellor, or by two of the judges of the courts at Weftminfter, to whom the confideration thereof fhall be referred by the Lord Chancellor · And the creditors fhall, if they think fit, be heard againft the making fuch certificate, and the confirmation thereof. 5 G 2. cap 30, fec. 10

Like claufe in the act of 4 and 5 Anne, cap 17.
Like claufe in the act of 5 Anne, cap 27.
Like claufe in the act of 5 G 0. 1. cap 24.

Every bond, bill, or other fecurity, given by any bankrupt to the ufe of any creditor, as a confideration to perfuade him to fign fuch allowance or certificate, fhall be void. 5 G 2. cap 30 fec 11
Like claufe in the act of 5 Anne, cap 13

I i

Like

Like clause in the act of 5 G o 1. cap 24

A certificate signed by a fictitious creditor, is void, unless the bankrupt discovers the fraud. 24 Geo. 2. cap. 57 sec 9

LORD CHANCELLOR, &c.

May enlarge the time for bankrupt's surrendering. 5 Geo 2. cap 30. sec 6.

Like clause in the act of 4 and 5 Anne, cap 17.

Like clause in the act of 5 Geo. 1. cap. 24.

The Lord Chancellor may vacate the first assignment of the bankrupt's estate, &c upon petition of any creditors, or make such order therein as he shall think reasonable 5 Geo 2. cap 30. sec. 21.

Like clause in the act of 5 Geo 1. cap. 24.

COMMISSION,

Of bankrupts to be sued out within five years after the person becomes a bankrupt 21 Jac. 1. cap. 19.

No commission of bankrupt shall be awarded against any person upon the petition of one or more creditors, unless the single debt of the petitioner do amount to 100l. or upwards, or the debt of two creditors to 150l or upwards, or the debt of three or more creditors to 200l. or upwards, and the petitioning creditor shall, before the same be granted, give bond to the Lord Chancellor, in the penalty of 200l conditioned for proving their debts, and the party a bankrupt at the time of taking out the commission, and the petitioners shall make oath, or (being Quakers) solemn affirmation in writing, before a Master in Chancery, of the truth and reality of their debts, which affidavit shall be filed

by

by the proper officer, and if such debts shall not appear
to be due, or the party shall not be proved a bankrupt,
but that such commission was taken out fraudulently or
maliciously, the Lord Chancellor, on the petition of
the party grieved may order satisfaction to be made
for the damages by him sustained, and for the better
recovery thereof, may assign the bond to the party petitioning, who may sue the same in his own name.
5 Geo. 2. cap 30 sec. 23.

Like clause (the oath, or affirmation, of the petitioning creditors excepted) in the act of 5 Anne, cap 13

Like clause (except as before excepted) in the act of
5 Geo. 1. cap 24.

If any bankrupt, after a commission is issued out
against him, shall pay to the person who sued out the
same, or deliver any goods, or give other satisfaction for
his debt, whereby such person shall privately have more
in the pound than the other creditors, such payment
&c shall be deemed an act of bankruptcy, whereby
such commission shall be superseded, and the Lord
Chancellor may award to any creditors petitioning for a
new commission   And the persons taking such goods, or
other satisfaction, shall pay back and deliver up the
same, or the full value, to such persons as the commissioners acting under such new commission shall appoint,
in trust for the other of the bankrupt's creditors 5 Geo. 2.
cap 30 sec. 24

Like clause in the act of 5 Geo. 1. cap 24.

The charge of issuing commissions to be paid by the
assignees. 5 Geo. 2. cap. 30. sec. 25.

COMMISSIONERS

To be chosen by the Lord Chancellor, have authority to imprison the body of the bankrupt, and also to

caufe his lands, gcods, &c. to be viewed, appraifed, and fold for the ufe of his creditors 13 *Eliz. cap.* 7.

The commiffioners are to appoint three feveral meetings within the time limited for the bankrupt to furrender himfelf, the laft of which fhall be on the forty-fecond day, by this act limited, for the bankrupt's appearance 5 *Geo* 2. *cap* 30. *Sec.* 2.

Are to attend bankrupts (if under execution) in prifon. *Sec.* 6.

Have power to examine bankrupts, as well by word of mouth as by interrogatories in writing, and alfo every other perfon fummoned before them, touching the trade and effects of fuch bankrupts, and may commit them to prifon upon non-compliance. *Sec.* 16.
Like claufe in the act of 1 *Jac* 1. *cap* 15
Like claufe in the act of 4 and 5 *Anne, cap.* 17.
Like claufe in the act of 5 *Geo.* 1 *cap* 24.

To give notice in the London Gazette when a perfon is declared a bankrupt, and appoint a time and place for the creditors to meet and prove their debts, choofe affignees, &c. 5 *Geo* 2. *cap.* 30. *fec.* 26.

May appoint affignees, who may be difplaced at the meeting of the creditors. *Sec.* 30.

To give notice in the London Gazette of the removal of the former affignees, and the appointment of new ones. *Sec* 31.

May fend their warrant to any gaoler to deliver up the body of a bankrupt, in his cuftody, to the perfons named in fuch warrant, and alfo to feize any goods or effects of the bankrupt which fhall be then in his cuftody, or in the cuftody of any other perfon, or in any prifon whatfoever. *Sec.* 14.

Like

Like clause in the act of 5 Geo. 1 cap 24.

Commissioners are impowered to administer an oath, or solemn affirmation, to any person authorized by letter of attorney from any creditor, touching the due execution thereof, and are to permit such person so authorized to vote in the choice of assignees. 5 Geo. 2. cap 30 sec 26

Like clause in the act of Geo. 1. cap 24.

To assign the bankrupt's estate to the assignees, chosen by the majority in value of the creditors. 5 G 2. 2. cap 30 sec 26

Like clause in the act of 5 G 1 cap 24.

To any action brought against them, for a thing done in pursuance of this act, may plead the general issue, and give this act, and the special matter, in evidence 1 Jac 1. cap 13

The like clause in the act of 5 Geo. 1 cap 24.

May proceed in execution upon the bankrupt's effects, notwithstanding the death of the bankrupt 1 Jac. 1. cap. 19.

May break open the house of a person declared a bankrupt 21 Jac 1 cap 19

Have power to send for and examine upon oath, or otherwise, any persons suspected of concealment of the bankrupt's effects, or of being indebted to him. 13 Eliz. cap 7.

Like clause in the act of 34 and 35 Hen 8 cap 4

Not allowed money for eating, drinking, &c out of the bankrupt's effects, or take too much for their fees for each meeting. Any commissioner offending against this clause to be disabled from ever after acting as a commissioner. 5 Geo. 2 cap 30 sec 42

No

No commissioner capable of acting as such till sworn
Sec 43

CONCEALERS of BANKRUPT's ESTATE, &c

Persons suspected of concealing any of the bankrupt's
effects, or of being indebted to him, may be sent for
and examined by the commissioners upon oath, or otherwise, and if upon examination they refuse to declare
the whole truth, on proof thereof made before the commissioners, they are to forfeit double the value of such
goods and effects to conceal d   34 and 35 *Hen* 8   *cap* 4
Like clause in the act of 1 *Eliz* *cap* 7.

Refusing to appear upon commissioner's summons, or
to answer to interrogatories, to be committed to prison
without bail, &c. till they submit   1 *Jac.* 1   *cap* 15.

Convicted of perjury, to incur and suffer the pains
and penalties imposed by the statute of 5 *Eliz* made
concerning perjury). 1 *Jac* 1   *cap* 15

Every person who has accepted of any trust, and shall
conceal any estate, real or personal, of any person becoming bankrupt, and shall not, within forty two
days after issuing of the commission, and notice thereof,
discover such trust and estate in writing to one or more
of the commissioners, and submit to be examined by
them, and truly discover the same, shall forfeit 100l.
and double the value of the estate concealed, for the use
of the creditors, to be recovered by an action of debt
in the name of the assignees, and cost shall be allowed
to either party, as in other cases 5 *Geo.* 2 *cap* 30
sec. 21.

CREDI-

CREDITORS

Claiming more than is justly due to them, to forfeit double the sum demanded 34 and 35 *Hen* 8 *cap* 4

May be heard against making and confirming the bankrupt's certificate 5 G. 2 *cap*. 30 *sec* 10.

Creditors petitioning for a commission, to give bond to the Lord Chancellor, conditioned to prove their debts and the party a bankrupt. *Sec* 23

Petitioning creditors to be reimbursed their expences of suing out commissions, by the assignees. *Sec*. 25

No creditor to vote in the choice of assignees, whose debt amounts not to 10l. *Sec* 27.

The creditors may appoint where the effects of the bankrupt shall be deposited, till a dividend is made thereof. *Sec* 32

DAYS TIMES.

The bankrupt is allowed forty-two days to appear in. *Sec* 1

The Lord Chancellor may enlarge the time for the bankrupt's surrendering, not exceeding fifty days, to be computed from the end of the said forty-two days, so as such order be made at least six days before the time on which such person was to surrender *Sec* 3

Persons who shall, within sixty days next after the time allowed a bankrupt to surrender, &c voluntarily make discovery of any part of the bankrupts estate, shall be allowed 3l per cent. &c 4 and 5 *Ann*, *cap*. 17.

Like

Like claufe in the act of 5 *Geo* 1 *cap* 24

Like claufe in the act of 5 *Gro.* 2. with the allowance of 5l. per cent. and no time limited *Sec.* 20

Bankrupt, after his certificate confirmed, fhall on fourteen days notice attend the affignees, &c. and fhall be allowed 2s 6d *per diem* for fuch attendance. 5 *G* 9 1. *cap* 24

Like claufe in the act of 5 *Geo.* 2. but no time limited for notice. *Sec.* 36.

The affignees appointed by the commiffioners fhall, within ten days after notice, deliver up to the affignees chofen by the creditors, all the effects of the bankrupt that fhall be come to their hands. 5 *Geo* 2 *cap.* 30. *fec. 30.*

DEBTS.

Creditors receiving debts or goods of bankrupts without notice, and in the courfe of trade, not obliged to refund, &c 19 *Geo.* 2. *cap.* 32

Where there are mutual debts between the bankrupt and any other perfons, contracted at any time before the perfon became a bankrupt, the commiffioners fhall ftate the account between them, and one debt may be fet againft the other, and no more fhall be paid on either fide than what fhall appear to be due on the balance of the account 5 *G* o 2 *cap.* 30 *fec* 28

Like claufe in the act of 4 and 5 *Anne, cap.* 17.

Like claufe in the act of 3 *G* 1. *cap.* 12.

Like claufe in the act of 5 *Geo* 1 *cap.* 24.

DISCHARGE.

Any one of the judges of the court, where judgment has been obtained againft a bankrupt before his certificate

cate was allowed and confirmed, taken in execution, and detained in prison, may, on such bankrupt's producing his certificate allowed and confirmed, order any sheriff, bailiff, or other gaoler, having a bankrupt in custody by virtue of such execution, to discharge such bankrupt out of custody without fee, and such sheriff, &c. is to discharge him accordingly, and is indemnified from any action for an escape in so doing 5 *Geo.* 2. *cap* 30. *ss.* 13.

Like clause in the act of 6 *Geo* 1 *cap* 22.

E Q U I T Y.

No suit in equity shall be commenced without the content of the major part in value of the creditors. 5 *Geo.* 2 *cap* 30 *ss* 38

ESTATE, EFFECTS, &c

Any estate or effects that shall descend, or by any means come to a bankrupt, before his debts are fully satisfied and paid, or otherwise agreed for, shall be expended and disposed of for the payment of the said debts.

Any lands assured by a bankrupt before he became a bankrupt, shall not be affected by this act, provided such assurance be made *bona fide*, and not to the use of the bankrupt or his heirs, and provided the parties to whom such assurance was made, be not privy to any fraudulent purpose of the bankrupt to deceive his creditors. 13 *Eliz* *cap* 7.

Any estate or effects in the possession of a bankrupt, whereof he is the reputed owner at the time of his becoming a bankrupt (although before assigned to other

K k

persons

perfons upon good confideration) fhall be fold for the ufe of the creditors

Any eftate or lands in remainder, or reverfion, belonging to a bankrupt, (except where the reverfion is in the king, &c) to be difpofed of for the benefit of his creditors

Conditional eftates granted or conveyed by a bankrupt, may be redeemed by the commiffioners before the time of the performance of fuch conditions, and fold for the ufes aforefaid 21 *Jac* 1 *cap* 19

All the eftate and effects of a bankrupt condemned as a felon fhall be divided amongft the creditors feeking relief under a commiffion of bankruptcy. 5 *Geo* 2. *cap* 30 *fec* 1
Like claufe in the act of 4 and 5 *Anne, cap* 24
Like claufe in the act of 5 *Geo* 1 *cap* 24.

No perfons difcharged upon a fecond bankruptcy, after the 24th of June, 1732, fhall be liable to arreft or imprifonment, but the future eftate and effects of fuch perfons fhall remain liable to their creditors as before, (the tools of trade, neceffary houfehold goods, and wearing apparel excepted) unlefs the eftate of fuch perfons, when under a commiffion of bankruptcy, was fufficient to pay their creditors 13s. in the pound 5 *Geo* 2 *cap* 30 *fec* 9.

EXCHEQUER BILLS

No governor, fub-governor, deputy-governor, or director of the South Sea Company, or any of the truftees or other perfons whatfoever, who fhall be entrufted, or any ways concerned in the circulation or exchanging of exchequer bills, purfuant to this act, fhall, for that offence only, be adjudged to be a bankrupt, within the meaning

meaning of any statute made against or concerning bankrupts. 6 Geo 1 cap. 4

No contractor for circulating the Exchequer bills, to be made to-th in pursuance of this act shall, for that cause only, be adjudged liable to be a bankrupt 2 Geo 1. cap 20

Like clause in the act of 9 Geo. 1 c p 18
Like clause in the act of 11 Geo 1 cap 17
Like clause in the act of 12 Geo 1 cap 4

FARMER, GRAZIER, &c.

No farmer, grazier, drover of cattle, or receiver general of taxes granted by parliament, shall be accounted as such to the intents of this act, or be deemed a bankrupt within this, or any of the statutes concerning bankrupts 5 Geo 2. cap 30 fe 40

Like clause in the act of 5 Ann c, caf. 15.
Like clause in the act of 5 Geo 1. cap 24.

FELONY.

If any person who since the 14th day of May, 1 became, or hereafter shall become bankrupt, and against whom a commission hath, or hereafter shall issue, whereon he shall be declared a bankrupt, shall not, within forty-two days after notice thereof in writing, left at his place of abode and notice in the London Gazette, of the time and place of meeting of the commissioners, surrender himself to them, and submit to be examined on oath, or (if a Quaker) upon his solemn affirmation and conform himself to the several rules concerning bankrupts and upon such examination discover how, and upon what consideration he hath disposed any of his goods or estate and disclose papers, and writings relative thereto, of which he, or any perſon in truſt for him, was poſſeſſed at the iſſuing out of the commiſſion, and deliver up to the commiſſioners all ſuch his goods, eſtate, &c. books, &c as, at his examination, ſhall be in his poſſeſſion (his and his wife's, and children's neceſſary wearing apparel only excepted) ſuch bankrupt, in caſe of wilful omiſſion of any or the premiſes, or in caſe he ſhall remove, conceal, or embezzle any part of his eſtate, real or perſonal, to the value of 20l or any books or writings relating thereto, with an intent to defraud his creditors, and being lawfully convicted, ſhall be deemed and adjuged guilty of felony, and ſuffer as a felon without benefit of clergy 5 Geo 2, cap 30. ſec. 1.

FORFEITURES.

The perſon of a bankrupt not liable to arreſt, and if any officer detains him, he ſhall forfeit to him 5l. per diem. 5 Geo. 2 cap. 30 ſec. 5

Gaoler ſuffering a bankrupt, or other perſon committed by the commiſſioners, to eſcape, or go without the walls of the priſon, forfeits 500l. to the uſe of the creditors Sec. 19.

Gaoler refuſing, on requeſt of a creditor, to produce and ſhew to him a bankrupt, or ſuch other perſon in his cuſtody, forfeits 100l. for the uſe of the creditors. Sec. 19.

The aſſignees choſen by the commiſſioners, refuſing to deliver and aſſign to the aſſignees choſen afterwards by the creditors all the eſtate and effects of the bankrupt which ſhall come to their hands, every ſuch aſſignee ſhall forfeit 200l for the uſe of the creditors. Sec. 31.

The

The like claufe in the act of 5 *Geo* 1. *cap*. 24.

Any creditor privately receiving of a bankrupt, any goods or fecurity whereby he fhall have more in the pound than the other creditors, in confideration of fuing out a commiffion, fhall forfeit the whole   5 *Geo*. 2. *cap*. 30. *fec* 24

GAMING.

Nothing in this act fhall extend to grant any privilege to a bankrupt who has loft in one day the value of 5l. or in the whole the value of 100l. within twelve months next preceding his becoming a bankrupt, in playing at cards, dice, tables, tennis, bowls, fhovel-board, or by cock-fighting, horfe-races, or any other paftime or game whatfoever, or by bearing a part in the ftakes or wagers; or by betting on the fides of fuch as do play, act, ride, or run, or by contracts for ftock, &c   5 *Geo*. 2 *cap* 30. *fec* 12

Like claufe in the act of 5 *Ann*. *cap*. 17.
Like claufe in the act of 5 *Geo* 1. *cap* 24.

IMPRISONMENT

Upon certificate under the hands and feals of the commiffioners, that a perfon is proved a bankrupt, the judges of the courts of Weftminfter, and all juftices of the peace, are to grant their warrant for apprehending fuch perfon, and to commit him to the giol of the county where taken, there to remain, till relcafed by the order of the commiffioners by warrant under their hands and feals The gaoler is required to receive fuch perfon into his cuftody, and forthwith to give notice thereof to one of the commiffioners, who are to fend their warrant for the delivery of fuch bankrupt to the perfons authorized

rized thereby, to convey him to them to be examined
5 Geo 2. cap 30 fec 14.

A like claufe in the act of 1 *Jac* 1 *cap* 15

Perfons fummoned to appear before the commiffioners
to be examined as witneffes, and refufing to appear, or
appearing, refufe to be fworn (or if Quakers) to take the
affirmation, or being fworn, &c. refufe to anfwer, the
commiffioners may commit fuch perfons to prifon without bail or mainprize, till they fubmit to anfwer upon
oath, &c. 5 Geo 2 cap. 30 fec 16

If a bankrupt after his certificate figned and confirmed,
fhall, on reafonable notice given him, neglect or refufe
to attend the affignees or order to fettle accounts between him and his creditors, or to attend any court of
record to be examined touching the fame, on proof
thereof made by the affignees before the commiffioners,
they are to iffue a warrant for apprehending fuch
bankrupt, and commit him to the county gaol without bail or mainprize, till he fubmits to be examined,
and duly conform to the fatisfaction of the faid commiffioners, and be by them, or by fpecial order of the Lord
Chancellor, or otherwife by due courfe of law difcharged, and the gaoler fhall keep fuch bankrupt in clofe
cuftody within the walls of the prifon till difcharged,
under the pains and penalties before mentioned for fuch
gaoler's fuffering fuch prifoner to efcape and go at large
Sec 36.

Every perfon that fhall willingly help to embezzel or
convey away any of the bankrupts goods, knowing
him to be a bankrup, fhall fuffer fuch penalties by imprifonment, as the Lord Chancellor fhall think fit   34
and 35 *Hen* 8 *cap* 4

Every perfon that fhall wittingly conceal or receive a
bankrupt after he is demanded by proclamation, fhall
                                      fuffer

suffer such penalties by imprisonment as the Lord Chancellor, &c. shall think fit. 13 *Eliz. cap* 7.

It a bankrupt refuse to be examined, or to answer fully to the interrogatories of the commissioners, they may commit him to prison there to remain till he conforms himself. 1 *Jac.* 1 *cap.* 15

If a bankrupt or other person committed to prison by the commissioners be removed by habeas corpus, the gaoler of the prison to which he shall be committed, shall keep such prisoner within the walls of the prison till discharged. 5 *Geo.* 1 *cap* 24

If any person be imprisoned by the commissioners for refusing to answer, &c. the commissioners are in their warrant of commitment particularly to specify the question or questions. 5 *Geo* 2. *cap* 30 *sec* 15

If a habeas corpus be brought upon such commitment, the judge may re-commit the prisoner. *Sec.* 18

MARRIAGE CONTRACT.

This act shall give no benefit or advantage to a bankrupt, who on marriage of any of his children hath given above the value of 100l. unless he can prove by his books, fairly kept, or otherwise upon oath that he had at the time thereof, over and above the value given, in goods, wares, &c. or other estate, real or personal, sufficient to satisfy his creditors their full debts. 5 *Geo* 2. *cap* 30 *sec* 12

Like clause in the act of 13 and 5 *Ann. cap* 17.
Like clause in the 5 *Geo* 1 *cap* 24.

MASTERS IN CHANCERY.

Impowered to adminifter oath to the bankrupt 5 *G.* 9. 2. *cap* 30. *fec.* 4

To the petitioners for a commiffion of bankruptcy. *Sec* 23.

To perfons acting by letter of attorney from any creditor. *Sec* 26

To fettle bills of fees. *Sec* 44.

OATH

Bankrupt's wife to be examined upon oath. 21 *Jac* 1, *cap* 19

Bankrupt fhall fubmit to be examined upon oath. *5 Geo.* 2. *cap* 30

The firft part of this claufe in the act of 1 *Jac.* 1 *cap*, 15

The firft part of this claufe in 4 & 5 *Anne, cap* 17.

The commiffioners may examine witneffes on their oaths. *5 Geo.* 2. *cap.* 30. *fec* 16.

Bankrupts to make oath, that the certificate of his having conformed, &c. was obtained fairly and without fraud. *Sec.* 10.

The affignees fhall make proof upon oath before the commiffioners, of the bankrupt's refufing to attend them in order to fettle accounts *Sec* 36

The commiffioners fhall admit the proof of any creditor's debt, who lives remote from the place of their meeting, by affidavit. *Sec* 26.

Proof

Proof must be made upon oath (either before a master in chancery, or before the commissioners, viva voce) of the due execution of a letter of attorney from any creditor, to authorize another person to vote for him in the choice of assignees. *Sec.* 45

No commissioner capable of acting till sworn. *Sec.* 43.

The form of the oath.

Which oath any two of the commissioners may administer to the others in the same commission named, and they are to keep a memorial thereof signed by themselves, among the depositions, and other proceedings on each commission.

Like clause in the act of 5 *Geo* 1 *cap* 24

Books of accounts to be delivered to the assignees upon oath. 5 *Geo* 2 *cap* 30. *sec* 4

Creditors petitioning for a commission, shall make oath or affirmation, in writing, of the truth and reality of their debts. *sec.* 23.

Assignees to deliver in their accounts of the bankrupt's estate upon oath, if required. *Sec.* 33

PARTNERS.

The discharge of a bankrupt by virtue of any act relating to bankrupts, shall not discharge any person who was his partner in trade at the time he became bankrupt, or who stood jointly bound, or had made any joint contract with him for the same debt from which he was discharged, but notwithstanding such discharge, such partner shall stand liable 10 *Ann, cap* 15

RECORD

On the petition of any perfon, the Lord Chancellor may order the commifsion, the depofitions proving the bankruptcy, the proceedings thereupon, the certificates, and other matters, to be entered of record, and in cafe of the death of witnefses, or if the commifsion, &c. be loft or miflaid, a true copy of the record may be given in evidence, and be a full and effectual bar and difcharge of any action brought by any creditor of a bankrupt for any debt or demand due before the ifsuing of the commifsion, unlefs the creditor can prove that fuch certificate was fraudulently obtained. 5 *Geo* 2. *cap*. 30. *fec*. 41.

Like claufe in the act of 5 *Geo* 1. *cap*. 24

SECURITIES

Of any kind given to a creditor, to induce him to fign the certificate, fhall be void. 5 *Geo*. 2 *cap* 30 *fec*. 11.

SEIZURE.

The commifsioners may by warrant feize the goods, wares, merchandizes, and effects of a bankrupt (his necefsary wearing apparel, and that of his wife and children only excepted) and all his books, papers, and writings, in his own, or any other's cuftody, or in any prifon whatfoever. 5 *Geo*. 2. *cap*. 30 *fec*. 14

See the act of 34 and 35 *Hen*. 8. *cap*. 4.
See the act of 13 *Eliz*. *cap*. 7.
See the act of 1 *Jac* 1. *cap*. 15.
Like claufe in 21 *Jac*. 1. *cap*. 19.
Like claufe in 4 & 5 *Anne*, *cap*. 17.
Like claufe in 5 *Geo*. 1. *cap*. 24.

VOID.

VOID.

Every bond, bill, note, contract, agreement, or other fecurity given by a bankrupt for the ufe of any creditor, or for the payment of any debt due from fuch bankrupt at the time of his becoming bankrupt, between that time and his difcharge, as a confideration, or with intent to perfuade fuch creditor to fign his allowance or certificate, fhall be void, and the money agreed to be paid, fhall not be recoverable, and the perfon fued on fuch bond, &c may plead the general iffue, &c 5 Geo. 2. *cap.* 30. *fec* 11.

Like claufe in 5 *Anne, cap.* 22
Like claufe in 5 *Geo.* 1 *cap* 24.

WITNESS.

Allowed cofts 1 *Jac.* 1 *cap.* 15.

Convicted of wilful perjury to fuffer fuch penalties as are limited by the ftatute of 5 *Eliz cap* 9.

The commiffioners may fend for and call before them by warrant, fummons, or otherwife, as they fhall think fit, fuch perfons as they are informed or believe can give information of any act of bankruptcy committed by any perfon againft whom a commiffion is iffued, and examine them on their oaths, or otherwife; and if any perfon, upon payment or tender of reafonable charges, fhall neglect, or refufe to appear, or being come, fhall refufe to be fworn, or (being a Quaker) to take the folemn affirmation, or being fworn, or having taken fuch affirmation, fhall refufe to anfwer, the commiffioners may by warrant commit fuch offender to prifon, there to remain without bail or mainprize till he fubmit to anfwer. 5 *Geo* 1 *cap* 30 *fc* 16

Like claufe in 4 *and* 5 *Ann* *cap* 17.
Like claufe in 5 *Geo.* 1. *cap* 24

Witnefs to fign their examination taken before the
commiffioners. 5 *Geo.* 2. *cap.* 30 *fec.* 16.

If a witnefs committed by a warrant from the commiffioners, bring a habeas corpus to be difcharged from
fuch commitment, the judge, before whom the party
fhall be brought, may remand him back to prifon, unlefs it be made appear, that the party fo committed, has
anfwered all lawful queftions of the commiffioners, or
has a good and fufficient reafon for not figning his examination. 5 *Geo.* 2. *cap.* 30. *fec.* 18.

F I N I S.

CPSIA information can be obtained at www.ICGtesting.com
Printed in the USA
LVOW120259200812

294896LV00003B/262/P